Typorama

Edited by Tino Grass   with contributions by Ellen Lupton and Alice Morgaine

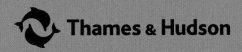 Thames & Hudson

The Graphic Work of

Philippe Apeloig

TYPORAMA

Contents

Foreword

If Philippe Apeloig is familiar with museums, his work is equally familiar to the many museums and cultural institutions with which he has been closely linked since the start of his career. It all began at the Musée d'Orsay in 1985. Ever since, he has been designing brochures, posters, exhibition catalogs, and logos for museums and institutions around the world. In 1980, while still at secondary school, Apeloig visited an exhibition dedicated to the work of Tomi Ungerer, which was held at Paris's Union centrale des Arts Décoratifs (now known simply as Les Arts Décoratifs). Apeloig recalls being struck by the illustrator's graphic approach and commitment, and the popular appeal of his drawings. He was especially thrilled by a poster that featured an elephant, seen from behind, dipping its trunk into a pot of green paint. Over thirty years later, in 2013, Les Arts Décoratifs would celebrate the work of Philippe Apeloig in his own exhibition, "Typorama: Philippe Apeloig, Graphic Design."

It is unusual for a graphic designer to reveal his visual references and sources of inspiration, and even more unusual for him to invite the public to fathom the private depths of his creativity. Such is the aim and originality, however, of this publication and its corresponding exhibition. Apeloig has an insatiable appetite for art, photography, cinema, architecture, literature, dance, and music, all of which he draws upon in his work. Rising to the challenge that he set at a young age, he has dedicated himself to graphic design with sensitivity and enthusiasm. The result is this visual testament to his work.

Apeloig first thought to create a monograph of his work after patiently carrying out detailed research in his studio archives; the exhibition, with its own logic and set of constraints, came later. Both book and exhibition present Apeloig's finished projects alongside their numerous preparatory sketches. Some of these sketches are drawings on paper, some are collages, while still others are entirely digital experiments. As collected here, Apeloig's works illustrate the development of graphic design's tools and techniques over the last four decades, as well as the revolution brought about by computer-aided design, which Apeloig first discovered when an intern at Total Design in Amsterdam. Ever-evolving digital tools continue to open up new techniques and avenues of enquiry for Apeloig. Let us hope this will be the case for a long time.

Many sponsors chose to support this book and its accompanying exhibition. We should like to take this opportunity to express our sincerest thanks to all of them.

Jean-Jacques Aillagon

Preface

I first met Philippe Apeloig in 2006 while helping prepare "22. Bundestreffen Forum Typografie," a typographic forum in Düsseldorf that brought together the most influential graphic designers and typographers working in Europe at the time. The forum led to my book *Schriftgestalten* (Designing and Handling Type; Niggli, 2008), which contains works exhibited at the forum, as well as participants' interviews and statements on contemporary typography and the numerous fields to which it can be applied. Philippe liked the book and asked me to help him create one about his own work.

At first I was unsure about accepting his invitation as I am not a great fan of monographs, insofar as they are frequently filled with images but no real content. Yet when Philippe showed me his project sketches dating all the way back to the 1980s, I realized that this archival material could be an extraordinary resource. I suggested that the book focus on the processes that underpin graphic creativity and present the different stages that lead to a work's realization, helping to make these processes easier to understand.

At the end of 2007, I moved to Paris from Cologne, not speaking a word of French and little English. Coming to terms with the essence of Philippe's work took me a year. The most difficult task was selecting the projects of another graphic designer with a view to interpreting his career. A lot of initial research was necessary in order to give me a precise understanding of Philippe's inventiveness, rigor, diversity, and scope. My role was more similar to that of an archivist or a historian of graphic design than an editor, which is what I was supposed to be.

The following year, in 2008, I helped organize an exhibition of Philippe's posters at Espace Topographie de l'art, a gallery in the Marais district of Paris. Planning the exhibition was easy; finding and assembling the exhibits was quite another matter. It took two people a month to track down the selected posters within the studio's vast archive. Thereafter, I established a simplified archival system that allowed easy access to each poster, and which I subsequently applied to the other different types of works in the archive. When Philippe asked me at a later date to help him organize another solo exhibition for the Université du Québec in Montreal, I was able to gather all the materials for the show in a single day. Nowadays, the way projects are archived in Philippe's studio is entirely different; the systematic filing of posters, sketches, books, printed works, and press articles has become an automatic reflex.

This book brings together a selection of Philippe's most significant designs. It showcases his completed projects and explains how each one came about, revealing their sources of inspiration and various stages of conception, from initial sketch through to realization. The publication is divided into two parts. The first is organized into thematic chapters that bring together a wide range of works in order to show Philippe's artistic references. Each project is accompanied by a text explaining its history and the rationale behind the graphic solutions employed. The second part presents preparatory drawings, photographs, collages, photocopies, and laser prints. These materials are reproduced in reverse chronological order, starting with the most recent. Studying Philippe's initial research materials allows us to comprehend how each project evolves, as well as to appreciate the number of false starts, rejected ideas, and dead ends that have to be faced before the final product can be achieved. How a graphic designer's work develops and the influence of new technology on his or her career are also revealed through the display of these sketches and working methods.

Despite our differences in age, experience, and education, Philippe and I enjoyed a fruitful collaboration. Our confrontations, even conflicts at times, helped us move forward. It is through dialogue and exchange that I have come to understand what is so unique about Philippe's work and just how unusual he is as a person. We wanted this book to bring to light the graphic processes involved in designing works as varied as a logotype, a poster, a page layout, or an animation. A brief for any one of these projects brings its own constraints, not least that of challenging the client's expectations in order to obtain the best results. The sinuous path that has to be taken through one's own thoughts and imagination is what makes a graphic designer both strong and vulnerable, and thereby a fully-fledged artist. This path is always an opportunity for discovery and digression. We have to accept we must lose ourselves in order to find ourselves!

I would like to thank Philippe for putting his trust in me throughout this entire project. Without his support, it would not have been possible. I am grateful to Anna Brugger and Yannick James in the Paris studio, and to Andreas Körner for all the photographic sessions in Stuttgart. Finally, my thanks to all those who have helped me and whose energy, patience, and knowledge supported this publication, from beginning to end.

Tino Grass

Signs of Life
Alice Morgaine

"I began my life as I shall surely end it, surrounded by books," wrote Jean-Paul Sartre in *Les Mots* (Words) in 1972.[1] Some forty years on, the endurance of print is no longer a given. From the inventions of block printing and the printing press to the dematerialization of the book today, can the printed word withstand the latest technological revolution? In 2003, the Musée des Arts et Métiers (Museum of the Arts and Trade) in Paris weighed in on this question with the following sentence (which appeared alongside a fossil of a leaf, the detail of its veins preserved forever in stone): "Nature invented print and man has used it as his memory." It is a statement that raises its own worrying questions about the function of print at a time when technological advances, some of which may be more fundamental than those of the Industrial Revolution, are scrambling and remixing communications as never before. Thousands of as yet undiscovered inventions will continue to open up endless possibilities for the written word. Nobody knows where they will lead. One of France's largest publishers has seen downloads of its texts expand tenfold in the past year without denting its paperback sales. Mainstream culture, at any rate, is sufficiently pragmatic and has learned to adapt. And though we may mourn the disappearance of bindings and gilt-edged pages, books have found other ways of appealing to the public as vast libraries and heavy encyclopedias readily lodge on laptops and smartphones.

Graphic designers are among the pioneers of this new world of signs and meanings and have enthusiastically embraced the infinite possibilities afforded by these up-to-the-minute tools of progress. Liberated by computer software that allows them to easily shape letters and treat images, designers are able to do, redo, and undo at will. They are masters now of every stage of the creative process, as if entire orchestras unto themselves, and free from the rigorous production line of yesteryear when they were dependent upon an industry of photocomposers, photoengravers, and printers. As working methods have developed, designers have taken on new responsibilities and once again acquired the status of artist – as in the past, when it was accorded to the early poster designers of the nineteenth century. Philippe Apeloig, now mid-career, is one of those to have acquired this status. He has successfully integrated print – supposedly in the process of being abolished – with digital design and has been using many of its tools for decades.

Most people do not think about which typeface they are deciphering when reading. Typography belongs to the world of things that pass by unnoticed. Behind each font, however, lies an unimaginable amount of work. As the raw material for communicating, typography is used on a daily basis in a neutral, modest, noble fashion, assisting man in his everyday exchanges. Stirring up the reader's interest in typography can transform the way he reads, inviting him to notice letters and signs as forms and thereby encouraging him to explore the text further. Typographic design is not just a mechanical procedure; the designer's aim is to make any new type as intelligible, self-explanatory, and striking as possible. Apeloig explains: "When traveling in countries where we are unable to decipher the writing, we feel lost and are forced to focus our attention on the shape of the letters and their beauty. We are frequently amazed by Japanese, Arabic, or Cyrillic script. But the Latin alphabet is just as wonderful and a source of continual invention."

For over thirty years, Philippe Apeloig has thrown himself into disrupting and experimenting with accepted forms. His unusual surname – with its German etymology: *Apfel* (apple) and *Auge* (sight or eye) – could have been handpicked for the graphic artist he has become. Apeloig's grandparents both fled the anti-Semitic pogroms in Poland to take refuge in France (in 1904 on his father's side, and 1930 on his mother's side). Apeloig was born in Paris in 1962 and should, by rights, have enjoyed a carefree, tranquil childhood in an era free from war. But a heightened sensibility and countless readings about the Holocaust and the historical persecution of Jews meant that in his youth Apeloig felt weighted down by these past traumas. A visit to Kazimierz Dolny, the Polish village of wooden houses where his carpenter grandfather had lived on the right bank of the river Vistula, devastated him. He found it devoid of its historical identity and language (Yiddish), with a cinema now in place of its synagogue. Similar to Daniel Mendelsohn, the author of *The Lost: A Search for Six of Six Million*, he determined that as a child of survivors, the memory of memories, he must speak out on behalf of all those who had been silenced. Apeloig has expressed his identification with the orphaned infant in Sergei Eisenstein's *Battleship Potemkin*, who, its mother only just shot dead, finds its pram hurtling down a flight of steps, before rolling to a stop between corpses. Surrounded by death, the innocent baby survives. For Apeloig, this scene represents "the victory of life over annihilation." "Nevertheless," he continues, "the future of this

1   Sergei Eisenstein (1898–1948)
    Battleship Potemkin, 1925
    Film still

2   Marcel Camus (1912–1982)
    Black Orpheus, 1959
    Film still

3   Federico Fellini (1920–1993)
    8½, 1963
    Film still

child is irreparably weakened. Everything has to be rebuilt." Apeloig experienced none of the atrocities of the Holocaust firsthand but in order to share this history with others he has learnt as much as possible about his ancestors' experiences and determined "to construct my life with elements that leave a lasting trace (painting, literature…)." That pledge brings other cinematic moments to mind, including the scene in Federico Fellini's film *8½* when the characters, some alive some dead, descend the steps in a magnificent hymn to life, and the conviction shared by the three slum children in Marcel Camus's film *Black Orpheus* that it is their guitar music and dancing that cause the sun to rise.

During his childhood in Vitry-sur-Seine and Choisy-le-Roi, two working-class neighborhoods near Paris, Apeloig saw himself as Dumbo, the flying elephant, who is rejected by others for being different. Classmates mocked him for choosing to play quietly and for his love of drawing and reading. Encouraged by his French teacher, however, he chose to embrace these differences and to lead a life founded on tolerance and respect for others. He also attended painting classes organized by the municipality.

3

1

One day his teacher, Maria Dèze, shared with the class Jean-Baptiste-Camille Corot's painting *The Bridge at Mantes*. Apeloig was delighted by the serenity of the landscape and the delicacy of the artist's palette, and he immediately adopted Corot as a model. He discovered Ingres, van Gogh, and Picasso around the same time. Picasso died in 1973 when Apeloig was ten years old. He still remembers the emotion in Madame Dèze's voice when she told her students the news. He asked his parents to buy him the special edition of *Paris Match* devoted to Picasso – he still owns his copy today.

As a teenager, Apeloig immersed himself in books and films, especially those of the Marx Brothers, as well as *West Side Story*, which was a real culture shock for him. Above all, he loved to dance. The local academy offered classes in classical and modern dance, jazz, and even folk dancing, and Apeloig became an ardent follower of the Indian, African, and American dance companies that performed at the Théâtre Jean Vilar in Vitry. The choreography of Martha Graham, Alwin Nikolais, and Merce Cunningham also thrilled and inspired him, and later, as a young season-ticket holder at the Théâtre de la Ville in Paris, he would lap up the performances of Pina Bausch, whose bold artistic vision he admired enormously. Apeloig seriously considered becoming a professional dancer but was aware that his competence as a dancer extended only so far (the famous Peter Principle). He did not want to remain mediocre so sought a different path. Despite the "special rapport with others that they implied, transmitting an emotion and communicating a message," he left dance and theater behind, in order to live as a typographer, surrounded by books.

After graduating from high school, Apeloig chose to study *expression visuelle* (visual expression) at Paris's École supérieure des arts appliqués (School of Applied Arts). While studying under the eminent calligrapher Roger Druet, he was made to copy page upon page of calligraphy, first in Caroline (the Gothic script used by the Carolingians, imposed by Charlemagne in the eighth century, and revived by the Florentine Humanists in the fifteenth) and then in the more gentle-looking Uncial, which is similar to the romance style (the earliest transformation of Roman capital letters into round writing). It served as a useful apprenticeship – a sort of music theory for graphic design – because you have to be able to excel technically in order to play freely with typography to the point of turning it into art, as did Max Bill and Richard Paul Lohse in Switzerland, and the brothers

Vladimir and Georgii Stenberg in Russia. "In lieu of becoming a dancer or a choreographer," Apeloig says, "I began to use graphics to re-transcribe movement, aware of the potential of manipulating typography as something alive and experimental, removed from all technical constraints." Dance and movement would always influence his work. For his final project at the École nationale supérieure des arts décoratifs (Ensad; National School of Decorative Arts), he sought "to write dance" and "make note of movement" by taking inspiration from Rudolf von Laban's notation system, which the dance theorist had invented in 1928 in Leipzig. Von Laban had built his system around the four elements that constitute movement: space, time, weight, and force. Positioned along a vertical stave, his various notation marks provided a visual indication of the duration, direction, and distances traveled in any sequence of movement, creating a "legible choreography." Laban's notation soon became the accepted reference for dance and he wrote several books on the subject, including *The Mastery of Movement* (1950), one of his last.

4 "La vie fabuleuse de Picasso"
Paris Match, April 21, 1973
Magazine

5 Jean-Baptiste-Camille Corot
(1796 – 1875)
The Bridge at Mantes, c. 1868 – 70
Oil on canvas
Musée du Louvre, Paris

5

4

6

7

8

9

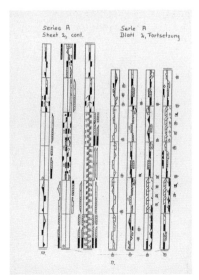

10

11

6 **Eadweard Muybridge (1830–1904)**
Running athlete, photographed
simultaneously from two viewpoints
(0.42 seconds), 1907
Photograph
Archives Kunst und Geschichte, Berlin

7 **Barbara Morgan (1900–1992)**
Martha Graham performing
Lamentation, 1941
Photograph
Barbara Morgan Archive
Courtesy of Bruce Silverstein Gallery,
New York City

8 **Pina Bausch (1940–2009)**
Nelken, 1982
Choreography
Photograph by Ulli Weiss

9 **Alwin Nikolais (1910–1993)**
Tensile Involvement, 1955
Premiere at Henry Street Playhouse,
New York City.
Choreography, costumes, music,
lighting, and sets by Alwin Nikolais
Interpreted by the Ririe-Woodbury
Dance Company
Photograph by Fred Hayes

10 **Albrecht Knust (1896–1978)**
Movement Notation:
Reading Exercises for Beginners
(Series A), c. 1931
After Rudolf von Laban's notation
system
Multimedia Center, Centre National
de la Danse, Pantin
The Albrecht Knust Collection,
donated by Roderyk Lange

11 **Jerome Robbins (1918–1998),**
Robert Wise (1914–2005)
West Side Story, 1961
Film still

12

13

14

15

16

17

18

The prints of Japanese *ukiyo-e* artist Hiroshige and Guillaume Apollinaire's poem "Il Pleut" (1918), handwritten in lines of rainfall, would further alter Apeloig's perception of how movement can be conveyed visually. He began to choreograph letters and entire words in a way similar to how the German Bauhaus painter, sculptor, and director Oskar Schlemmer had reconfigured the human form in geometric terms. "When one creates a poster, a logo, or a typeface," says Apeloig, "one is constantly referring back to the Bauhaus in one way or another."

When working at the Musée d'Orsay some years later, Apeloig came across the photographs of Étienne-Jules Marey and Eadweard Muybridge, which deconstruct the process of walking and running via a series of freeze frames. Movement and the passing of time, the links between the past and the future, have remained an integral part of Apeloig's work.

Total Design

The library at the School of Applied Arts had only three books on contemporary graphic design – two didactic works and a copy of Milton Glaser's *Graphic Design* (1973) with a psychedelic portrait of Bob Dylan on its cover – so Apeloig began to build his own collection. His first purchase was English designer F.H.K. Henrion's *Top Graphic Design* (1983), which introduced him to Roman Cieślewicz, Odermatt & Tissi, and, most importantly, Wolfgang Weingart. Apeloig dreamed of studying under Weingart, who, he later said, "turned Swiss graphic design on its head. As the pioneer of all that would subsequently be achieved through the use of computers, he is the spiritual father of contemporary graphic design."

Roger Druet was aware of his student's reading materials and interest in graphic design and suggested that Apeloig apply for an internship with the Dutch design studio Total Design during his second year. Apeloig applied and landed a three-month placement at this important design studio on the banks of Amsterdam's Herengracht canal. The summer of 1983 he worked as part of Daphne Duijvelshoff-van Peski's team, surrounded by fellow students from Switzerland, Germany, and America, all of whom were better trained. He soon familiarized himself with the work of Piet Mondrian, Kazimir Malevich, Gerrit Rietveld, Theo van Doesburg, Piet Zwart, and the Dutch De Stijl art movement, and he began to work on various poster projects and annual reports, while also learning about the fundamentals of page layout, including the grid.

Abstract graphic designer Wim Crouwel and five peers had founded Total Design in 1963. Crouwel was fascinated by the possibilities offered by computers and in 1967 designed the audacious typeface New Alphabet, an early attempt at a digital type. It consisted only of straight segments, similar to architectural elements. The computerized geometry of the letters served as a springboard for creativity. The following year, Crouwel designed a totally novel black-and-white typographic poster for the exhibition "Vormgevers" (Designers) at the Stedelijk Museum in Amsterdam and left the construction grid visible (page 208). In his brochure *New Alphabet*, published in 1967, Crouwel explained the origins and guiding principles of his almost elemental graphic approach. The brochure remains an essential read for anyone designing characters today – an introduction to the possibility of creating freely with letters. During his internship, Apeloig was lucky enough to try out Aesthedes, the latest and most sophisticated computer system available during the early 1980s. He was quick to recognize that computers would transform graphic design, both in practice and in outcome, as every aspect of typography would become easy to manipulate at will.

Total Design took a primarily functionalist approach to design but also nurtured the spirit and theories of the De Stijl movement, which could be applied to both industrial design and to typography. Crouwel himself was greatly influenced by contemporary art and he designed numerous exhibition posters for the Van Abbemuseum in Eindhoven between 1950 and 1960, and for the Stedelijk Museum between 1963 and 1985. His posters avoided the simple reproduction of a work of art, instead opting for an assertively modernist and analytically abstract typographical approach that still clearly reflected a modern aesthetic. Apeloig learned from this approach and from the questions forever being posed in the Total Design studio: "How can we turn something seemingly functional into something creative?" "How can we adjust typography to its correct scale, and intuitively manage to position and order everything perfectly, while retaining a specific emotional tension?" In 2010, aware of Apeloig's admiration for Crouwel and at the instigation of Unit Editions, the Design Museum in London invited Apeloig to create a limited-edition poster for its exhibition on the Dutch designer (page 209). The poster followed Crouwel's grid and orthodoxy to the letter. Total Design's conciseness, rigor, functionality, and highly original sophistication had a lasting influence on the idealistic, enthusiastic Apeloig, who remembers how he felt, even then, like "I was in the right place at the right time."

It was in Amsterdam that Apeloig also discovered the work of April Greiman in the book *Posters by Members of the Alliance Graphique Internationale 1960–1985*, edited by Rudolph de Harak. "Straightaway," says Apeloig, "I found a visual language that was totally different to that used by others. I didn't entirely grasp the meaning of April Greiman's 'Your Turn My Turn' poster, but it didn't matter, because its bold design was teeming with information, color, photos, textures, marks, dots, and abstract signs. The typography appeared to be floating in space in an acrobatic fashion. Furthermore, the poster was a true manifesto of creative freedom for it had been designed to be viewed in relief with special stereoscopic 3D glasses." Greiman's work, for all its imagination, sophistication, and technical and artistic achievements, was grounded in the purist, avant-garde teachings of Swiss graphic design: she had been a pupil of Wolfgang Weingart and Armin Hofmann at the Basel School of Design. Her decision to transgress their strict orthodoxy was conscious, a deliberate attempt to develop a personal style more in line with the progressive spirit of the west coast of America, where she had settled. The result was a hybrid style that combined typography, photographs, and color in collages that were free and unrestrained.

When Apeloig returned to Paris, he also returned to a training designed to prepare students for careers within advertising agencies and publishing houses. His teachers passed on insight that was generations old and assumed their students would be working with lead type. They taught the principles behind the "roughs" created for advertisements, book covers, and page layouts, how to mark up an author's typed copy, and how to order characters from a typesetter. Photography, photo-framing, and illustration were also taught. In short, the curriculum had been designed to produce skilled, professional technicians capable of transforming ideas into images using existing methods. Apeloig felt numbed and frustrated by all this technique. He also did not share the political motivations of his fellow students: "When I was a student…in Paris, the focus was mainly on socially engaged creativity, and I didn't feel at home with this dissenting manner of perceiving graphic design. At the end of the day, the visual communication issues we were presented with were exactly the same as those encountered by advertising agencies, but we were expected to take an ideological stand. I wasn't interested in becoming a political activist." He was far happier attending painting classes for sixteen hours a week: "Painting, theater, and dance were what made me dream." For Apeloig, it was the work itself that drove him, although his own moral anxieties also linked him, indeed positively strapped him, to the complexities of being Jewish, a position poignantly described by Georges Perec in *Ellis Island: A Reader and Resource Guide* as "something shapeless, almost unutterable…more of a silence, an absence, a question, a questioning, a hesitation, an anxiety: a disturbing certainty of owing one's life to chance and exile."[2] As Apeloig has confirmed: "I often have the feeling of being condemned to live on the edge of different human groups."

In 1984, Apeloig continued his education at the École nationale supérieure des arts décoratifs (Ensad), furthering his knowledge of Swiss graphic design and the work of Cieślewicz, Cassandre, and Paul Rand. In 1985, he returned to Total Design for a second internship, two years after his first, this time working under Jolijn van de Wouw. The internship coincided with the twentieth anniversary of Total Design, which was marked with an exhibition at the De Beyerd Center for Contemporary Art in Breda and the publication of an unusual trapezoid catalog, *Ontwerp: Total Design*, by Kees Broos. Soon after returning to Paris, Apeloig was hired as a graphic designer at the Musée d'Orsay, a new institution, yet to open, that would celebrate art created between 1848 and 1914, a period of transition for modern culture when both the artist's individuality and creative freedom were asserted, and numerous new techniques and approaches appeared. Apeloig joined a team of graphic designers that had worked with Bruno Monguzzi and Jean Widmer to design the museum's logo and branding. "I'll never forget that month of September 1985," says Apeloig. "Having been through an initial selection process, I found myself in the temporary premises of the public establishment that would become the Musée d'Orsay, facing a jury of well-known figures none of whom I knew. Among them, Jean Widmer, the talented graphic designer who I dreamed of having as a teacher." Apeloig was only twenty-three when his new employer dispatched him to Jean Widmer's studio for a few weeks to familiarize himself with the museum's brand and graphic approach.

The Musée d'Orsay's typeface, Walbaum (regular weight and italics only), was chosen to work with the logo because of its similarities with the nineteenth-century Didot typeface. It was only to be used in its lowercase form, except when capital letters were needed to make information clearer, as with the initials of the museum and artists' names.

19 **April Greiman (born in 1948)**
Your Turn, My Turn, 1983
Conference on interior design
Poster
Pacific Design Center

20 **Paul Rand (1914–1996)**
Dada, 1951
Book jacket of Robert Motherwell's
book *The Dada Painters
and Poets: An Anthology*, 1951
Yale University Library, New Haven

21 **Frans Lieshout (born in 1956)**
Ontwerp: Total Design, 1985
Catalogue cover for the exhibition,
20 years Total Design
Reflex, Utrecht
Center for Contemporary Art, Breda

Apeloig was put in charge of creating exhibit notices, information sheets, and educational panels, adapting them to the interiors of this former turn-of-the-century train station, which the Italian architect Gae Aulenti had transformed (pages 42–43). It was a fabulous opportunity for a young designer to work on such a prestigious national project and to collaborate with architects, art historians, and exhibition curators, all of whom were forever requesting new signs for the public, whether panels, private-view invitations, brochures, newsletters, or posters. Apeloig drew upon the historical heritage of the museum's building but endeavored to reinterpret it in as resolutely a contemporary fashion as possible. The challenge was to incorporate the uncompromisingly elegant graphic approach that had proliferated at the time the station was built (1898–1900) without succumbing to pastiche or to the re-creation of period rooms. "I was putting into practice what I had learned at Total Design," Apeloig says, "capturing people's attention by means of typography, grids, information layout, forms, and color alone."

19

20

21

Apeloig made one of his most famous posters while working at the museum: the 1987 exhibition poster "Chicago, Naissance d'une métropole" (Chicago: Birth of a Metropolis) (page 37). It was made by hand in a traditional fashion using an archival photograph placed at an angle, creating a sense of vertigo and an impression of the sheer size of the early skyscrapers. To produce the typography of the word "Chicago," Apeloig used Aesthedes software, which was then unavailable in France; he had to travel to Geneva to access the technology. He recalls:"I had already created photos of letters in perspective, but for this one I wanted a perfectly defined image. Thanks to this technology, I was able to create a sense of perspective for the typography without having to worry about the photographic process which inevitably left blurred areas on the text (due to the depth of field). What interested me in this poster was creating the illusion of a third dimension on a two-dimensional support (a flat, printed surface). I also wanted to capture movement, as if caught in mid-flight, to freeze a specific instant, a sort of gust of wind, that would sweep the text away, as if there was a before and an after this moment. 'Chicago: Birth of a Metropolis,' the first project I designed with the use of a computer, remains the most convincing poster I created for the Musée d'Orsay. I like the movement of the text which appears in the middle of the street and hugs the building as it rounds the corner at a crossroads. The syllable 'go' is intentionally provocative."

Los Angeles

Thanks to a timely grant from the French Ministry of Foreign Affairs, in 1986 Apeloig set out for the United States for the first time and arrived in Los Angeles with the intention of meeting the graphic designer April Greiman. He recalls the shock he felt on first encountering her working environment: "Upon entering her studio, I felt as if I was stepping inside one of her posters. There were colorful walls at an angle, large surfaces of fluorescent Plexiglas that projected patches of tangy colors, Mexican and Japanese objects, masks, odd pieces of furniture, shelves arranged in zigzags, phosphorescent tables that she had designed, and posters stuck up all over the place. I asked April Greiman to take me on as an intern for a year. She welcomed me at the end of 1987."

At the time, graphic designers throughout the world still worked with drawing boards, set squares, rulers, and Rotring pens, whereas in April Greiman's studio there was already a Mac Plus at each workstation. Greiman pioneered the introduction of computers as a working tool for designers. "April Greiman showed me that it was possible to be both a graphic designer and a fully-fledged artist," says Apeloig.

"She created her posters like paintings or 3D constructions. Postmodernism and Deconstructivism were all the rage in California at that time – buildings that defied weightlessness, and digital technologies that were shaking up graphic culture. Frank Gehry imposed his stamp by using cheap, poorly viewed materials such as corrugated iron, fencing, and chipboard. The magazine *Emigré* (designed and published by the Dutch graphic designer Rudy VanderLans) began circulating new typefaces in bitmap format entirely created on Apple Macintosh by Zuzana Licko. They were the work of young designers with little experience, and their letters reproduced the crude matrix of early computer screens. They opened up a new path, however, that at times contradicted the aesthetic and conceptual norms of classical typography which was still drawn with a manual, vectorial outline."

Apeloig admits, "At first, I found this new technology, which until then had been reserved for engineers, tricky. It was both disconcerting and fascinating, and led to countless blunders, but in the long run added enormously to my stylistic vocabulary." The Californians' use of computers and their consequent efficiency and turnaround speed would redefine the contours of the profession. New software meant new routes to creating page layouts, drawing, and image processing, and the rapidity and flexibility of computers introduced new working practices. Greiman was entirely at ease with all of this and did not allow herself to be put off by the pixelation of bitmap images. On the contrary, she made the geometric transformation of images and signs visible, allowing the pixels to show. She turned these micro-mosaics into typography, making the most of their roughness, erasing details, and treating them as pictorial matter. The early days of CAD (computer-aided design) were a far cry from today's high-definition technology. Printing a photograph and text in low definition, in rough-hewn fashion, and intentionally leaving the bitmap rendition in close-up was tantamount to the work of an artist. Every now and then, Greiman opted for more sophisticated equipment, including the famous Quantel Paintbox used by cinema technicians, among others. Her poster for "The Modern Poster" exhibition at New York's Museum of

Modern Art (MoMA) in 1988 was designed in ultra-sophisticated laboratories where she worked day and night, alongside technicians who shaped and perfected her images, scrupulously respecting the way her thoughts flicked back and forth, and her love of experimentation. Apeloig admired Greiman's approach and would be influenced by her aesthetic: "The construction of 'The Modern Poster,' with the rather vectorial appearance of its spiral based on the golden ratio, served as inspiration for my design for the limited-edition fine-art book titled *Comme un coursier indompté* (Like an Indomitable Racehorse) produced by the Imprimerie nationale (National Printers) in 1989 for the Bicentenary of the French Revolution (page 110). The 3D effects were created with computer software that also enabled a sense of transparency that would have been impossible to achieve otherwise. April Greiman adopted a technique of collages and overlaying grids similar to Wolfgang Weingart's use of photographic grids, but with images taken from TV screens that she reworked and distorted to the point of abstraction. Above all, she envisaged graphic design spatially: x and y coordinates were, for her, insufficient, and she inevitably added a third axis, z, which was that of depth, to create the illusion of perspective on the page, which itself remained flat but assumed volume, creating optical effects and an optical illusion. It was a case of 'seeing further.'"

22

23

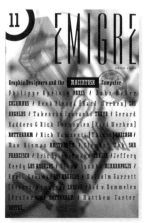

24

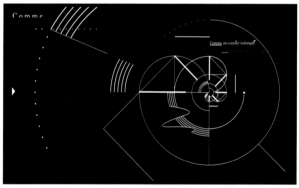

25

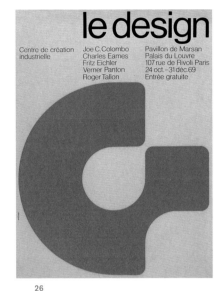

26

27

On returning to France, Apeloig opened his own small agency in Paris, determined to apply American dynamism to European thinking. In 1992 Richard Peduzzi, the director of Ensad, invited him to join the teaching staff of his former alma mater. Apeloig accepted and would teach at the renowned art school until 1998. Fellow teachers included the Swiss duo Rudi Meyer and Peter Keller, who had already trained a large number of students in the twenty or so years they had been teaching typography there. Jean Widmer had been recruited in the 1960s to modernize the graphic design curriculum, first as a professor and later as director of design studies. Inspired by the Ulm School of Design, he introduced the idea of interdisciplinary learning, touching on the theories of Johannes Itten, and invited other Swiss graphic designers to come and share their knowledge in Paris. The influence of these Swiss instructors on French graphic design cannot be understated but, fifteen years on, the French were clearly uncomfortable with this dominance and began to react against the severity of teaching practices in which typography always took pride of place. For the Swiss, the aim of page layout was first and foremost to convey information in a clear and legible fashion, and students had to learn that even the most beautiful of characters, if laid out badly or spaced awkwardly, were at best unpleasant to read, at worst illegible. In contrast, Apeloig wanted typography to be viewed and taught in an experimental fashion that could enable freedom of expression, as with any other artistic medium. It was not a question of undermining the importance of drawing, or the way in which characters and the page layout were created, but of showing that with computers changing working practices and making things quicker and more accurate many more options were now available.

In 1993, Apeloig became involved with two projects with clearly defined specifications. He was invited to design the logo and visual identity of the Carré d'Art in Nîmes, for which he was obliged to use the Rotis typeface designed in the 1980s by the German graphic designer Otl Aicher (page 224). (Norman Foster, the museum's architect, insists that this typeface accompany all his architecture.) At the same time, thirsty for new experiences, Apeloig accepted the artistic directorship of the women's fashion magazine *Jardin des Modes*, for which Milton Glaser had designed the logo and layout (page 115). That same year the French Ministry of Culture awarded him a fellowship at the French Academy of Art at the Villa Medici in

28

Rome, where he soon locked horns with the powers that be over their prevarication in getting computers up and running. The highly ambitious project that Apeloig had set himself while there – creating a new typeface, maybe even several – made no allowance for delays. Of typography, Apeloig says: "Typography is the very essence of drawing: a balance between full and empty, light and shadow. Midway between science and art, it is a discipline that is both functional and poetic – a precise yet arbitrary subject. I like it to be modern, experimental, almost clumsy. Typography is more alive when it is slightly awkward and fragile, for it is the original and radical expression of the artist's unfettered feelings. A balance has to be found between the freedom to create and the functional role of graphically designed objects. My early characters were thickset and sculptural, like monoliths pierced with lines and hollowed out here and there to form recognizable signs. These openings were what enabled the letters to be differentiated from each other, and their broad silhouettes made them legible from afar, perfect for the titles of posters. These characters were designed in a free and easy fashion, without all the stress that a specialist designer would normally have to cope with in conforming to countless technical issues regarding legibility and durability. However, I did not wish to break up the delicate balance between form, meaning, and usage (see pages 162–163). To this end, I designed the typeface Octobre, named after the festival for which I designed it: 'Octobre en Normandie' (page 85). I bought a school notebook with small squares and quite simply began to blacken in some of the squares until a letter formed, then another, and so on (page 358). I started putting squares and rectangles together, or broke them up to form random typographic signs. Pure geometry can be applied to designing letters just as it is applied to design and the visual arts. It was an experimental, heterogeneous, mechanical, and truly unpredictable process that involved following the crisscross pattern of a grid, in keeping with everything I had gleaned in Holland, and from observing the amazing pioneering work of Jurriaan Schrofer."

Apeloig's time at the Villa Medici provided a welcome break from his regular workload and allowed him to concentrate on his own project uninterrupted by other jobs and commissions. "I drew a few letters, progressing from paper to computer screen. However, I soon woke up to the enormity of the task I had undertaken, realizing that it would take considerably more than a year to create a new typeface. Such an undertaking is, nonetheless, a unique opportunity for carrying

out research unfettered by constraints. I have found myself disorientated on a number of occasions when creating typefaces, not knowing exactly where things would lead me. With such a vast and complex subject, I try to approach it freely, at times ignoring basic typographic rules in order to pursue an experimental path more appropriate to the project. I think typography is capable of distancing itself from the constraints of realism. I force myself to rationalize the letter designs, compressing them into geometric forms. The primitive appearance of my typographic characters refers back to early computer drawings, before the days of curves and diagonals. I have returned to these early letter designs on a number of occasions and am still perfecting them even now. Thanks to the inestimable assistance of young typographers, highly skilled in computing, my typefaces continue to be modified. This process includes certain technological adaptations and the addition of new glyphs. I comment on and correct the detailed designs before they are converted into vectorial files, the aim being to design characters that can be circulated and made available to other graphic designers, because I believe that is important. After my stay at the Villa Medici, I continued to design typographic characters whenever I had the opportunity of creating a visual identity." One such opportunity came from the French librarians' association, the Association des Bibliothécaires de France (ABF); since 2006 Apeloig has been responsible for their graphic identity (pages 260–265). The academic journal *Afrique contemporaine* (Contemporary Africa) offered another (pages 204–205). The process is the same each time: a few hand-drawn lines, and then forms start to appear based on architecture, sculpture, furniture, or other objects.

Sources

Upon his return from Rome, recently crowned with glory on two fronts – a new member of the elite Alliance Graphique Internationale (an association for the world's leading graphic artists and designers) and artistic consultant to the Louvre – Apeloig began to forge a path whose impact originates in flashes of thought, deep reflection, and his unusual and atypical literary and visual background. With his very short blond hair, thin face, and slender, austere build – similar to that of Le Corbusier – Apeloig has a slightly Jansenist look about him, and his way of working echoes that of the Dutch theologian: constant questioning interspersed with moments of self-doubt,

26 Jean Widmer (born in 1929)
    Le design, 1969
    Poster
    Musée national d'Art moderne –
    Centre Georges Pompidou, Paris

27 Rudi Meyer (born in 1943)
    23e Festival du Marais, Paris, 1986
    Poster

28 Peter Keller (1944 – 2010)
    SNCF Timetable, 1976
    Brochure

self-criticism, and hesitation, but nurtured by numerous cultural sources. In short, a far cry from his youthful fits of laughter, lyrical enthusiasms, and passion for chocolate. Apeloig shares his working methods with the four or five graphic designers and interns in his studio (he carefully avoids the use of the word "agency") at any one time. They all eat together in the middle of the day, taking time out to debate and discuss ideas gleaned from people the world over in the tranquil and harmonious light-filled space.

Some of the younger designers in the studio are not always so keen on this form of phalanstery and remain unconvinced by Apeloig's proselytizing and his insatiable appetite for books, films, and exhibitions. But Apeloig is undeterred and considers such sustenance essential (in the etymological sense of the word) and not to be dissimulated. He acknowledges his sources openly, referencing them with enthusiasm and admiration. For him, creativity is born from engaging with the creative output of others, enriched by history, the spirit of the times, and the subtle differences of the past. The result is either blindingly simple or spectacularly modern depending on the case. Apeloig confides that "Matisse's painting *The Dance* combines everything I love about art: movement, rhythm, areas of solid color, simplified forms, and the notion of scenic space." He is also deeply moved by Joan Miró's work, with its naïve, poetic, childish vision of the world – an aesthetic often found in contemporary graphics. The works of Eileen Gray and Carl Andre, as well as some of the drawings of Sol LeWitt, with their repetitive systems and geometry, have also influenced Apeloig's typefaces. Interestingly, none of this thinking and studying of art and literature, always undertaken in an unhurried, leisurely manner, is immediately visible in Apeloig's works, which appear to have been perfectly thought through and structured, then assembled like high-precision machines. First, there's the impact, then a feeling of surprise, a smile… Only later, upon scrutiny and closer analysis, does the work start to reveal his utopian dreams for a just and peaceful world.

There's something quixotic about Apeloig's drawings, words, and motivations, as well as something that has come from afar – wounds never received, wars never known, organized massacres from which he was spared, a totalitarianism never suffered. A personal and universal sense of responsibility for every being on earth pervades his work. As Antoine de Saint-Exupéry said in his book *Flight to Arras*: "Each of us individually is responsible for everyone." [3] This sentiment also appears in the works of the Russian Constructivist artist El Lissitzky, who illustrated Ilya Ehrenburg's short story "Shifs karta" (Boat ticket) by sticking Hebrew characters onto a handprint. "Lissitzky's use of an outstretched hand in guise of a refusal", says one of the artist's biographers, "matches Malevich's statement, 'That the rejection of the old world of arts be marked on the palm of your hands' (from Unovis leaflet No. 1)." [4] Apeloig looked to this hand and to Chagall's *Self-Portrait with Seven Fingers* when designing the logo for the Musée d'art et d'histoire du Judaïsme (Jewish Art and History Museum) in Paris. The museum chose not to go with this symbol, however, preferring Apeloig's 1997 black-and-white stylized design of a lit menorah, which is evocative of a seal, an ancient coin, or a hallmark (page 230).

Apeloig has, from the outset of his career, worked predominantly on cultural projects, particularly institutional ones. Pierre Rosenberg, curator-in-chief of the paintings department at the Louvre, chaired the scholarship selection jury that sent Apeloig to the Villa Medici in 1993. Later, as director of the Louvre, he entrusted Apeloig with the upkeep of the museum's visual identity, which was originally designed by Grapus in 1989. Apeloig's first poster, celebrating the 100th anniversary of the Society of Friends of the Louvre in 1996, featured close-ups of twenty artworks from the museum's seven departments, a sort of photographic who's who (page 51). Over the next nine years, Apeloig's collaboration with the Louvre grew even closer, with the new director, Henri Loyrette, appointing him artistic director with his own in-house team. In 2013, Apeloig created the logo for the Louvre Abu Dhabi and designed its signage in collaboration with the architect Jean Nouvel (page 279).

In July 2011, the French Ministry of Culture commemorated the 450th anniversary of the death of typographer-publisher Claude Garamont and invited a number of graphic designers, including Apeloig, to design personal tributes. Apeloig rarely uses the Garamond typeface in his work but explains: "I chose Garamond for the visual identity of the Conservatoire National Supérieur d'Art Dramatique (National Academy of Dramatic Arts) because it echoed the literary education given to the students there, a combination of contemporary and classical French theater (page 90). The version of Garamond I chose was the one designed by Robert Slimbach for Adobe in 1989, which harks back to classicism while using contemporary forms.

29 **Henri Matisse (1869–1954)**
The Dance, 1909
Oil on canvas
The Museum of Modern Art, New York

30 **Max Bill (1908–1994)**
Konkrete Kunst, Kunsthalle, Basel, 1944
Poster
Museum für Gestaltung, Zurich

31 **Sol LeWitt (1928–2007)**
All Single, Double, Triple, and Quadruple Combinations of Lines and Color in Four Directions in One-, Two-, Three-, and Four-Part Combinations, 1970
Ink on paper
The Museum of Modern Art, New York

32 **Eileen Gray (1878–1976)**
Screen, 1922
Victoria and Albert Museum, London

The drawing of the characters is remarkable, and the proportions of the letters in relation to each other are the work of a
genius. The fact that it has been adapted for new technology is
also very helpful. I admire and respect Garamond, but it is
complete in itself. I can't see what one can add to it without
disfiguring or mistreating it. After the modernist era, it was
seemingly impossible to neglect the wealth of grotesque
and sans serif typographic characters; it would have been
tantamount to wiping out an entire facet of art history.
Personally, I've always found their geometric construction
rather charming. Graphic design and typography can be used
for artistic expression in the same way as *haute couture*
and architecture. Every period has its own requirements,
trends, developments, and schisms. Typography belongs to
this evolving world, sometimes in a brutal fashion but more
often in a silent or transparent manner." The upheaval of
a profession awash with new technologies has encouraged
graphic designers to expand their areas of intervention, from
designing a logo to creating film sets, from theater design
to applying one's color expertise to architecture.

29

30

31

32

Cooper Union

Philippe Apeloig's logical turn of mind and Surrealist flashes of inspiration are clearly suited to teaching and have successfully captured the attentions of the young ever since he started at Ensad in 1992. In 1999, he took on a lifetime professorship at the Cooper Union School of Art in New York, while also being appointed curator of its Herb Lubalin Study Center of Design and Typography. At the same time as carrying out these two roles, he organized a number of exhibitions, including ones on Otl Aicher, contemporary Chinese graphic design ("Chinese Graphic Design towards the International Sphere"), Massin ("Massin in continuo"), and, notably, curated one on the work of Jean Widmer ("A Devotion to Modernism") (pages 118–119). Apeloig also initiated a lecture series, "Graphicooper," which ran until 2003 and involved graphic designers from all over the world (page 117).

Apeloig was surprised by his American students from the outset, both as a teacher at the Rhode Island School of Design, where he was invited to teach during the winter of 1998, and at Cooper Union the following year. Their principal references were advertising and popular culture, and, naturally, a multimedia patchwork. Surrounded by impenetrable, aggressive visual pollution, they had internalized the brash language of advertising and Apeloig wondered how amid all this urban distraction they could possibly incorporate other references. In contrast, his Ensad pupils in Paris had been exposed to a more cultivated aesthetic environment. The French education system had put the emphasis on theory and the development of their critical faculties, whereas his American students were the children of Pop Art and embraced consumer society in their work, as if entering a world of undiluted sensations.

Their fearlessness meant that everything that passed between their hands or in front of their eyes could be made their own. This approach was better suited to diversification and had a profound influence on Apeloig's teaching style. His American students were not afraid of transgressing the rules of "proper drawing," or of pairing Western methods with those from other cultures. "I really liked my American students," Apeloig says. "At times, I was scared by their thirst for knowledge because they gave absolute credence to what I was transmitting to them. They were ambitious, hard-working, and open to debate, and took their studies very seriously."

A Conscientious Approach

Since 1997, Apeloig has been creating graphics for the posters and programs of the Fête du livre, an annual book festival dedicated to foreign literature in Aix-en-Provence. Faced with the daunting but enjoyable challenge of producing graphics to accompany the words of major writers from around the world, Apeloig has immersed himself in the writing of authors such as Philip Roth, Toni Morrison, and Kenzaburō Ōe, experimenting with ways of transcribing their literary universe through graphic design (pages 176–189). The portraits and themes he has devised for the festival over the years – for example, "Lire la Caraïbe" (Reading the Caribbean), "L'Asie des écritures croisées" (An Asia of Intersecting Writing: A Real Novel), and, more recently, "Bruits du monde" (Noises of the World) – have become iconic to us today and were the result of intense intellectual research.

Similar consideration led to Apeloig's 2004 brand work for the Istituto Universitario di Architettura di Venezia (University Institute of Architecture, Venice), in which the school's initials, IUAV, were symmetrically placed one on top of another like the floors of a building. The resulting logo, which is legible recto or verso, is deceptively simple, as if it had always existed, and constitutes an important benchmark in the work of Apeloig's studio (page 236). He devised a similarly harmonious and coherent logo two years later for the Direction des musées de France, the organization in charge of administering France's public museums (page 226).

The layout of any art book tells a story, with a beginning, a climax, and an ending. Its cover acts like a trailer for a film: it has to make you want to discover its contents straightaway. "When I design a book," says Apeloig, "I transform myself into a fashion designer, clothing the book in keeping with its format, letting myself be won over by the complete range of materials and finishing techniques available." Guided by his love of the written word, he tries to explore unusual publishing genres and sometimes designs limited editions. The book's contents have to be dramatized, its design sparking off a sense of familiarity in readers that will make them want to read it. A graphic designer must anticipate the reader's gestures and glances, using the rhythm of the page layout and visual accents to lead the gaze in what could be described as controlled improvisation.

Of course, graphic design can be seen as an art form, but, as Apeloig points out, "Talent is used to help put across a message or piece of information for a client. The graphic designer's vocation is similar to that of an actor whose task it is to create a character and to recite an author's text in the clearest and most personal way possible. His interpretation reveals his genius. If the text is incomprehensible and the role barely credible, one might say he had performed badly and that the piece was a failure. Similarly, the graphic designer must respect his client's requirements. His task is to interpret them visually. If he changes direction or monopolizes the argument, rendering it indecipherable, he has failed. He has to take account of the way the public perceives his images. A graphic designer's skill consists of finding a visual concept that makes [his] presence felt in an obvious yet original way, and that is, of course, easy to remember."

It is unusual for a graphic designer to have prior knowledge of a subject when he first meets with a client. Everything has to be learned, "and I adore that," says Apeloig. Restraint, simplicity, and complexity are the key words here, but the thought process is long and winding. Apeloig therefore often uses old film-editing techniques: "I cut ideas into pieces, putting them back together in a different order. I play around with them, constructing my indecision until the composition looks strong enough to work its way into the public's visual memory. My job is to perturb."

The poster, in terms of ideas, intrigue, and visual impact, has its own status within the world of graphic design. It is as if its exposure to the popular approbation of the street has made it more universal, elevating it onto a pedestal and thereby confirming the graphic designer's status as artist. The poster tradition was shaped first by the early French poster designers – Henri de Toulouse-Lautrec, Pierre Bonnard, Jules Chéret – who were first and foremost painters, followed by the artists of the Vienna Secession movement, Cassandre, and, later, the famous Swiss designers who created posters that were more technical and informative, less decorative and lyrical. Poster design is a relatively free form of expression that clearly illustrates its maker's talent and provides instant visibility. Nowadays, with mass communication and marketing techniques increasingly controlling our imagination's freedom to roam, graphic designers continue to produce posters for cultural institutions and community services, but the days of the printed poster are under threat. Giant screens increasingly

appear in public spaces throughout cities, gradually replacing billboards. They have already changed the urban landscapes of certain American cities (for example, Times Square in New York and Las Vegas). The existence of interactive masterpieces may indicate the emergence of an entirely new digital art form. Apeloig himself has been creating animations in increasing numbers: for the *New York Times Style Magazine* ("T Constructivist") (page 143), for a graphic design festival in Échirolles ("Les écritures"), and especially for New Year's e-cards (pages 222–223, 265, 268–269). The use of new technologies does not, however, alter his creative process, which still depends entirely on the imagination and, sometimes, on the relationship with the client.

It goes without saying that the appropriate spark of creative genius can only be found if there is complete trust between designer and client. A client who is not prepared to take risks and constantly seeks the advice of others will inevitably compromise the result, which will lose intensity if it becomes a work of consensus. Apeloig has successfully carried out many collaborative ventures with, among others, the French Institute Alliance Française (FIAF) in New York, the Voies navigables de France (Navigable Waterways of France), the silversmiths Puiforcat, Moeller Fine Art, and the team behind the 2010 Yves Saint Laurent exhibition. Little is routine in the graphic designer's work. Apeloig is accustomed to being thrown into wildly divergent fields where he has to adapt quickly to disparate commissions.

In line with his all-consuming cultural appetite, Apeloig is a discerning and compulsive reader. Particular favorites include Claude Lévi-Strauss's *A World on the Wane* (1955) and *The Raw and the Cooked* (1964), which brought him face to face with other world cultures, *One Hundred Years of Solitude* (1967) by Gabriel Garcia Márquez, as well as works by Michel Tournier, Franz Kafka, Guy de Maupassant, Simone de Beauvoir, Jean-Paul Sartre, and Raymond Carver. His taste in art is equally eclectic, ranging from Carpaccio, Velázquez, Zurbarán, and Holbein to Bonnard, Matisse, Mondrian and Rothko to Ellsworth Kelly, James Turrell, Walter De Maria, and Bill Viola. Apeloig knows how to make sense out of the apparent chaos of all these influences: go straight to the point; make light of the constraints of the commission; stay subtly subversive; and, every now and then, sneak off to make a drypoint print. Apeloig is fascinated by certain tightrope walkers such as Philippe Petit, who in 1974 walked across the space between the twin towers of New York's World Trade Center. He frequently merges features of graphic design with these dangerous lines, associating this ephemeral activity, performed without a safety net, with graphic design, which in urban environments also disappears almost as quickly as it appears. This is the case for posters, newspapers, magazines, flyers, and all kinds of printed publicity material. Logos, signs, and books stay with us for longer, but new technologies have sped up the production rate of instantaneous graphics and considerably reduced their lifespan. If printed matter endures, its contents frozen, the screen image lacks such permanence. It is extremely versatile, and the information it contains can be altered at any time. Impermanence can be reassuring. A poster rarely remains visible for more than a week or two before it is covered over with another poster. This echoes the way our visual memory works for which image, symbol, or message will remain forever engraved upon the collective unconscious? Yet Apeloig is not averse to looking back to his earlier works. His posters may not all be equally powerful, but he considers them all as he would a painting. Occasionally, therefore, he will reprint one to give it a second life as a limited-edition print (printing forty at most). Apeloig confides: "I end up finding the time, freedom of mind, and financial means to alter the poster design and print it as I imagine it." *Mutatis mutandis* (changing those things that need to be changed). The lengthy process of redesigning posters and reprinting them contributes to the transformation of the graphic designer into an independent author, as well as a producer.

In 2005, Apeloig designed the poster for "De La Lorraine: Histoire, mémoires, regards contemporains" (Of the Lorraine: History, Memory, a Contemporary Look), an exhibition devoted to this northeastern region of France that was held at the Musée des Beaux-Arts in Nancy and the Musée de la Cour d'Or in Metz (page 169). The poster's abstract typeface was inspired by the region's textile industry, specifically the embroidery work from the Vosges area to which Apeloig added a somewhat harsh, contemporary dimension. The embroidery on this poster is just one example of how fabrics have inspired Apeloig to create a handmade jumble of graphic spontaneity and minutely plaited typographic elements (the posters for "Typo/Typé" and "Wole Soyinka" are two other examples; pages 170 and 184). Indeed, some of his work could even be described as typographic tapestries. To create the woven grids that appear

on his "Vivo in Typo" poster (page 173) and his poster for the 2010 Crossing the Line Festival (page 173), Apeloig overlapped punctuation marks and abstract letters selected for their forms: the vertical stroke of a capital *I*, the square shape of a capital *L*, and the almost perfect circle of a lower-case *o*. He repeated these letters several times, varying their weights and point sizes, blending and overlaying them, intervening with their kerning and line spacing, all in order to create dense meshes – surfaces that play with light and shadow as if drawn on grainy paper with a Conté crayon. Where there's texture, there can also be transparency, and words can be erased or super-imposed to grasp their meaning. This impression of thickness or intangible fiber – the "special link" – produces a powerful and poetic visual effect as light emanates from the white paper through the weave of letters, allowing them to appear and disappear. Apeloig claims this framework is the very foundation of his work and thus the perfect analogy for his commitment to weaving together ideas and language into a cohesive social fabric – to intertwining in all his work the threads of teamwork with the sharing and generosity of spirit that smooth our passage through life.

—

1 All the quotation translations in this essay are the work of the present translator.

2 Georges Perec, *Ellis Island: A Reader and Resource Guide*, New York, The New Press, 1997.

3 Antoine de Saint-Exupéry, *Flight to Arras*, New York, Reynal & Hitchcock, 1942.

4 Unovis leaflet No. 1, 1920.

33 Philippe Petit (born in 1949)
Tightrope walking at the
World Trade Center, New York, 1974
Photographs

34 Philippe Apeloig
Vis pour nous/Vis sans nous, 2001
Poster made for the exhibition entitled
"Au cœur du mot" (At the heart of
the word) held at the Galerie Anatome
in 2001, based on a family photograph
taken in Paris circa 1938, showing
Philippe Apeloig's maternal
grandparents, the Rozenbergs, and
their children, a few years after their
arrival in France.
Silkscreen poster
118 × 176 cm (46½ × 69¼ in.)
Printer: Arts Graphiques de France
See page 323

34

33

A is for Apeloig
Ellen Lupton

A consistent vision pervades the design endeavors of Philippe Apeloig. Like a body of water, his body of work is an ever-moving mass that supports diverse forms at levels both macro and micro, its surface shimmering with possibility. The flash of a discordant influence, the damaged skin of an historical photograph, a classic detail borrowed from a traditional letterform: such specks of otherness glint with their own energy from within the slick molasses of Apeloigian time and space. Through a restless process of searching and sketching, Apeloig explores concepts in multiple directions, moving from software to pen, and back again. In his search for a moment of resolution, he generates dozens of variations, splintering text across complex grids, slicing, grafting, and obscuring letterforms in his quest to learn how far beneath the plane of familiarity a shape can plunge before it loses its power to communicate. His creative process most closely resembles that of a painter who returns again and again to certain themes and techniques, each time armed with new content and experiences.

Apeloig's career began in earnest when he was very young – a student, really – and he was able to develop his own style, while still generously acknowledging the forces that shaped his outlook. Over time, he has crafted a visual language strongly connected with rhythm, structure, pattern, and choreography. Many graphic designers avoid conceding direct sources of influence from within the design world; they might speak of architects, filmmakers, or philosophers, but not reference their own peers – or even their own teachers – as touch points in their development. Not so for Apeloig, who carries around his admiration for a few key figures as a story he must tell. His frank confessions are warm with gratitude and convey no urge to assert his own triumphs over those of his mentors. And yet triumph he has, forging his own voice out of the systems and structures of graphic design.

What did it mean to become a designer in France during the early 1980s? Apeloig describes the decade as a "manifesto break" for graphic designers as technological innovations forced practitioners to learn – and invent – new skills without any established basis in methodology or theory, or even in standards of beauty and appropriateness. Apeloig recalls: "Even if we were full of political hopes for a better world, ready to change society, the birth of computer graphics had turned the practice upside down for any young designer arriving on the working scene." Prior to transitioning from the confines of art school into the heady rush of this rapidly changing work environment, Apeloig's training and education were traditional, his interests intellectual; he learned to craft calligraphy by hand and studied the theories of Roland Barthes and Jean Baudrillard.

Within the French design establishment of Apeloig's youth, many of the leading figures were Swiss, including Adrian Frutiger, Jean Widmer, and Peter Knapp. They had moved to France during the late 1950s and early 1960s and brought with them a structured modernity that offered an alternative to the prevailing aesthetic and practice of the French poster artists. These artists include Raymond Savignac, Bernard Villemot, and A. M. Cassandre, robust picture-makers who worked similarly to painters and whose mastery of the arts of reproduction resulted in images with dramatic graphics and maximum impact. In book publishing, the designers Massin and Pierre Faucheux developed their own French touch for pocket books and the publications of the big publishing houses, from Gallimard to Le Club Français du Livre.

The dominance of Swiss rationalism had begun to rupture by the 1970s. The May 1968 protests in France had infused the arts with an attitude of resistance, while Polish poster art, with its fearless questioning and clever iconography, had opened up a fresh vein of practice in graphic design. Roman Cieślewicz had come to work in Paris from Poland during the early 1960s, becoming a French citizen in 1971. Just as the Push Pin Studio in New York was forging a Pop mentality in graphic design, Cieślewicz used painting, drawing, collage, and photomontage to challenge the international Swiss style (though in a less commercial and cheerful manner than his American counterparts). In 1970, the French design cooperative Grapus formed, its founders united by the teachings of the Warsaw-based designer Henryk Tomaszewski. Grapus pioneered a graphic language that used hand-lettering and raw production methods to foreground political ideas in the public sphere.

In 1977, Jean Widmer created the iconic logo for the Centre Georges Pompidou, which became the starting point for the French tradition of designers creating sophisticated branding for museums and cultural festivals. Thereafter, the majority of influential graphic design commissions in France came

1 Jean Widmer (born in 1929),
   Ernst Hiestand (born in 1935)
   Centre Georges Pompidou, Paris, 1977
   Logotype

2 Jean Widmer,
   Bruno Monguzzi (born in 1941)
   Musée d'Orsay, Paris, 1986
   Logotype

3 Roman Cieślewicz (1930–1996)
   Paris-Moscou 1900–1930, 1979
   Poster
   Centre Georges Pompidou, Paris

1

from the cultural sphere. Posters were typically produced for theaters, museums, and arts organizations, a situation that holds true today, as is evident in Apeloig's own career.

Coming of age in the 1980s, Apeloig belonged to a generation of designers educated in tools and methods that were no longer of much use in the professional world. Technology pushed designers to experiment in new ways and to generate a self-made process. Apeloig may have been a child of the utopian 1960s but he made the most of the challenge, looking left and right to understand the French design context while bringing to the table techniques learned during internships in Amsterdam and Los Angeles. "We had to invent a new method of working with new tools. We were at the hinge of a radical turn," Apeloig notes. "We had no other choice than to become mutants. Perhaps unconsciously, we form (or sculpt) day after day the transformation of graphic design. Perhaps we move forward like blind people without knowing clearly how our practice will evolve." Apeloig's distinct approach to graphic design reflects his fascination with modernist systems, as well as his need to rattle the apple cart. His creative process of constant searching defies stasis and rest.

Apeloig was hired by the Musée d'Orsay in 1985 following two internships at the legendary studio Total Design in Amsterdam that had given him training wholly different to that of other young French designers. While design education in Paris was one part critical theory and one part handicraft, working at Total Design was hands on and technical. Immersed in the day-to-day workings of the office, Apeloig absorbed a function-al mindset whereby typography, grid systems, and early computer-graphics software defined the daily rigors of design. In Amsterdam, he also discovered the Dutch De Stijl movement and the abstract paintings of Kazimir Malevich, then on display at the Stedelijk Museum.

One of Apeloig's most famous posters is among his earliest and was created for the 1987 exhibition "Chicago, Naissance d'une métropole" (Chicago: Birth of a Metropolis) at the Musée d'Orsay (page 36); Apeloig had been recently appointed an in-house designer for the new museum. On the poster, the word "Chicago" turns a corner, so to speak, wrapping itself around a long urban block in that great wind-swept city. The folded text foregrounds the syllable "go," emphasizing the city's dynamism. Apeloig performed this act of magic using an early CAD (computer-aided design) typesetting system, which

he had seen in action at Total Design. To bend the type around the right angles of architecture, he used an algorithm that distorted the shape of each character, thinning out the strokes in the vertical axis. This technical solution was part of a longer process that began with drawing and sketching and ended with a composite of the digitally manipulated type, a duotone photograph, and other conventional graphic and typographic elements. At the time, such diverse elements could not be handled within a single software environment so Apeloig worked in a manner both old and new, assembling his components via technological means and creating a mockup by hand; he even shaded a black-and-white photocopy with a brown pencil to simulate a duotone photograph (page 374).

Compelling as the poster is, it remains something of an anomaly for Apeloig, a one-time solution to a singular problem rather than an open avenue of inquiry. Apeloig would find those avenues elsewhere, discovering a set of techniques that he could work and rework into his own signature. Though he continued to make software his ally, never shying away from its constructive and destructive potential and always pressing against the constraints of two-dimensional space, he would come to use digital tools in a more painterly, less illustrative, style. His logo for the festival Octobre en Normandie (October in Normandy; 1990) used digital distortion to blur the massive pixels of the letterforms, creating layers of depth that lie parallel to the picture plane (page 78). This blurring across multiple planes recurs in Apeloig's stunning graphics for "Bewegte Schrift" (Moving Type; 2011), an exhibition held at the Museum für Gestaltung (Museum of Design) in Zurich. Here, Apeloig used stacked grids of glowing pixels to portray distance and change (page 206). In a lengthy process of development, he tested different levels of sharpness to achieve this impression of movement and multiple dimensions, while preserving readability. The design adapted gracefully from print to motion: animated graphics appeared on a giant screen in the Zurich train station and at the museum.

Few structures are more ingrained in a designer's vocabulary than the grid, the network of coordinates that organizes nearly every page of content, whether actively or indifferently. The Swiss rationalist designers endowed the grid with a utopian edge in the 1950s and 1960s and it later became the restrictive vernacular of desktop publishing, whose graphical interfaces offer instant gutters, guidelines, and columns. Apeloig's grids are more dynamic, complex, and overt; they

often sit on top of the page rather than in the background and drive forward the construction process rather than supporting it.

Apeloig discovered the potential of the grid during his internships at Total Design, where he worked directly with Daphne Duijvelshoff-van Peski and Jolijn van de Wouw, who in turn assisted the studio's founder, Wim Crouwel. Designers at the firm produced their sketches by hand on tracing paper, always with a sheet of Rotring graph paper underneath. All solutions were pursued typographically, in contrast with French designers' reliance on illustration and lettering. The preferred typeface was Univers, and nearly always sans serif. For Apeloig, "This strict approach was a symbol of modernity."

Inspired by Crouwel, Apeloig embraced the grid as both a generative tool and system of organization. While Crouwel's grids are largely rational in their outcome, however, Apeloig's structural nets seek out a greater diversity of forms and relationships, openly embracing that which is awkward, mismatched, or disjunctive. The grid serves not only to control and regulate but also to splinter, deform, and dissolve. At its finest grain, the grid becomes a filter or screen that decomposes shapes and surfaces into bits. The collision of strange shapes in the poster for the 2010 exhibition "Radical Jewish Culture: Scène musicale New York" (The New York Music Scene) finds an arrhythmic oddity and persistent order in the mechanical heartbeat of the grid; modular letters float over hand-scrawled notes by composer John Zorn (page 202). To give the lettering a sense of depth, Apeloig produced a laser-cut stencil of the custom-drawn characters. Spraying the stencil with powdered charcoal, he created drawings that were later digitally retouched and overlapped to produce shadows inside the letterforms, enhancing a sense of three dimensions. Life seeps in through the cracks in the grid.

In Apeloig's poster for the 2007 exhibition "Wole Soyinka: La maison et le monde" (Wole Soyinka: The House and the World), the usually transparent, ethereal grid becomes physical and opaque (page 184). To celebrate the work of this esteemed Nigerian author, Apeloig applied the traditional weaving techniques of West Africa's Yoruba people to the writer's portrait, slicing two copies of the image into narrow strips of contrasting color and tone and then methodically weaving them together by hand. The material pixelation resulting from this process added layers of depth and disturbance to the author's

unwavering gaze. Apeloig created numerous variations of the underlying image and its typographic overlay before arriving at the final poster. His sketches show how he experimented with different levels of abstraction and ways of incorporating typography on the surface of the image, shuttling between physical and digital manipulations.

Apeloig's fascination with deformed and overlapping grids reflects the influence of the Swiss designer Wolfgang Weingart, who subverted the tradition of Swiss rationalist typography beginning in the late 1960s. Weingart would seed the global movement of Postmodern typography by using the modernist vocabulary of type, line, shape, and grid in complex and contradictory ways. His students include April Greiman – the California-based designer with whom Apeloig interned in 1987 and 1988. From Greiman, Apeloig learned to embrace software as a source of unexpected errors and strange new forms of beauty. With its layered grids and eccentric curves, Apeloig's 1990 calendar for "Bussière arts graphiques" (Bussière's Graphic Arts) recalls the work of Wolfgang Weingart (page 114). His design of the 1989 book *Bilan et perspectives '89: les arts plastiques* (Balance and Perspective '89: Visual Arts) incorporates Greiman's more spontaneous, digitally liberated sensibility, and her full-on rebellion against the laws of the grid (page 108).

Apeloig would go on to author his own distinctive voice, one that embraces constraints while allowing abstract systems to collide with the particularities of content and context, language and gesture. The grid is mother to the module; across Apeloig's work, letterforms emerge in bits and pieces from the matrix of x and y. For dozens of alphabets, posters, and logotypes, Apeloig has used the implicit crossings of the grid to build modular components. Like a sculptor, he employs methods both additive and subtractive, building shapes and defining edges while also cutting, clipping, and cropping to reveal form by destroying it.

In 1993, Apeloig won a fellowship to pursue independent work at the French Academy in Rome's Villa Medici. Working in the manner of a studio artist, he immersed himself in the task of designing a series of modular typefaces: Carré, Aleph, Octobre, and Cursive (page 163). Built by filling in the squares of a grid-paper notebook, these typefaces appear frequently in Apeloig's body of work and function similarly to a painter's brushwork or a raftsman's marks. Whereas many

4

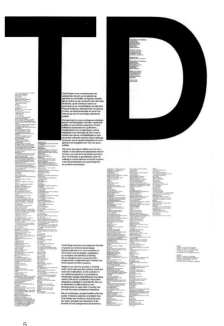

5

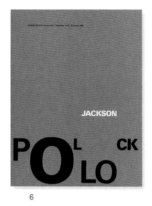

6

the
architectonic
in
graphic
the design
concert
poster
series
december 16, 1980–
january 24, 1981
reinhold-brown gallery
tel. 212/734-7999
tuesday–saturday
10:30–5:00
26 east
78 street
of
josef
müller-
brockmann

7

designers forge their sensibilities slowly as they sift through the infinite archive of new and historical typefaces, Apeloig constructed his typographic arsenal early on in his career. Sometimes he draws upon typography's shared tradition, embracing classic typefaces, from Frutiger to Akkurat, but more often he draws from his own library of letterforms.

He does not claim to be a master type designer and calls his own early alphabets "innocent, clumsy, and playful." Since then, however, he has turned that clumsiness into an elegant and enabling signature, and continued to refine and deploy self-authored modular forms as a structural frame-work and source of pictorial elements. An irrational and erratic quality pervades these custom characters. The eccentric shapes assembled in his typeface Ndebele, created in 2010 for the journal *Afrique contemporaine*, recall the toys, textiles, and ceramics of the Ndebele people of South Africa (page 204). In a work produced for the Sounds French music festival in New York in 2003, Apeloig foregrounded the figurative quality of his letterforms; here, experimental fonts appear together in singular roles, each one becoming an icon or found object with its own voice and personality.

This type-as-artifact spirit also animates Apeloig's 2006 logotype for the Association des Bibliothécaires de France (Association of French Librarians): characters reference the modular furniture used in libraries, as if depicted from above, with small, round forms that resemble patrons circulating among chairs, tables, computer monitors, and volumes of books, bringing the library to life (page 260). Apeloig's sketches reveal his struggle to create a feeling of movement and variation within the confines of an otherwise geometric system. By settling on components that contrast in scale, he was able to create an active, accidental feeling that defies the origins of the typeface in a restricted set of modules. This typeface has provided the ever-mutating DNA for an ongoing series of posters for ABF's annual conferences. In 2009, for the 55th Congress in Paris, Apeloig built heavy shadows around the letterforms to suggest the architectural context of the library (page 262). The next year he dissolved the letters into fragile lines and quirky pie charts to represent economic crisis and uncertainty. The typeface, ABF Linéaire (used on the cover of this book), was released as a digital type family by the Zurich-based foundry Nouvelle Noire in November 2013 (page 264).

8

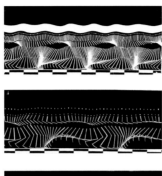

9

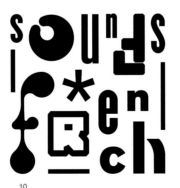

10

In addition to creating typefaces from geometric parts, Apeloig draws modules from the existing elements of typography. His Lorraine alphabet is a touchstone for this technique as each letter consists of dozens of smaller elements, including slash marks and punctuation, that mass together to form the strokes and crossbars of letterforms (pages 168–171). Entering these bits via keystroke, Apeloig adjusts the size and weight of characters and the spaces above, below, and between them in order to alter the texture and cohesion of the whole. He has thus used typographic conventions to build a new typography all his own. A similar technique appears in his exhibition poster for "Alfred Nobel: au service de l'innovation" (Alfred Nobel: In the Service of Innovation; 2008), in which letterforms emerge from a grid of dots (page 200). The dots change weight from letter to letter, creating subtle shifts in transparency. In the background, photographic orbs of light create an organic pattern of dots at a wholly different scale.

Apeloig also mines letterforms from typography's rich existing discourse. For his 1992 poster for the exhibition "Henry Moore intime" (Henry Moore Up Close), Apeloig produced a graphic sculpture by building a dense mound of characters in an overweight setting of Gill Sans (page 158). The poster speaks to Moore's English heritage through the choice of typeface, as well as through the photograph of the artist's house – Apeloig traveled to the house with a photographer in order to experience the landscape firsthand and shoot an original image. To create the final poster, he manipulated the resulting photograph into a low-resolution bitmap, a technique he had learned in April Greiman's studio. This was a new idea at the time and reflected his fearless attitude toward photography as yet another medium due for transformation. Apeloig softened the photograph into a soft, shadowy backdrop on which the massive letters loom in the front garden.

For his 2004 logotype for the Istituto Universitario di Architettura di Venezia (IUAV; the University Institute of Architecture, Venice), Apeloig exploited the symmetry of the institute's four letterforms by stacking them one above the other (page 236). He stabilized this precarious tower by using the monospaced typeface Fago, designed by Ole Schäfer, in which each letter has the same width. The simple symmetry of the final logotype emerged from a long process of study in which Apeloig sought to unlock motion and change from the characters' underlying geometry. A more recent poster for the annual book festival "Bruits du monde" (Noises of the World; 2012) features heavy lowercase letters – in the typeface Taz – that sit estranged and adrift across a flat sea of azure (page 189). Rotations and misalignments give spatial complexity and depth to these stranded characters. Blotches of ink – smeared and finger-printed – read as shadows, blurs, and motion tracks, burdening each letter with a sluggish, ominous life force.

An artist will return again and again to a way of working, a way of marking, a way of pulling form and movement out of the shallow reservoir of the image. Ideas rebound across the planes of Apeloig's works, from year to year, decade to decade. In a technique inspired by the photography of Étienne-Jules Marey, Apeloig often stacks and repeats forms in order to evoke motion and depth. Transposing this basic principle of anima-tion onto the printed page, he constructs abstract references to time and space. Viewed across his many sketches and digital revisions, his life's work reveals itself as a body in constant motion, a singular entity that holds together even while enduring endless transformations. Like a painter, Apeloig immerses himself in the mysteries of two-dimensional space, honoring its capacity to harbor stunning illusion and exploiting its status as a thin and brittle shell, an ephemeral husk of the real. He never rushes to penetrate that shallow skin with a single bold message or a clever "big idea." Instead, he invites us to wander through a thicket of letters, lines, and shapes that coalesce, at the end of our journey, into something magical.

8 **Philippe Apeloig**
Typo/Typé, 2005
Poster for a personal exhibition
Carré Sainte-Anne, Montpellier
Silkscreen poster
118.5 × 175 cm (46⅝ × 68⅞ in.)
Printer: 5ᵉ Couleur
See pages 170–171

9 **Étienne-Jules Marey (1830–1904)**
Chronophotographic Study of Human Movement, 1886
Photograph
Musée des Beaux-Arts, Beaune

10 **Philippe Apeloig**
Sounds French: A Festival of New Music from France, 2003
Logotype
New York

Museums

Musée d'Orsay

In 1985, the transformation of an obsolete railway station into one of Paris's premier museums, the Musée d'Orsay, was nearing completion. The museum organized a search for an in-house designer to create promotional materials incorporating the institution's trademark logo. In consultation with Bruno Monguzzi, Jean Widmer's Visuel Design Studio had created a way-finding system, the corporate identity and the graphic charter which the newly hired designer would complete. Twenty-two-year-old Philippe Apeloig was the finalist of the search. While still a student at the École nationale supérieure des arts décoratifs, he had responded to the posted listing and was prepared for the challenge, having already completed two internships at Total Design in Amsterdam, one in 1983, the other in 1985.

Chicago, Naissance d'une métropole 1872–1922

The Musée d'Orsay's first exhibition focused on interests far beyond the new museum's renowned Impressionist paintings and other traditional art forms. Co-curated by the Art Institute of Chicago, the exhibition was titled "Chicago, Naissance d'une métropole, 1872–1922" (Chicago: Birth of a Metropolis) and its subject was the architecture and urban design of Chicago at the turn of the twentieth century. After a fire destroyed much of the city in 1871, Chicago came to symbolize the "new world," providing architects with the unparalleled opportunity to rebuild the city and design buildings using the latest engineering technologies.

Apeloig's promotional poster captures the Windy City's progressive architecture and jazzy vibe and features an archival photograph by J. W. Taylor from the Art Institute's holdings. The long shutter speed employed by the photographer has frozen the people on the streets below in motion; they seem to be pushing against the famous Chicago winds. The entire image is tilted to create a sense of vertigo.

The innovative shape and placement of the text are the result of experimentation and of numerous hand-drawn sketches, photographs, and Polaroids. The typeface is the Musée d'Orsay's official font, Walbaum. The final print was assembled using the Aesthedes graphic-design workstation. For the first time, the revolutionary development of computer-aided design (CAD), introduced in 1982, made it possible for graphic designers to explore three dimensions in their two-dimensional compositions. The word "Chicago" runs between the skyscrapers, folding to follow the direction of the streets, culminating with a capital *O* that emphasizes the O in "d'Orsay." The poster's design effectively beckons visitors to the exhibition with its dynamic text, tilted eagle's-eye view, and sense of bustling movement and energy.

J. W. Taylor (1846–1918)
Panorama of Chicago, 1913
Photograph
Burnham Library of Architecture
The Art Institute, Chicago

Poster
Chicago
Naissance d'une métropole
1872 – 1922
Musée d'Orsay, Paris
150 × 100 cm (59 × 39⅜ in.)
Printer: Jacques London/Bedos
Typeface: Walbaum
1987
See pages 374 – 75

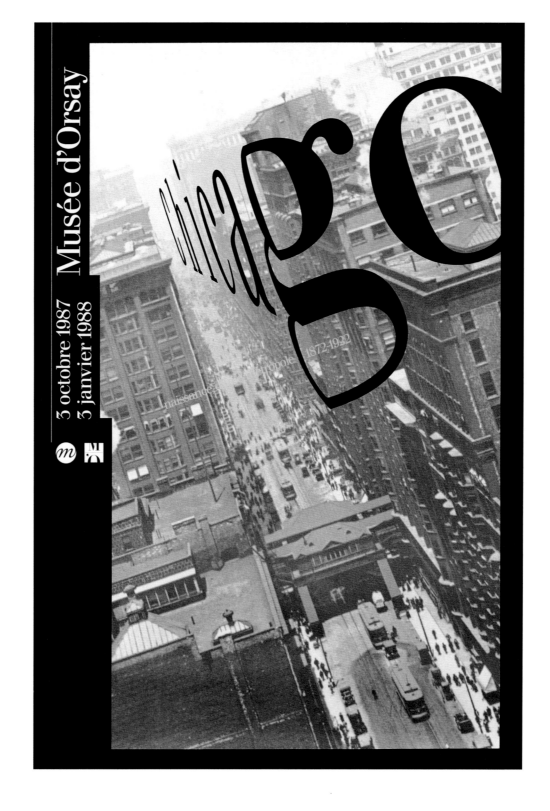

comique muet

Journées
du comique muet
cinéma
de France et d'ailleurs

du 11 au 18 juin 1987

Musée d'Orsay
Auditorium

Comique muet
Journées du comique muet
Cinéma de France et d'ailleurs

The first poster designed for a cultural event at the Musée d'Orsay promoted the silent film festival Comique muet (Mute Comic). The poster features an early twentieth-century newspaper clipping of French actress Sarah Duhamel, who performed as the heroine Rosalie in thirty-five short films produced between 1911 and 1914. Her funny, pop-eyed mugging is typical of the exaggerated expressions that silent actors used to convey character. The original photograph was printed using a newspaper-scale screen and is heavily inked. The large screen was retained for the poster but printed in dual tones to mimic the bluish tones common in films from this era.

The foil-printed type evokes the techniques and magic of cinema. The upside-down letter *i* in the word *"comique,"* running vertically along the left edge, winks at a 1960s French TV show about the silent film industry called *Histoires sans paroles* (Stories Without Words). In borrowing elements from both cinema and television, the poster provides historical context but is forward-thinking, integrating past with present.

Poster
Comique muet
Journées du comique muet
Cinéma de France et d'ailleurs
Musée d'Orsay, Paris
70 × 50 cm (27⅝ × 19⅝ in.)
Offset and hot foil
Printer: Union
Typeface: Walbaum
1987

Program
Comique muet
Journées du comique muet
Cinéma de France et d'ailleurs
Musée d'Orsay, Paris
21 × 10.5 cm (8¼ × 4⅛ in.)
Printer: Jacques London
Typeface: Walbaum
1987

Chicago et le cinéma

The *"Chicago, Naissance d'une métropole"* exhibition was accompanied by a film festival celebrating the city. Its poster is based on a black-and-white still from the 1949 film *The Fountainhead*, starring Gary Cooper. The film, based on the book by Ayn Rand, models its central character, Howard Roark, on the architect Frank Lloyd Wright.

The irregular shape of the poster is the result of a special die cut and simulates two overlapping posters. These are linked together visually by large punctuation marks that accentuate the astonishment on the faces of the actors who lean toward the festival's title below them.

The festival program was cut into an irregular shape so that it folded in such a way as to emphasize the architectural theme of the exhibition and film festival.

Expositions-dossiers
Concerts

The promotional poster for "Musée d'Orsay: Expositions-dossiers" (Exhibition Files) uses a detail from Olympe Aguado's 1860 photograph *Admiration!* as its central image. The photograph gently mocks the reverent attitudes of a group of Second Empire swells assembled around a painting in a gallery. The poster "Musée d'Orsay: Concerts" promotes the museum's classical concert series and features a carefully composed photograph depicting a sculpture within the galleries. Framed by a tall vertical opening in a gallery wall, the marble sculpture is isolated on a metaphorical stage. We see it from the viewpoint of the spectator: one exquisite piece embodying the beauty and genteel surroundings in which the viewer will be entertained.

These two posters challenge the museum-world convention of reproducing one work to market the entire collection. In the "Concerts" poster, the designer co-opted that tradition to establish the mood and tone of the concert series.

In both, Apeloig respects the grid by aligning the text with the internal guides provided by both of the central images: in "Expositions-dossiers" the edge of the painting frame; in "Concerts" the sides of the break in the wall and the walls' outer edges. The images determine the compositional balance. Each image is framed by a black border, which harmonizes the classical imagery and proportions with the more modern elements and influences.

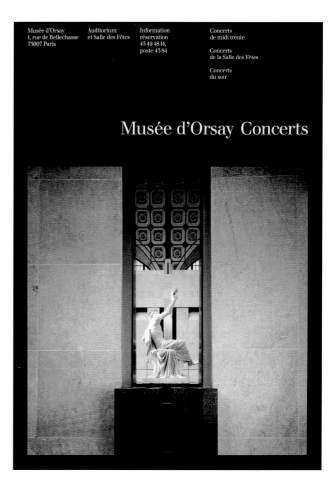

Poster
Chicago et le cinéma
Musée d'Orsay, Paris
70 × 50 cm (27⅝ × 19⅝ in.)
Die cut
Printer: Union
Typeface: Walbaum
1987

Leaflet
Chicago et le cinéma
Musée d'Orsay, Paris
21.5 × 38 cm (8½ × 15 in.)
Closed: 21 × 10.5 cm (8¼ × 4⅛ in.)
Printer: Union
Typeface: Walbaum
1987

Poster
Musée d'Orsay, Paris
Expositions-dossiers
70 × 50 cm (27⅝ × 19⅝ in.)
Printer: Union
Typeface: Walbaum
1988

Poster
Musée d'Orsay, Paris
Concerts
70 × 50 cm (27⅝ × 19⅝ in.)
Printer: Union
Typeface: Walbaum
1988

Passage des dates
Passage de la presse

Two historical displays were designed for the arched glass-walled passageways behind the Musée d'Orsay's signature clock, a vestige of its former life as a train station. Presented on separate floors, the displays were laid out similarly. Both hallways were lined with one-meter-deep, metal-framed display cases designed by Gae Aulenti, the architect behind the museum's interiors. (The cases no longer exist.) The interiors of these glass-fronted display cases were fitted at an angle, top to bottom, with translucent white fabric. Light streaming through the building's glass walls illuminated the cases from behind. Photographs and text were silkscreened onto the glass.

The "Passage des dates" profiled watershed events – artistic, technological, political, and cultural – from 1848, a time of revolution and the year that France's Second Republic was founded, to 1914 and the outbreak of World War I. Each panel held approximately six dates, beneath which were listed the most significant events of that year. The texts were accompanied by reproductions of historical photographs and artworks.

While harmonizing and systematizing the tenets of design, Apeloig added elements such as double lines and dropped capital letters. It was important to create a stimulating experience for the viewer, who needed to absorb copious amounts of information. Apeloig organized the lists of historical dates, inventions, events, and illustrations using horizontal hairlines and bold vertical lines.

"Passage de la presse" examined the journalistic trade and its impact on cultural and social affairs during the industrial, early-modern era in France, a time of rapid change and political tumult, when censorship of the press was a hot topic. The exhibition focused on writers such as Émile de Girardin, caricaturist Honoré Daumier, and Émile Zola, whose 1898 "J'Accuse," an open letter addressed to the French president during the Dreyfus Affair, was published in the newspaper *L'Aurore* and spawned an entirely new way of spreading ideas on a mass scale. A shadow effect was used on the first letters of headings, such as the *P* in "Presse." A three-dimensional effect was created by silkscreening these letters twice, in yellow on the display-case glass and in gray on the angled fabric panels inside.

Panels
Passage des dates
Musée d'Orsay, Paris
Screen print
Typeface: Walbaum
1986

Panels
Passage de la presse
Musée d'Orsay, Paris
Screen print
Typeface: Walbaum
1986

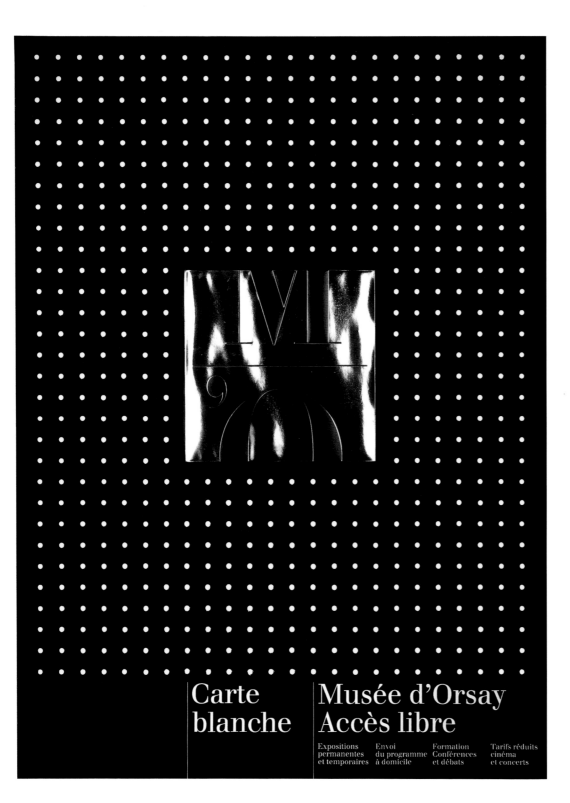

 Musée d'Orsay | Service culturel Relations extérieures

A Avantages de la Carte blanche

pour les Correspondants

E Ensemble des avantages consentis aux adhérents

Un programme de formation comprenant des cycles de visites thématiques des collections du musée

des cycles d'initiation au langage plastique à travers les collections du musée

Une présentation spéciale des expositions temporaires en avant première

La gratuité sur les affichettes et les catalogues de certaines expositions temporaires

Par ailleurs, le Service culturel envisage de proposer aux correspondants la visite d'un site, d'une ville ou d'un musée ayant des collections en rapport avec la période 1848-1914.

 Musée d'Orsay | Service culturel Relations extérieures | 62, rue de Lille 75007 PARIS Tél. : 45.40.48.14 Poste 4580 | Carte blanche 1988

Adhésion

Votre Carte blanche vous sera adressée à domicile. Pour l'obtenir, remplissez ce formulaire, sans oublier de cocher la case tarif correspondant à votre type d'adhésion.

| | Monsieur ☐ | Madame ☐ | Mademoiselle ☐ |

Nom, Prénom

Adresse

Code postal   Ville

Pays   Année de naissance

Téléphone pers. :   prof. :

● Tarifs individuels

Votre Carte blanche est valable un an à compter de votre adhésion.
Remettez votre formulaire avec votre règlement à la caisse des adhésions (tous les jours de 10 h à 17 h 00 sauf le lundi, jeudi jusqu'à 20 heures) ou adressez-le au Service culturel, Relations extérieures.

111 ☐ ☐ Tarif individuel : 250 F

112 ☐ ☐ 18-25 ans et plus de 60 ans : 150 F

Les moins de 18 ans bénéficient de l'accès gratuit au musée

● Tarifs collectivités

Votre Carte blanche est valable jusqu'au 31 décembre 1988 quelle que soit la date de votre adhésion.
La formule collectivités est réservée aux adhésions de 10 personnes minimum regroupées par un correspondant.
Remplissez votre formulaire et remettez-le à votre correspondant qui nous le transmettra.
Vous recevrez à domicile une Carte blanche individuelle.

711 ☐ ☐ Tarif collectivités : 150 F

911 ☐ ☐ Correspondant : 150 F

Paiement joint à l'ordre de l'agent comptable de la réunion des musées nationaux

☐ Chèque bancaire

☐ Chèque postal

☐ Espèces (uniquement pour les paiements sur place). Tarifs valables jusqu'au 31 décembre 1988

Votre correspondant

Nom

Prénom

Numéro

Vos centres d'intérêt

1 ☐ ☐ Peinture
2 ☐ ☐ Sculpture
3 ☐ ☐ Objets d'art
4 ☐ ☐ Photographie
5 ☐ ☐ Architecture
6 ☐ ☐ Histoire de la période 1848-1914
7 ☐ ☐ Littérature
8 ☐ ☐ Musique
9 ☐ ☐ Cinéma
2 ☐ ☐ Conférences et débats
8 ☐ ☐ Activités jeunes visiteurs
9 ☐ ☐ Formation adultes

Votre profession ou activité principale

1 ☐ ☐ Scolaire, étudiant
8 ☐ ☐ Enseignant, animateur
2 ☐ ☐ Agriculteur, ouvrier
3 ☐ ☐ Commerçant, artisan
4 ☐ ☐ Employé
5 ☐ ☐ Cadre moyen
7 ☐ ☐ Cadre supérieur, profession libérale
6 ☐ ☐ Profession artistique
3 ☐ ☐ Sans profession
8 ☐ ☐ Autre, précisez

**Carte blanche
Musée d'Orsay Accès libre**

When the Musée d'Orsay opened in December 1986, it offered a special "Carte blanche" annual pass that provided members with open admission (no waiting), access to free lectures and symposiums, unlimited visits, and reduced rates for film screenings, festivals, concerts, and other ticketed events.

Apeloig was asked to design the identity for this initiative. In response, he perforated the surface of an opaque, double-printed black poster with die-cut holes, creating a virtual wall with a grid of minuscule circular windows. His inspiration for this design was seeing his *Comique muet* poster installed on the large glass windows of the museum's main lobby. Daylight shining through the paper made it slightly transparent, integrating the poster with the architecture and allowing him to see through it into the building. He deliberately played with this idea in the "Carte blanche" identity. The central foiled logo creates a mirrored surface in which visitors can see their own reflections as they peek through the holes. The strong contrast between the black background and the effects of light on the logo is a metaphor for the brilliance of the brand-new Musée d'Orsay.

Other aspects of the museum's identity were subject to a similarly experimental approach. The subscription forms had innovative, unusual shapes that reveal an attraction to abstract swirling curves, cut letters, and curving type. These designs were created through painstaking manual labor, but just a few years later would be easy to produce using a computer.

**Musée d'Orsay,
10 ans après**

For its tenth anniversary in 1996, the Musée d'Orsay commissioned Apeloig to create a commemorative poster. His design is a spare update of the museum's core identity, with the logo as its centerpiece: fragments of the logo can be glimpsed inside a monumental, extra bold number ten. Inside the digit *1*, "Musée d'Orsay, 10 ans après" (10 years on) is printed in small, soft yellow type. The occasion – a moment to celebrate and an opportunity to expand the public's awareness of the museum – is marked by the use of sober aluminum tones. Darker for the background and lighter for the digits, the solid color gives the 10 the aura of an architectural fragment, bringing materiality, light, and scale to the piece. Both the massive and tiny typographic elements are subtly combined, causing the present to speak to the past.

Poster
**Carte blanche
Musée d'Orsay, Paris
Accès libre**
70 × 50 cm (27⅝ × 19⅝ in.)
Hot foil, perforation
Printer: Jacques London
Typeface: Walbaum
1987

Subscription form
**Carte blanche
Musée d'Orsay, Paris**
29.7 × 21 cm (11⅝ × 8¼ in.)
Typeface: Walbaum
1987

Poster
**Musée d'Orsay, Paris
10 ans après**
70 × 50 cm (27⅝ × 19⅝ in.)
Printer: Blanchard
Typeface: Walbaum
1996

Musée de Picardie

Housed in a Second Empire building, with murals by Pierre Puvis de Chavannes in the main staircase, the Musée de Picardie in Amiens is one of the largest provincial museums in France. It has prehistoric and medieval holdings, as well as Flemish, Dutch, and French art from the seventeenth through to the nineteenth centuries, and a collection of modern art by artists from around the world. Located not far from the magnificent Amiens Cathedral, its architecture resonates in the same gothic style.

The museum's logo, designed by Apeloig in 1993, consists of a vertical line of type set in Hollander, a typeface designed in 1983 by Gerard Unger. The font carries global connotations suitable for the museum's international scope and is reminiscent of seventeenth-century Dutch typefaces in its interplay between thick and thin parts, its tall X height, and generous proportions. The simple but elegant vertical logo consists only of the names of the city (Amiens) and museum (Musée de Picardie), separated by a thin horizontal line.

Puvis de Chavannes,
Sol LeWitt
Dessins

In 1994, curators at the Musée de Picardie staged an encounter between Puvis de Chavannes's lavish decorative nineteenth-century frescoes and Sol LeWitt's brightly colored, precisely geometric twentieth-century wall drawings. While de Chavannes's paintings fit right in with the museum's Second Empire architecture, the stark modernity of LeWitt's installation provided a jolting contrast to their surroundings.

LeWitt completed a permanent site-specific wall drawing for the museum's rotunda in 1992 that plays off of the circular space in its lines, shape, and distribution. In practice, LeWitt's modern, conceptual approach and de Chavannes's classical technique are nearly identical: both drew and painted their works directly onto walls, integrating them with a building's architecture, and both began with a grid system onto which preliminary sketches were overlaid for easy enlargement. The graph lines are hidden in de Chavannes' final paintings, however, while LeWitt's wall drawings reveal the underlying grid. The act of graphing, which connects the two artists, inspired Apeloig's poster design. The background is a deep blue overlaid with thin, light blue gridlines. Slight color variations suggest traces of the artists' hands.

Pierre Puvis de Chavannes
(1824–1898)
Man seen from the right in three-quarters view, hands folded at his waist…, c. 1881
Black pencil on tracing paper
Musée du Louvre, Paris

Sol LeWitt (1928–2007)
Schematic Drawings of Open Cubes,
1974
Invitation to exhibition opening
John Weber Gallery
LeWitt Collection, Chester, Conn.

Poster
**Puvis de Chavannes
Dessins: 1856 – 1896
Sol LeWitt
Dessins: 1958 – 1992**
Musée de Picardie, Amiens, France
175 × 118.5 cm (68⅞ × 46⅝ in.)
Screen print
Printer: Graphicaza
Typeface: Hollander
1994

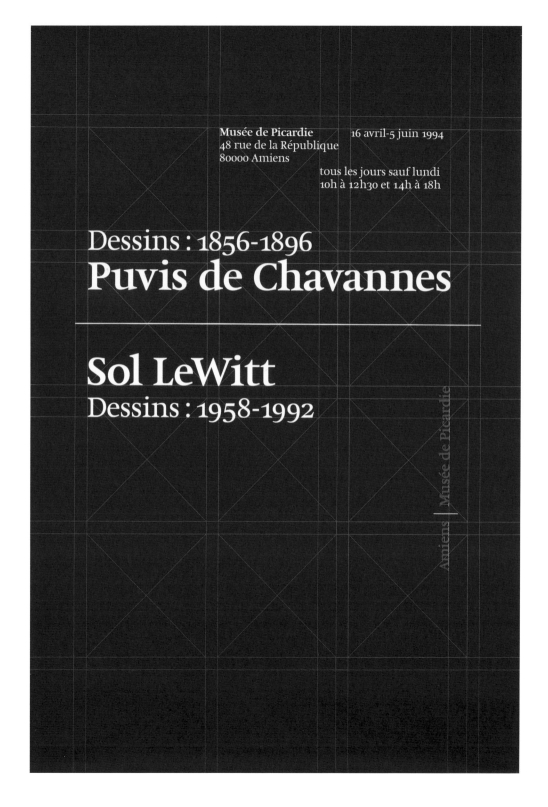

Années 30

In 1997, in a collaborative initiative called Années 30 (The Thirties), three institutions in Paris's sixteenth *arrondissement* celebrated the cultural, technological, and artistic advances of the 1930s. The Musée d'Art moderne de la Ville de Paris organized a survey of the visual arts, the Cinémathèque française a comprehensive series of films, and the Musée des Monuments français an overview of architecture and design. The accompanying poster, "Années 30, Colline de Chaillot," celebrates this collaborative program. The logo vertically groups "années" and "30" using a free interpretation of A. M. Cassandre's 1929 typeface, Bifur. The colors are typical of the 1930s, as are the stylized geometric shapes: rounded, sweeping curves, interlocking forms, and massive proportions. Furniture, architecture, textiles, and graphics from the 1930s all share these traits. The lower parts of the *3* and the *0* resemble the spinning wheels of a locomotive or automobile.

Every aspect of the poster for the exhibition "Années 30, L'architecture et les arts de l'espace entre industrie et nostalgie" (Between Industry and Nostalgia: Architecture and the Spatial Arts in the 1930s), held at the Musée des Monuments français, was carefully researched: the photographs, the muted three-tone palette (the silver, black, and brown reference old press images), the arrangement of the typography, and the proportions of the logo. The typography is partly rotated on a 90-degree angle, giving it a Constructivist look and feel. Using the technique of photomontage (one he rarely uses), Apeloig combined images of industrial turbines, the architecture of the Palais de Chaillot (built for the 1937 International Exhibition), the magnificent iron and glass dome of the Grand Palais, and a glimpse of the Eiffel Tower. He reversed the tonality of some of the photographs by playing with the halftone printing process so that one melds into the next. His poster creates a layered, dynamic space that foregrounds industry as an engine of progress and a sign of cultural transformation in the 1930s. The use of Futura for the informational text also evokes the period.

Poster
Années 30
Colline de Chaillot
Musée d'Art moderne de la Ville de Paris
Musée des Monuments français
Cinémateque Française Palais de Chaillot
175 × 118.5 cm (68⅞ × 46⅝ in.)
Screen print
Printer: Arts Graphiques de France
Typefaces: original creation, Futura
1997

Poster
Années 30
L'architecture et les arts de l'espace
entre industrie et nostalgie
Musée des Monuments français, Paris
175 × 118.5 cm (68⅞ × 46⅝ in.)
Printer: AGF/Blanchard
Typefaces: original creation, Futura
1997

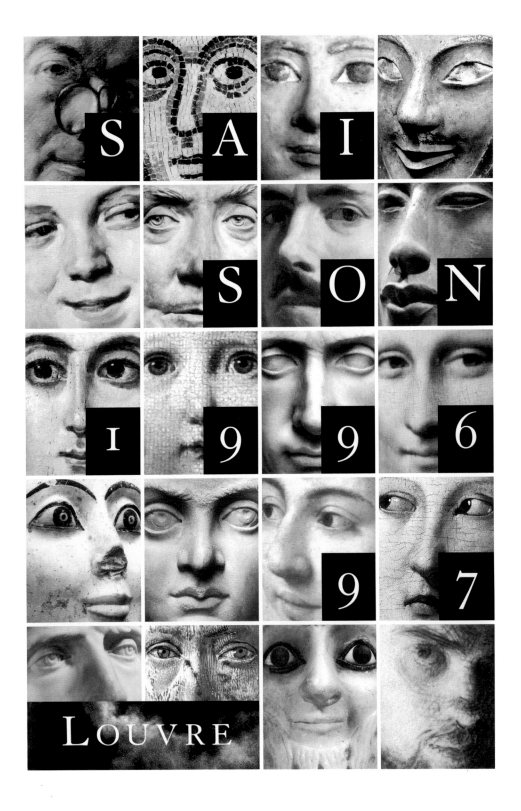

Poster
Saison 1996 – 97
Musée du Louvre, Paris
150 × 100 cm (59 × 39⅜ in.)
Printer: Blanchard
Typeface: Granjon
1996
See page 354

Poster display
in the Paris subway
Saison 1996 – 97
Musée du Louvre, Paris
150 × 100 cm (59 × 39⅜ in.)
Printer: Blanchard
Typeface: Granjon
1996
See page 354

Musée du Louvre

In 1994, Pierre Rosenberg, president of the Louvre, approached Apeloig to strengthen and clarify the museum's visual identity. The collective Grapus had created the original branding in 1989, the year I. M. Pei's glass pyramid was constructed.

Apeloig wanted to honor and preserve the original logotype, as well as the contributions of others, but saw the need for more structure. He created templates that developed a unified look using a series of flexible grid systems for informational text. These were the foundation for all promotional material.

Later on, in a consulting capacity, Apeloig updated the design manual. He retained the two original typefaces: Granjon and Univers. Through 2009, Apeloig was responsible for global art direction under Henri Loyrette, the Louvre's new president, and worked in tandem with the curatorial, marketing, and design teams. He also continued to design individual pieces for exhibitions and special programs.

Saison 1996 – 97

In 1996 and 1997, the Louvre celebrated the centennial anniversary of La Société des Amis du Louvre (The Society of Friends of the Louvre), an association that upholds the museum's mission to build and enrich the collection.

Apeloig's yearbook-like poster design revolves around twenty portraits selected from the Louvre's seven permanent collection departments. The faces span continents and millennia, and include details of works in all mediums: painting, sculpture, printing, drawing, and the decorative arts. Some are famous: *The Mona Lisa*, *The Seated Scribe*, the woman in Georges de La Tour's *The Cheat with the Ace of Diamonds*. Others are less recognizable. By framing each portrait as a close-up and using a grid to democratize the group, Apeloig helped the masterpieces gain new life.

This gallery of Louvre inhabitants emphasizes community, a perfect way to celebrate the society. Each letter of the word "saison" and each numeral of "1996 – 97" is contained in a black rectangle intermixed within the mosaic, adding depth and another perceptual layer to the composition. This design identity, based on the grid, was the template for other materials, such as invitations and programs.

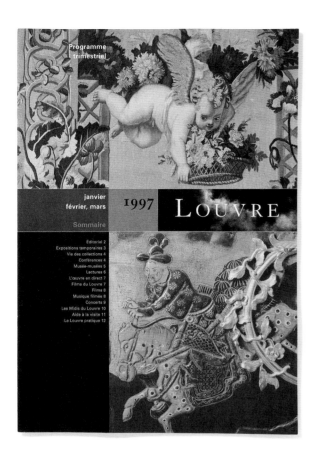

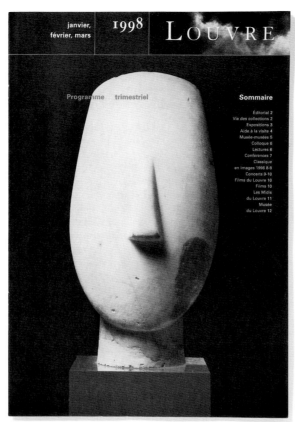

Quarterly programs
Musée du Louvre, Paris
42 × 29.7 cm (16½ × 11⅝ in.)
Typefaces: Granjon, Univers
1997 and 1998

Program festival sleeve
Leoš Janáček
Auditorium du Louvre, Paris
22 × 21.5 cm (8⅝ × 8½ in.)
Typeface: Univers
1998

Poster
Saison 1997 – 98
Musée du Louvre, Paris
150 × 100 cm (59 × 39⅜ in.)
Typeface: Univers
1997

Saison 1997 – 98

The 1997 to 1998 season at the Louvre focused on the installation of the Egyptian collections. The promotional poster was divided into two parts, each featuring an object that would capture the public's fascination with ancient Egypt and its hieroglyphic writing system. One is a detail of a wooden coffin depicting the eyes of the god Horus. This iconic image at the top of the poster represents protection and good fortune. Horus's gaze confronts the viewer directly, the past reaching into the present. At the bottom of the poster is a cropped fragment of a granite funerary stele, which plays with the grid, placing the roman informational text inside the vertical columns of the hieroglyphs.

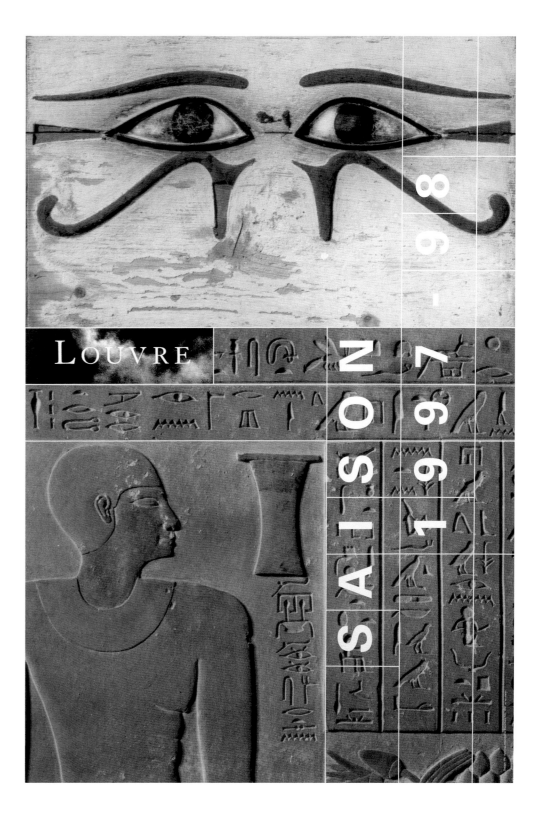

Louvre
Dix ans de la pyramide
Saison 1998 – 99

In 1999, the tenth anniversary of the addition of
I. M. Pei's glass pyramid to the Louvre's existing
architecture was celebrated and a poster was created
to commemorate the event. Since its inauguration,
the pyramid had been documented in countless
photographs. To show it in a new light, the poster
focused on its essential infrastructure and its spirit:
transparency, economy, and brilliance.

The diamond-shaped design, built of identical
squares reminiscent of the pyramid's glass panels,
was inspired by an original drawing by Pei. The poster
implies two simultaneous views: a cross-section
as seen from the courtyard and the whole as seen
from above. Metallic ink is used for the lines defining
the squares, representing the pyramid above ground.
The shimmering color evokes the play of light on
glass, through which the structure and potency of
the architecture are seen and felt.

With a letter at each corner of each square, the words
read on diagonal lines slanting to the upper right-
hand corner on a 45-degree angle. Reaching the end
of a line, information continues on the next to create
a continuous stream of letters. The alternating
black-and-white words and the visual threads connec-
ting the structure direct our reading from bottom left
to top right.

Poster
Louvre
Dix ans de la pyramide
Saison 1998 – 99
150 × 100 cm (59 × 39⅜ in.)
Screen print
Printer: Sérica
Typeface: Granjon
1998
See page 336

Ieoh Ming Pei (born in 1917)
Sketch for the Louvre pyramid, 1983

Yann Weymouth (born in 1941)
Sketch for the pyramids, courtyard,
and ornamental ponds of the Louvre,
1984

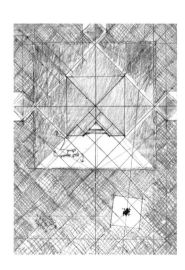

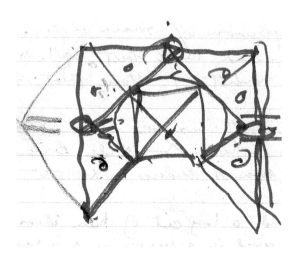

SAISON LOUVRE 1998-99

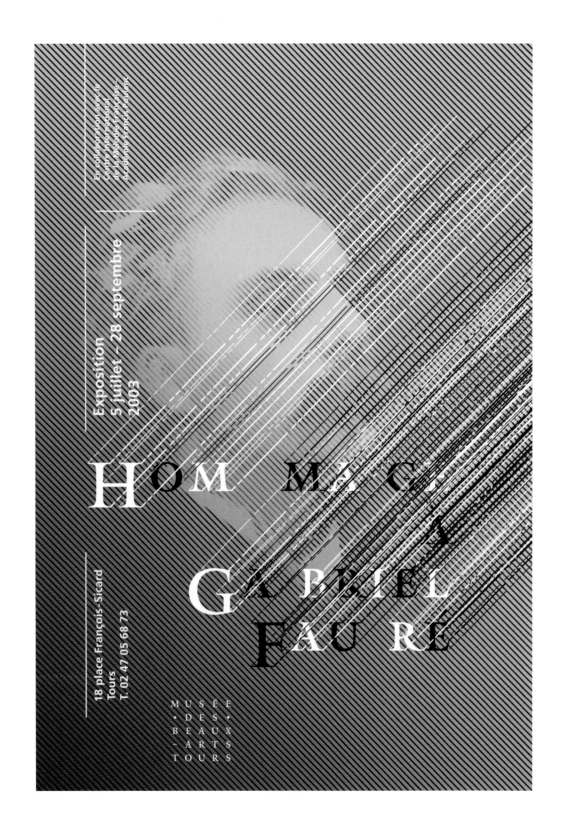

Musée des Beaux-Arts
de Tours

The Musée des Beaux-Arts in Tours, housed in an eighteenth-century former archbishop's palace, has a wide-ranging collection, from seventeenth- and eighteenth-century French furniture and paintings to Italian Primitive art and more contemporary works. The masterpieces, however, are two 1459 panels by Italian painter Andrea Mantegna from the predella of the San Zeno altarpiece.

Saison 2003–2004

The first poster that Apeloig produced for the museum promoted its 2003–2004 season. His logotype uses the classical font Mantinia, designed in 1993 by Matthew Carter, who drew his inspiration from the painted and engraved letterforms of Mantegna. Mantinia evokes both Classicism and the Musée des Beaux-Arts's prestigious collection, while "Saison 2003–2004," printed in white, fits within the rhythm of the grid, its placement dictated by the order and regularity of the logo. Placed inside the logo, the white text produces a magical, almost hypnotic visual illusion.

The poster's design derives from the museum's flooring and its ordered, geometric motif of square white tiles against octagonal black cabochons – a classic French design of diamonds with squared-off edges. The composition builds on this innate grid structure to create a balanced geometric composition that is both rich and decorative. Instead of using bullets, the square grid is completed by little cabochon shapes that echo the Mantinia font.

Hommage à Gabriel Fauré

This poster was created for an exhibition dedicated to the French composer Gabriel Fauré. A portrait of him by American artist John Singer Sargent is presented in shades of gray and given a ghostly quality through the layering of faded lines that make the three-quarters view of his face and head recede. Typography is used playfully for the exhibition title – the alternating colors of the letters recall piano keys, and their varied spacing sets up a musical rhythm. The composer's gaze follows the slanting diagonals emanating from each title letter. The lines traverse the surface, calling to mind sustained notes that linger in the air.

Poster
Hommage à Gabriel Fauré
Musée des Beaux-Arts, Tours
175 × 118.5 cm (68⅞ × 46⅝ in.)
Screen print
Printer: Dubois Imagerie
Typefaces: Mantinia, Galliard
2003

Poster
Saison 2003–2004
Musée des Beaux-Arts, Tours
175 × 118.5 cm (68⅞ × 46⅝ in.)
Screen print
Printer: Dubois Imagerie
Typefaces: Mantinia, Galliard
2003

Musée Rodin

The Musée Rodin in Paris is dedicated to the work of French sculptor Auguste Rodin and contains the largest collection of his works in the world. It is housed in the Hôtel Biron, an eighteenth-century townhouse where Rodin lived and worked. The rest of the collection resides in the artist's former country estate, now a museum-studio, in Meudon. For two years, Apeloig was head of design for the museum's exhibitions and public programs. He selected one unique font, Brauer Neue, set in bold capital letters with round angles and a heavy silhouette, which serves as a metaphor for sculpting.

La passion à l'œuvre
Rodin et Freud collectionneurs

The Musée Rodin organized an exhibition titled "La passion à l'œuvre: Rodin et Freud collectionneurs" (Passion at Work: Rodin and Freud as Collectors) that assembled a collection of objects evidencing a passion for antiquity. A marble relief from the first half of the second century, known as the *Relief of Aglaurides*, was chosen for the poster. Called *La Gradiva* by the Romans and a source of inspiration for Freud and generations of artists and writers, it was on loan from the Vatican's Chiaramonti Museum.

A photograph of the relief fills the background of the poster. Over it, an assemblage of uniformly sized text in a contemporary typeface creates friction between the old and the new. Because some parts of the halftone lettering are almost transparent, the poster appeals to both sight and touch.

Poster
La passion à l'œuvre
Rodin et Freud collectionneurs
Musée Rodin, Paris
150 × 100 cm (59 × 39⅜ in.)
Printer: Arts Graphiques de France
Typeface: Brauer Neue
2008

Poster
Matisse & Rodin
Musée Rodin, Paris
150 × 100 cm (59 × 39⅜ in.)
Printer: Arts Graphiques de France
Typeface: Brauer Neue
2009

Matisse & Rodin

The "Matisse & Rodin" exhibition provided a face-to-face encounter between two master artists a generation apart. Henri Matisse discovered Rodin's drawings and working methods at the turn of the twentieth century. Like Rodin, Matisse preferred the malleability of clay to the hardness of stone when sculpting. The exhibition uncovered other points of convergence and divergence in their works.

The exhibition poster and communication materials were conceived in a nontraditional manner. The title is built as if a modern sculpture and sits in the center of the design. The two artists' names, in capital letters, are rotated vertically and the addition of the ampersand – a glyph designed for the poster that does not exist in the original font – makes for a compact grouping, to which "Musée Rodin" is added in smaller type. Around this sculptural shape, five female forms – sculptures by Rodin and Matisse – stretch, arch, and pose. Their poses allude to Matisse's famous 1910 painting *La Danse*. The grouping seduces the viewer into a game of guessing which artist created which sculpture, hinting at the discoveries to be made in the exhibition.

Yves Saint Laurent

A retrospective of Yves Saint Laurent's fashion designs at the Petit Palais, organized and curated by the Fondation Pierre Bergé – Yves Saint Laurent and Paris-Musées, was entitled "Yves Saint Laurent, 40 ans de création" (40 Years of Creation). In Apeloig's design solution, the title was shortened to the name alone and broken down into two parts. Early on in the design process, Apeloig realized that Cassandre's famous *YSL* logotype would provide the main graphic element. His challenge was to overlap visual layers without creating a cluttered look, in keeping with Saint Laurent's reductive style. Apeloig wanted to express the soul of the designer, not promote the brand. In a meeting room at the Fondation, Apeloig spotted a gouache-and-ink drawing of the 1961 logo in photographs of Saint Laurent's studio. This original Cassandre drawing hung on a wall behind his worktable. Handmade, with discernible, delicate brush marks, it was easily differentiated from the stamped commercial logo. Apeloig brought it to life by reversing the color shading, which also gave the brushstrokes the illusion of three dimensions. The palette's proportions and yellow, red, and blue color scheme derive from a 1965 Yves Saint Laurent "Mondrian" dress. The new rendering of the intertwined *YSL* integrates Cassandre's design with Saint Laurent's *haute couture*.

A detail of a 1960s photograph of Saint Laurent by Pierre Boulat was used for the poster's background. It was reproduced using a large dot screen, evoking not only newsprint but also silkscreen – specifically, Andy Warhol's emblematic 1972 portrait of his friend. Over the image, in large white bold capitals, lays the word "YVES." The use of his first name made the designer accessible. "Saint Laurent," in smaller red type, sits across the bridge of Saint Laurent's nose, drawing the viewer's eyes to his gaze.

Informational text, placed vertically along the left edge of the poster, follows the proportional coloring established in the logo. The font is Avenir, designed by Adrian Frutiger in 1988, which Apeloig selected for its geometric aspect and subtle variations in weight. It provides superb readability, matching the clarity of Saint Laurent's style. Uppercase letters are used for the title, poster, and book layout.

Poster
Yves Saint Laurent
Petit Palais, Paris
175 × 118.5 cm (68⅞ × 46⅝ in.)
Screen print
Printer: Sérica
Typeface: Avenir
2010

Adolphe Jean-Marie Mouron,
known as A. M. Cassandre (1901–1968)
Yves Saint Laurent logotype, 1961
Gouache on paper

Pierre Boulat (1924–1998)
Yves Saint Laurent, 1961
Photograph

Yves Saint Laurent (1936–2008)
Haute couture Collection
Fall/Winter 1965
Hommage to Piet Mondrian
Ecru wool jersey

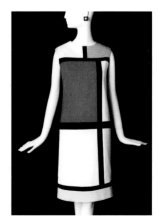

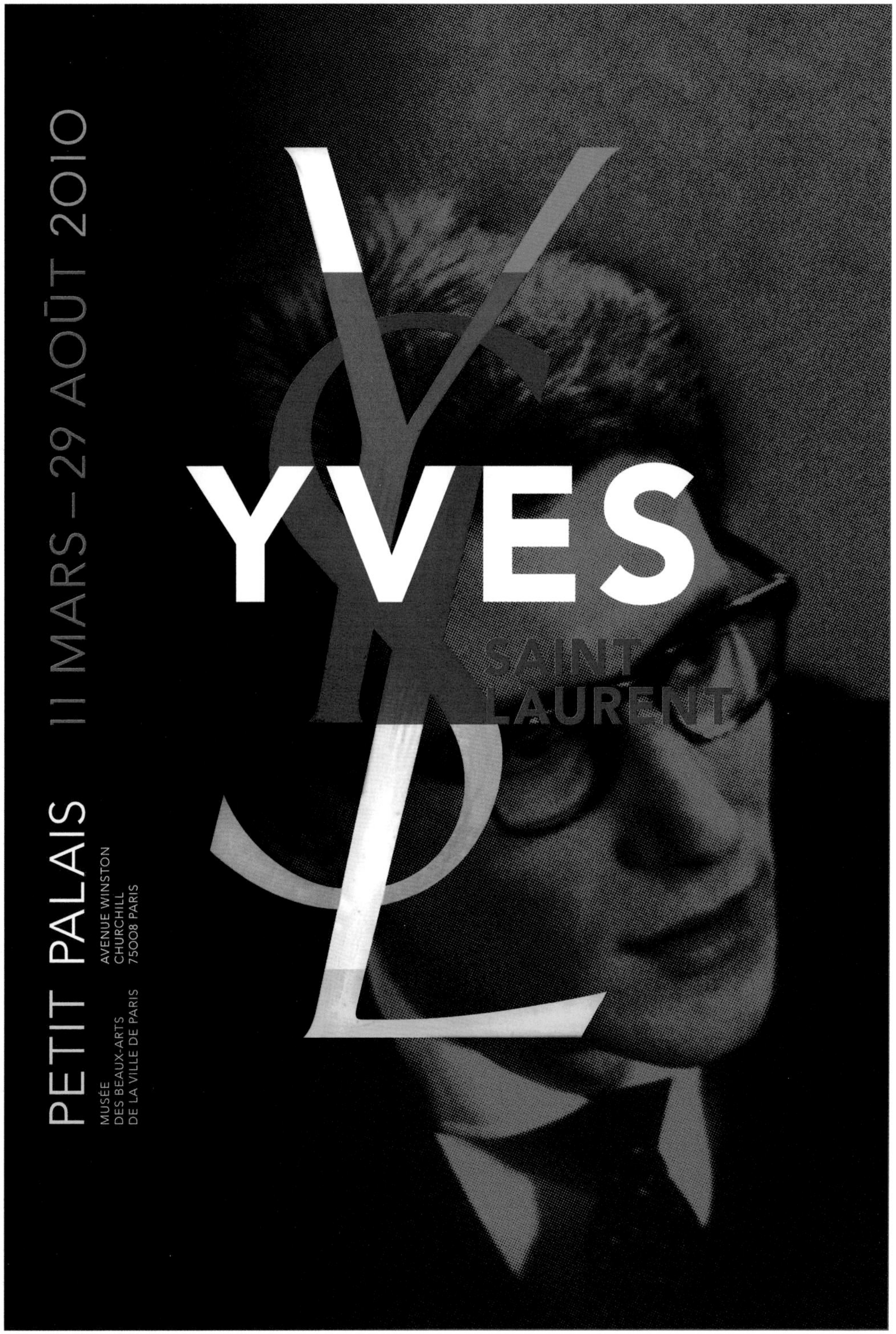
YVES
SAINT
LAURENT
11 MARS – 29 AOÛT 2010
PETIT PALAIS
MUSÉE
DES BEAUX-ARTS
DE LA VILLE DE PARIS
AVENUE WINSTON
CHURCHILL
75008 PARIS

YVES
SAINT LAURENT

I LOVED RENOVATING
THE MAJORELLE GARDEN.
NO ONE KNOWS WITH
ANY CERTAINTY WHAT
THE EXACT COLORS
WERE ORIGINALLY.
I SCRATCHED THE WALLS,
BUT I NEVER FOUND
ANY OF THE FAMOUS
MAJORELLE BLUE.
IT WAS PROBABLY LESS
ELECTRIC. MAJORELLE
WAS A MATISSE;
THAT'S MY PASSION.

GLOBE, 1986

LE NOIR EST UNE
COULEUR. IL EST LE TRAIT
DE CRAYON QUI DESSINE
LA LIGNE SUR LA FEUILLE
BLANCHE.
LE NOIR EST LA COULEUR
DES PORTRAITS
DE LA RENAISSANCE,
DE CLOUET, D'AGNÈS
SOREL, DE LA COUR
DES VALOIS, DE FRANS
HALS, DE MANET.

YVES SAINT LAURENT

Exhibition catalog
Yves Saint Laurent
Éditions de La Martinière
27 × 22.5 cm (10⅝ × 8⅞ in.), 388 pages
Typefaces: Avenir, Miller Text
2010

1984–1994
MADAME DE
STAËL: "FAME
IS A GLITTERY
BEREAVEMENT
FOR
HAPPINESS."

ABILLER LE TEMPS
RÉSENT :
ES «VÊTEMENTS
SSENTIELS»
YVES SAINT LAURENT.

Geoffroy Tory
Imprimeur de François Ier
Graphiste avant la lettre

Geoffroy Tory was a prolific sixteenth-century engraver, author, humanist, and proponent of a standardized system of writing. He had a major impact on the French Renaissance style of book decoration and led the effort to use roman instead of the prevailing gothic lettering and the French language over Latin in printed texts. He was appointed printer to King François 1st of France in about 1530. His most influential publication was *Le Champfleury* (1529), in which he proposed using simple punctuation marks – accents, the apostrophe, the cedilla – leading to the standardization of French publishing.

The exhibition on Tory's work, "Geoffroy Tory, imprimeur de François Ier, graphiste avant la lettre" (Geoffroy Tory, Printer of François 1st, A Graphic Designer Before His Time) was curated by the Musée national de la Renaissance and the National Library of France. The exhibition poster was inspired by *Le Champfleury,* the first typographic treatise to include philosophical content and to introduce innovative characters derived from the proportions of the human body. The background is a reproduction of a page from this work. The strong black shapes of Tory's historic experimental *abécédaire* (alphabet) have a surprisingly contemporary quality.

The poster layout acts as a vertical rupture, with new type confronting the old. A layer of transparent rectangles is placed on top of the old alphabet, with each letter of Tory's name positioned in a rectangle, observing the golden proportions suggested in *Le Champfleury*. Dark gray stripes give texture to the transparent blocks of text, which mimic the frames around the letters and illustrations in Tory's book. The placement of the letters within the rectangles echo the layouts generated by Tory's early system.

The delicate color palette helps balance the composition: soft gray and ivory, with touches of gold and red taken from Tory's color scheme for the subtitle.

Poster
Geoffroy Tory
Imprimeur de François Ier
Graphiste avant la lettre
Musée national de la Renaissance,
Écouen
150 × 100 cm (59 × 39⅜ in.)
Typeface: Akzidenz Grotesk
Bold Condensed
2011
See page 291

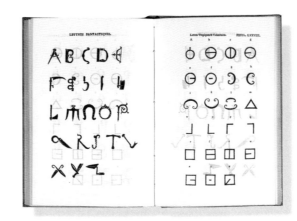

Geoffroy Tory (1480 – 1533)
"Lettres fantastiques"
in *Le Champfleury*, **1529**
Imprimerie nationale, Paris

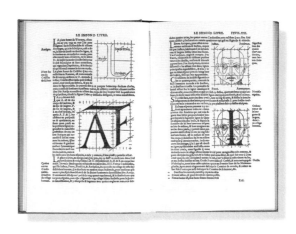

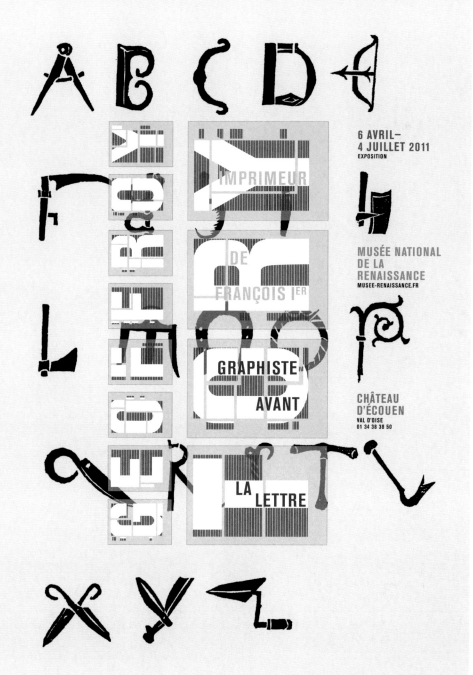

L'Art de l'automobile
Chefs-d'œuvre
de la collection Ralph Lauren

Fashion designer Ralph Lauren's collection of vintage and new sports cars, dating from the 1930s on, were put on view for the first time in Europe at the Musée des Arts Décoratifs in Paris. The exhibition provided an overview of European automotive history, showing an industrial art form forged from innovative engineering.

The exhibition was titled "The Art of The Automobile: Masterpieces from the Ralph Lauren Collection." Long titles can be problematic, since an immediate impact is necessary to grab attention. For the designer, the problem is one of creating subtlety while organizing information in a limited space.

The poster features the Jaguar XKD, the car that catapulted the British brand to fame in the 1950s. Three photographic perspectives of the XKD imply movement and speed, as its sleek fragmented body appears to zoom across the surface.

The typographic placement underscores this visual movement through a zigzag reading pattern. In this configuration, the length of the word "automobile" is no longer an obstacle. Cut in half and reading right to left, the title text counterbalances the car's crosswise motion. The elegant, light construction of the stenciled letters – with differently sized vowels and consonants and missing parts – references the brand's status, as well as its cars' lavish aesthetics and inventiveness.

The design of the exhibition title was adapted for the cover of the catalog and fabricated in three dimensions for the exhibition, where it was suspended in mid-air over one of the cars. The installation drew attention to industrial art and to the beauty of the cars in Lauren's collection.

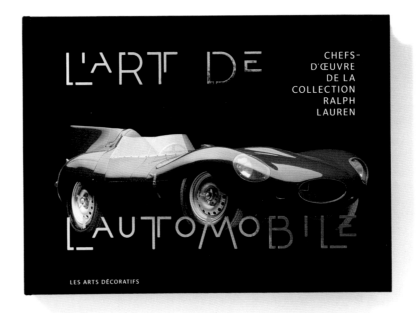

Catalog
L'Art de l'automobile
Chefs-d'œuvre
de la collection Ralph Lauren
Les Arts Décoratifs, Paris
27 × 35.2 cm (10⅝ × 13⅞ in.), 160 pages
Printer: Mondadori Printing
Typefaces: original creation,
Foundry Sterling
2011

Poster
L'Art de l'automobile
Chefs-d'œuvre
de la collection Ralph Lauren
Les Arts Décoratifs, Paris
175 × 118.5 cm (68⅞ × 46⅝ in.)
Screen print
Printer: Sérica
Typefaces: original creation,
Foundry Sterling
2011

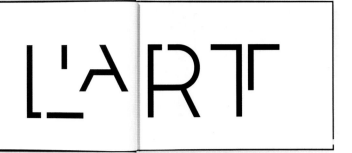

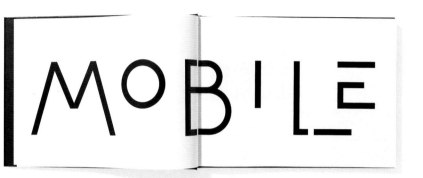

Catalog
**L'Art de l'automobile
Chefs-d'œuvre
de la collection Ralph Lauren
Les Arts Décoratifs, Paris**
27 × 35.2 cm (10⅝ × 13⅞ in.), 160 pages
Printer: Mondadori Printing
Typefaces: original creation,
Foundry Sterling
2011

Panel
**L'Art de l'automobile
Chefs-d'œuvre
de la collection Ralph Lauren
Les Arts Décoratifs, Paris**
Typeface: original creation
2011

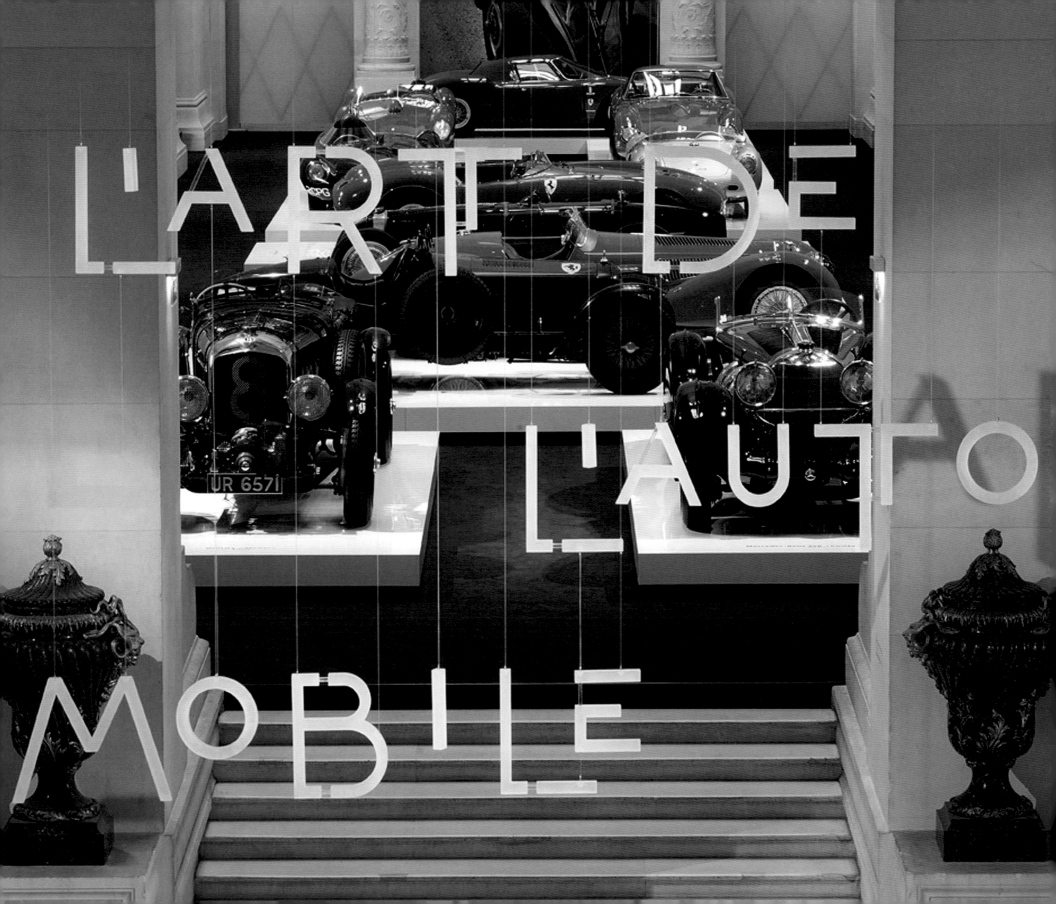

Performing Arts

Festival d'été
de Seine-Maritime

For its 1986 season, Normandy's Festival d'été de Seine-Maritime, an avant-garde summer arts festival, sought to redesign its visual identity. The new logo uses a combination of two typefaces, Times Italic and Univers, reflecting the festival's mixture of classical and contemporary programming. The festival's 1987 New Year's greeting card, responding to the logo's intrinsic geometry, takes the form of a folded triangle featuring enlargements of the punctuation and the name, reduced to its first two letters. The capital *F* represents tradition, while the lowercase *e* projects modernity. Their dynamic juxtaposition captures the spirit of the festival.

Apeloig recognized the graphic potential of the accent marks and punctuation in the title and assigned each mark a different color. A gray acute accent, yellow apostrophe, and red period inform the color palette of the identity and connote the three artistic disciplines showcased in the festival: theater, music, and dance. The vivid, abstract punctuation causes the eye to jump around, creating an almost musical rhythm. These three elements add a playful dimension to the design identity and inspire various iterations of the logo.

Festival programs and promotional materials expanded and explored the potential of the bold identity. Produced during the early age of computers, the sweeping curves and free-form shapes reflect Apeloig's interest in experimentation and ideas of "randomness" and "meaninglessness" as design concepts and tools.

Festival d'été.

Fé

Rouen le,

Folded card
New Year's greeting card 1986
Festival d'été de Seine-Maritime
17.5 × 12.5 cm (6⅞ × 4⅞ in.)
Typefaces: Times Italic, Univers
1985

Letterhead
Festival d'été de Seine-Maritime
1985

Folded card
New Year's greeting card 1987
Festival d'été de Seine-Maritime
Triangular fold
16 × 16 cm (6¼ × 6¼ in.)
Open: 31.5 × 31.5 cm (12⅜ × 12⅜ in.)
Typefaces: Times Italic, Univers
1986

Hôtel du Département
76101 Rouen Cedex
Tél. : 35.71.15.08
Télex : 771 972 F

Conseil Général de Seine-Maritime

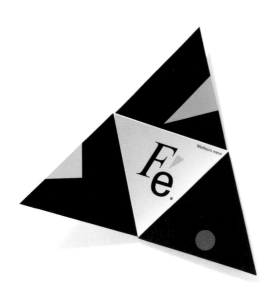

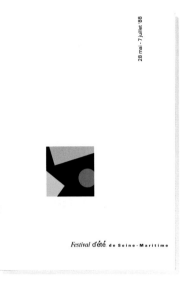

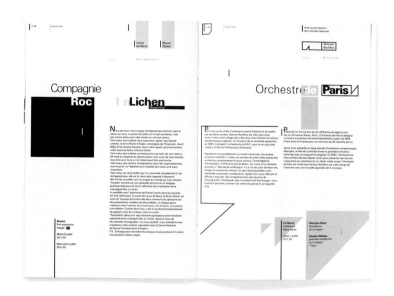

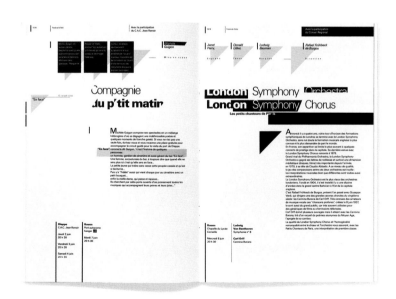

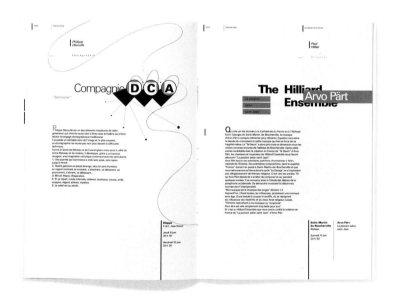

Program
Festival d'été de Seine-Maritime
29.7 × 21 cm (11⅝ × 8¼ in.)
Typeface: Univers
1988

Folded card
New Year's greeting card 1990
Festival d'été de Seine-Maritime
22 × 14.8 cm (8⅝ × 5⅞ in.)
Printer: Bussière
Typeface: Univers
1989

Program
Festival d'été de Seine-Maritime
21 × 15 cm (8¼ × 5⅞ in.)
Typeface: Univers
1986

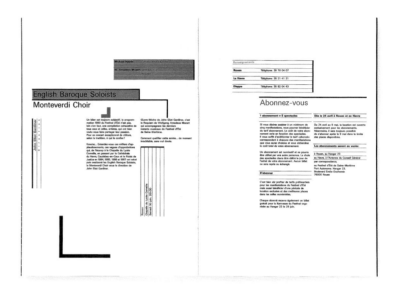

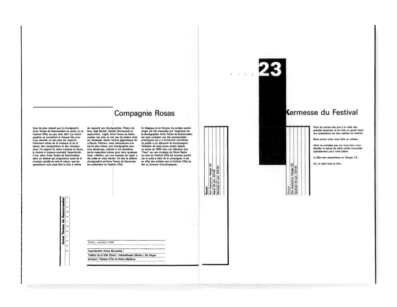

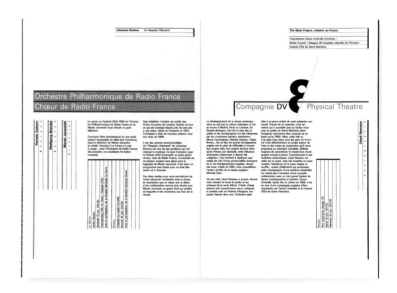

Program
Festival d'été de Seine-Maritime
29.7 × 21 cm (11⅝ × 8¼ in.)
Typeface: Univers
1990

Poster
Wolfgang Amadeus Mozart: Requiem
Festival d'été de Seine-Maritime
80 × 60 cm (31½ × 23⅝ in.)
Typeface: Univers
1990

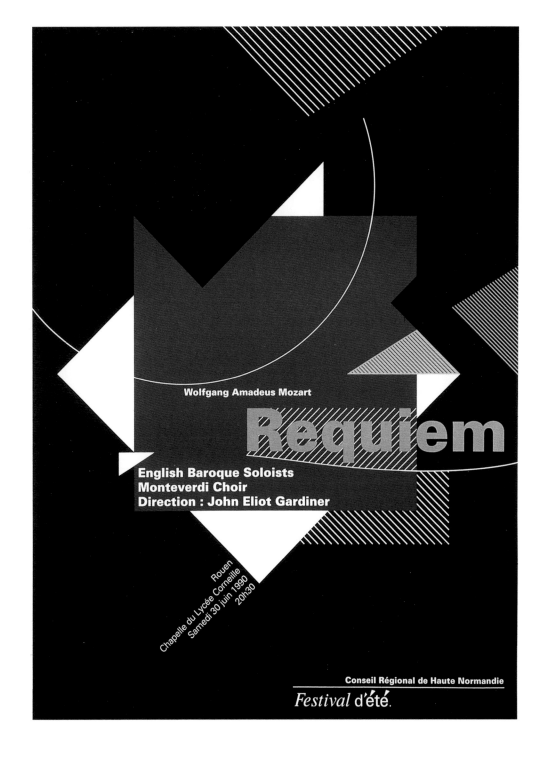

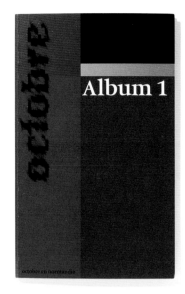

Album 1

Album 2

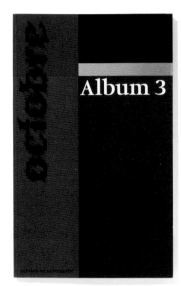

Album 3

Album 4

Album 5

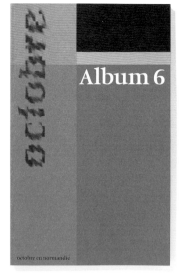

Album 6

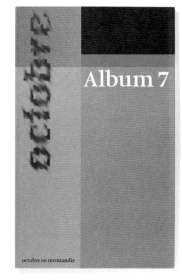

Album 7

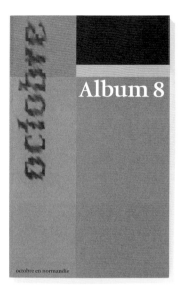

Album 8

Album 9

Octobre en Normandie

In 1990, the Festival d'été de Seine-Maritime, faced with major competition from other summertime events, moved its schedule to October and rebranded itself. The new festival name, Octobre en Normandie (October in Normandy), capitalizes on the appeal and history of the region and the month. Not only is the weather in Normandy better suited to the fall, but the festival's avant-garde audience is also more attuned to the northern European arts scene at this time of year.

Apeloig's updated logo (the word "octobre") is in lowercase lettering and uses a computer-generated, screened font in bitmap resolution. Its streaked letters and grainy roughness were achieved using the eraser, smudge, and blur tools in PhotoShop. Applied to the bitmap, with its low-resolution font, the image seems to have been eroded by water and wind.

Booklet
Albums 1 to 9
Octobre en Normandie
29 × 18 cm (11³/₈ × 7 ¹/₈ in.)
Printer: Union
Typeface: Hollander
1991 – 95

Logotype
Octobre en Normandie
1991
See pages 366 – 67

Octobre en Normandie
Musique et danse

During the Octobre en Normandie rebranding process, the festival directors were drawn to Jacques Henri Lartigue's photograph *Sala, Rocher de la Vierge, Biarritz* of August 1927. It depicts a lone man, his back to the camera, contemplating a breaking wave at the edge of a jetty. Though his body appears fragile compared to the crashing wave, he observes it calmly at close hand. The destructive force of nature reverberates in the large screen of the poster's blurred logotype, laid vertically over the image. The poster has a solid black rectangle at its top, an expanse symbolizing the imagination, with an overlapping transparent brown border at the left edge.

The breaking wave, the overlapping transparent colors, and the suffusion of the scene with a subdued multidimensional light suggest the influence of William Turner and his paintings of the British landscape.

Two narrow white lines fly away in opposite directions, providing further direction and movement. Through its selective use of photography and typographic invention, the composition as a whole harnesses the forces of nature as metaphors for the dynamism and creativity of music and dance.

Poster
Musique et Danse
Octobre en Normandie
175 × 118.5 cm (68⅞ × 46⅝ in.)
Screen print
Printer: Arts Graphiques de France
Typeface: Hollander
1991
See page 367

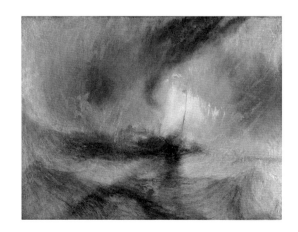

J. M. W. Turner (1775 – 1851)
Snow Storm, 1842
Oil on canvas
Tate, London

octobre en normandie
1er - 31 octobre 1991

Musique et Danse

Rouen, Le Havre,
Dieppe

locations:
35 70 04 07

Ers

Rosas
Anne Teresa de Keersmaeker

Chorals de Leipzig

Fase

Rosas
Anne Teresa de Keersmaeker

Rosas dans Rosas

Rosas
Anne Teresa de Keersmaeker

Mozart

Adagio et fugue

Les dix ans de la compagnie Rosas
1983–93

In 1993, for the tenth anniversary of the Belgian dance company Rosas, Octobre en Nomandie invited choreographer Anne Teresa De Keersmaeker to present a retrospective of her work. The book produced for the event was divided into six chapters, each dedicated to an individual composer. Color appeared only on the cover, in a still taken from a video of one of De Keersmaeker's performances, *Mikrokosmos*. Shot through an embossed glass, the wavy image captures the rhythmic rigor of her choreography.

The book's interior layouts are printed on thick, uncoated mat board, similar to sketch paper. The texture contrasts with the smoothness of the matte laminated cover, which uses a coated paper. All texts and images are in black and white with a horizontal layout, so the pages are flipped vertically. The text is laid out in narrow columns and responds to the content and composition of each image. By gradually increasing the leading, or space, between lines, Apeloig allowed blocks of text to acquire movement, mirroring the dancers' gestures.

Book
Les dix ans de la compagnie Rosas,
1983–93
Octobre en Normandie
36 × 24 cm (14⅛ × 9½ in.), 96 pages
Printer: Union
Typeface: Hollander
1993

Octobre ouvre la saison en musique
Octobre fait danser la saison

The events Octobre ouvre la saison en musique (October Opens the Season With Music) and Octobre fait danser la saison (October Makes the Season Dance) are both part of the Octobre en Normandie festival. For the first time in his collaboration with the festival, Apeloig was given free rein to play with pure abstraction and typography in designing these posters.

The experimental typeface he invented conveys the festival's essence, evoking the dance and music (both classical and contemporary) performed by well-known European conductors and orchestras. Apeloig created the font – called Octobre in honor of the festival – during his 1993 to 1994 residency at the French Academy of Art at the Villa Medici in Rome. The letters are a stencil shape: mechanical, massive, and designed as if sculpture, with each part emerging slowly from a solid form. The edges look as if they were generated from a bitmap image, with softly defined shapes and overlapping or enlarged pixels spread out on a grid.

The aesthetics of these two posters brought the public directly into the world of the avant-garde. Their daring, inventive style matched the ambitious level of the programming, and the slogans commenced a dialogue. Both express a "dance-writing" system, or method of transferring the abstract concept of movement to flat signs. Apeloig's design also evokes the style of Rudolf von Laban and Oskar Schlemmer, who treated human bodies in a two-dimensional, schematic fashion yet created spatially plastic costumes that moved in space like colored sculptures.

For the music poster, the letters are pasted like musical notes onto a partitioned grid. Their contrasting sizes suggest an undulating melodic line. The dance poster has a freer, more complex composition, yet it is still precise and balanced. Again, alternating small and large lettering suggests musical measures and dance moves. The letters are surrogates for the dancer's bodies, and the poster their stage.

These posters bring a poetic dimension to cultural promotion, thus redefining design's role. The series received the Gold Award from the Tokyo Type Directors Club in 1995.

Poster
Octobre ouvre la saison en musique
Octobre en Normandie
175 × 118.5 cm (68⅞ × 46⅝ in.)
Screen print
Printer: Arts Graphiques de France
Typeface: Octobre
1995
See pages 355, 358

Poster
Octobre fait danser la saison
Octobre en Normandie
175 × 118.5 cm (68⅞ × 46⅝ in.)
Screen print
Printer: Arts Graphiques de France
Typeface: Octobre
1995
See pages 355, 358

After Rudolf von Laban
Dance of the Ikosaeder, 1925
The Library, Kunsthaus, Zurich
Suzanne Perrottet Estate

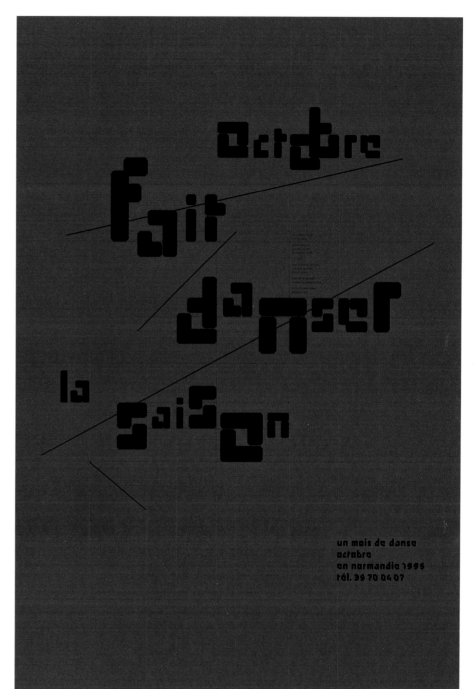

Théâtre des Amandiers

The Théâtre des Amandiers in Nanterre, led by director Patrice Chéreau, with set design by Richard Peduzzi, was a major player in the 1980s art scene in France. The theater's groundbreaking work featured nontraditional interpretations of contemporary and classic texts.

The annual brochure celebrates the Théâtre des Amandiers' founding spirit through its inventive approach to text. Angled letters set in Gill Sans typeface (designed by Eric Gill between 1927 and 1930) reside within an architectural grid system juxtaposed with thin white lines, creating a composition infused with movement. Like the theater's repertory, the graphic solution celebrates the text. The theater's unique personality is expressed through letters that behave like actors on a stage.

Compagnie Chopinot

Régine Chopinot's dance company came to the forefront of the dance field in the 1980s and was known for its radical choreography and fantastic costumes designed by Jean Paul Gaultier. The graphic identity for the company's letterhead and press kit captures this spirit of innovation. Neon pink and an uneven die cut of the inside flap give the piece its instant vibrant energy. The design establishes a dialogue between typography and choreography, with letter placement and style simulating movement.

The logo is set in Futura, a typeface designed in 1927 by Paul Renner. On a solid black background, dynamically cropped letters spelling out "Compagnie Chopinot" lean dramatically to the left. Intersecting with and layered over them are slanted open rectangles with thin pink and white borders. In an abstract way, the design evokes bodies in motion mid-improvisation – the letters tumbling, spreading, fragmenting.

Program
Saison 1986 – 87
Théâtre des Amandiers
Nanterre
21 × 15 cm (8¼ × 5⅞ in.)
Typeface: Gill Sans
1986

Press release
Compagnie Chopinot
39 × 65 cm (15⅜ × 25⅝ in.)
Closed: 31 × 22.5 cm (12¼ × 8⅞ in.)
Printer: Jacques London
Typeface: Futura
1990

Festival Rose et Fafner

Rose et Fafner, the title of a performing arts festival in Flamanville, a small village in Normandy, is layered with meaning. "Rose" refers both to the flower symbolizing love and beauty as well as to an actual woman who was a muse and friend of the festival. "Fafner" is the name of the giant-turned-dragon in Richard Wagner's epic opera *Der Ring des Nibelungen* (The Ring of the Nibelungen). In juxtaposing the sublime and the passionate, the festival title addresses its mission: to meld together and explore diverse approaches to theater.

The festival identity uses a single parenthesis – derived from the Letter Gothic typeface – repeated at many angles and in multiple sizes and weights to form varied groupings. The composition arranges them in a spiraling pattern that suggests both the curved neck of a dragon and a rose. It can also be seen as the center ring of a circus. Each parenthesis also represents a fragment of a continuing circle, visually underscoring the reference to Wagner's ring cycle in the festival's name.

Finally, creating subtle variations that breathe life into the design, Apeloig specified that the placement of each parenthesis should change every time the logo is used.

Leaflet
Festival Rose et Fafner
Flamanville, France
79.8 × 21 cm (31⅜ × 8¼ in.)
Typeface: Letter Gothic
2003

Logotype
Festival Rose et Fafner
Flamanville, France
2003
See page 329

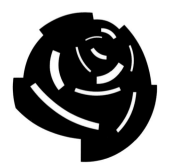

Compagnie Régis Obadia

In designing the graphic identity for Compagnie Régis Obadia, Apeloig was inspired by calligraphy. He created several brush-and-ink drawings. In the final design, a drawing of a group of abstracted figures overlaps a grid of linear elements that both frames them and implies that they exist within an orderly set of rules. The words "Compagnie," "Régis," and "Obadia" are dismantled, according to their respective syllabic division. The capital letters make up three parallel columns of type each within its own grid, and together, a larger grid. The wide, regular kerning between letters graphically represents space, and the grouping of letters a system of dance notation. While this complicates the visual inter-pretation, the deliberate segmentation of the type corresponds to the unique innovations that characterize the company and its contribution to experimental dance.

Centre national de danse contemporaine

French dancer-choreographers Joëlle Bouvier and Régis Obadia joined forces in 1980, emerging as leaders of a new wave of choreography. From 1993 to 2003, the two served as artistic directors of Centre national de danse contemporaine (CNDC; National Center for Contemporary Dance), an organization established in Angers in 1978 by the French Ministry of Culture to serve as a "university of contemporary dance." The CNDC is host to a prestigious artist-in-residence program.

The four-letter logotype expresses both the rigor and lightness of dance, and its organization references Apeloig's poster for the Octobre fait danser la saion event (page 85). Aligned along one of two crossed diagonals, the evenly spaced capital letters, *CNDC*, appear in choreographed formation. The composition can be seen as two crossed arms, two legs, or as stage directions, with a group of dancers awaiting the next step. The playful arrange-ment of text bounds across the page, creating lithe, agile rhythm and movement.

Le Lac des cygnes Opéra national de Paris

In 1994, the National Opera in Paris asked Apeloig to design the posters for two productions, including *Le lac des cygnes* (Swan Lake). His design for the production builds on a sepia-washed, out-of-focus photograph of ballerinas onstage. An overlay of classic uppercase characters – each letter printed in gold ink – creates a progressive formation that reflects ballet's pure, traditional choreography. Each letter is framed by precise diagonal lines, referencing the discipline involved in ballet. Additional light blue text cascades rhythmically on the diagonal, suggesting the delicate movements of a dancer *en pointe*.

Press release
Compagnie Régis Obadia, Paris
31 × 22.5 cm (12¼ × 8⅞ in.)
Typeface: Gravur Condensed
2004
See page 323

Program
Saison 1994 – 95
Centre national de danse
contemporaine, Angers
21.5 × 15.5 cm (8½ × 6⅛ in.)
Typeface: Foundry Sans
1994

Poster
Le Lac des cygnes
Opéra National de Paris
120 × 118 cm (47¼ × 46½ in.)
Screen print
Printer: Arts Graphiques de France
Typeface: Minion
1994

COM RÉ O
PA GI BA
GNIS DI
E A

Centre National de Danse Contemporaine d'Angers l'Esquisse

CNDC
l'esquisse
·9495

Le Ballet
de l'Opéra National
de Paris
Les Étoiles,
les Premiers Danseurs,
le Corps de Ballet
L'Orchestre
de l'Opéra National
de Paris

L	E
L	A	C
D	E	S
C	Y	G	N	E	S

Musique
Piotr Ilyitch Tchaïkovski
Chorégraphie
et mise en scène
Rudolf Noureev
d'après Marius Petipa
et Lev Ivanov

Direction musicale:
Sello Pähn/
Ermanno Florio

Décors: Ezio Frigerio

Costumes:
Franca Squarciapino

Bastille
Décembre 1994
9, 12, 13, 14, 15,
16, 19, 20, 21, 22,
23, 24, 26, 27, 28,
29, 30, 31 à 19h30
10, 17 à 14h30 et 20h

Réservations:

Tél. 47 42 53 71

Location:

Guichet Bastille

14 jours à l'avance

Places de 50F à 370F

Opéra
NATIONAL
DE PARIS

Conservatoire National Supérieur d'Art Dramatique

The corporate identity of the French National Academy of Dramatic Arts (CNSAD) reflects a modern vision of an aesthetic associated with classical and avant-garde French literature. Each year, the school produces a brochure identifying the enrolled students, as well as a series of invitation cards promoting its program.

CNSAD's traditional use of dark red Garamond type (designed in 1989 by Robert Slimbach for Adobe) was preserved for the brochure. The cover uses uncoated paper and red type on an ivory background. The cards use Taz type, designed in 1997 by Luc(as) de Groot, reflecting the contemporary repertoire of the school's program. The varied color palette allows for versatility and experimentation in the visual identity.

Brochures
Promotion 2000
Promotion 2001
Conservatoire National Supérieur d'Art Dramatique, Paris
15 × 11 cm (5⅞ × 4⅜ in.)
Printer: Floch-London
Typeface: Adobe Garamond
1999 – 2001

Invitations
Conservatoire National Supérieur d'Art Dramatique, Paris
14.8 × 10.5 cm (5⅞ × 4⅛ in.)
Printer: Nory
Typeface: Taz
2005 – 07

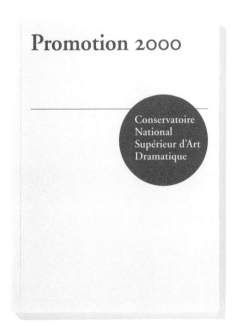

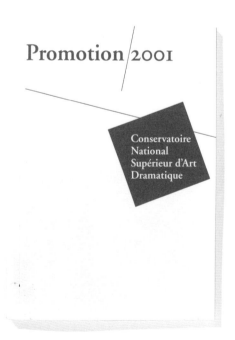

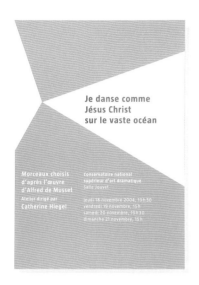

Je danse comme
Jésus Christ
sur le vaste océan

Morceaux choisis
d'après l'œuvre
d'Alfred de Musset
Atelier dirigé par
Catherine Hiegel

Conservatoire national
supérieur d'art dramatique
Salle Jouvet

jeudi 18 novembre 2004, 19 h 30
vendredi 19 novembre, 15 h
samedi 20 novembre, 19 h 30
dimanche 21 novembre, 15 h

Anna Tommy

Texte — Musique — Danse
création de
Caroline Marcadé
Atelier Danse de 3e année dirigé par
Caroline Marcadé

Conservatoire national
supérieur d'art dramatique
Théâtre du Conservatoire

mercredi 9 février 2005, 19 h 30
jeudi 10 février 2005, 19 h 30

Songe, Tempête
(fragments Shakespeare)

Atelier de 3e année dirigé par
Georges Lavaudant

Conservatoire national
supérieur d'art dramatique
Théâtre du Conservatoire

mercredi 6 avril 2005, 19 h 30
jeudi 7 avril 2005, 19 h 30
vendredi 8 avril 2005, 19 h 30

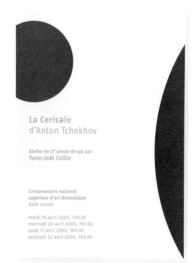

La Cerisaie
d'Anton Tchekhov

Atelier de 3e année dirigé par
Yann-Joël Collin

Conservatoire national
supérieur d'art dramatique
Salle Jouvet

mardi 19 avril 2005, 19 h 30
mercredi 20 avril 2005, 19 h 30
jeudi 21 avril 2005, 19 h 30
vendredi 22 avril 2005, 19 h 30

Journées de Juin 2005
Brecht | Eisler | Weill

Atelier de 3e année
co-dirigé par

Julie Brochen
assistée de Sabrina Delarue

et par
Françoise Rondeleux
assistée de Vincent Leterme

Conservatoire national
supérieur d'art dramatique
Théâtre du Conservatoire

lundi 27 juin 2005, 19 h 30
mardi 28 juin 2005, 19 h 30
mercredi 29 juin 2005, 19 h 30
jeudi 30 juin 2005, 19 h 30

Journées pédagogiques
de Juin 2005

2e année, classes de

Muriel Mayette
Daniel Mesguich
Nada Strancar

Conservatoire national
supérieur d'art dramatique

Conservatoire
National
Supérieur d'Art
Dramatique

Atelier de 3e année
dirigé par
Alain Françon

Tailleur pour dames
Léonie est en avance
ou le mal joli
Dormez, je le veux !
Georges Feydeau

Lundi 19, mardi 20,
mercredi 21, jeudi 22,
décembre 2005
à 19h30

Conservatoire
National
Supérieur d'Art
Dramatique

Atelier Masque
de 3e année dirigé
par
Mario Gonzalez

Samuel Beckett

Lundi 10 et mardi
11 avril 2006 à 19h30
mercredi 12 avril 2006
à 15h

Conservatoire national supérieur de musique et de danse de Paris

The Conservatoire national supérieur de musique et de danse de Paris (National Conservatory of Music and Dance) was established by Louis XIV as a royal singing school. Its current home, designed by Christian de Portzamparc, opened in 1990 in Paris's nineteenth *arrondissement*. Apeloig designed the 2011–12 brochure for which photographer Ferrante Ferranti supplied photographs of the building and the school's day-to-day life. The acronym CNSMDP appears on the front and back of the cover, but on the front these letters – in bold black letters – are set within the full name of the school. The other letters form a hypnotically regular schema, alternating between red and light purple, with the preposition "de" (of) set in smaller letters and disrupting the grid. The visual effect is of a dance notation or a musical score. Two flaps create a proscenium: the front opens to reveal a photograph of dancers, the back an image of the school's organ.

The texts are printed on uncoated paper, the photographs on coated. The use of a complex grid with multiple columns provides flexibility, allowing for numerous insertions and fluid reading.

Program
Saison 2011–12
Conservatoire national supérieur de musique et de danse, Paris
20.9 × 13.7 cm (8¼ × 5⅜ in.), 232 pages
Printer: Snel
Typeface: DTL Prokyon
2011

Program
Saison 2006 – 07
Châtelet, Théâtre musical de Paris
21 × 5.5 cm (8¼ × 2⅛ in.)
Printer: Stipa/PLJ Édition Communication
Typeface: Akkurat
2006

Program
Saison 2008 – 09
Châtelet, Théâtre musical de Paris
14.5 × 9.5 cm (5¾ × 3¾ in.)
Printer: Stipa/PLJ Édition Communication
Typeface: Akkurat
2008

Program
Saison 2011 – 12
Châtelet, Théâtre musical de Paris
14.5 × 9.5 cm (5¾ × 3¾ in.)
Printer: Stipa/PLJ Édition Communication
Typeface: Akkurat
2011

Châtelet
Théâtre musical de Paris

Founded in 1862, the Théâtre du Châtelet gained fame during the first half of the twentieth century for operettas featuring the most famous artists of the day. After undergoing a major renovation, the Châtelet reopened in 1980 under the name Châtelet, Théâtre musical de Paris. Today, it presents musicals, opera, and dance, as well as classical, jazz, and pop concerts. The organization's logo, designed by Apeloig in 2006, draws attention to music, which lies at the heart of both the theater program and its language. It uses the font Akkurat, created by Laurenz Brunner in 2004. The design cuts "Châtelet" into three syllables, stressing the sonority and rhythm of the word. Apeloig plays with the theater's evolving identity by stacking the fragments "châ," "te," and "let" in large, bold lowercase type and by sandwiching "Théâtre musical de Paris" in small uppercase letters between them. Lines around the central second syllable "te" suggest a note dissected from a score.

The first printed program was designed to emulate a Pantone color fan, giving the public a tactile and visual understanding of the season's offerings. The use of bright colors – hot pink and neon yellow – shocks the eye. The narrow pages flip freely, creating a sense of rhythm, repetition, and surprise.

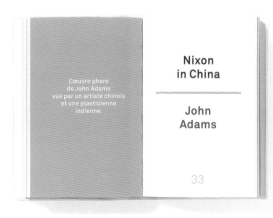

Les Paladins

—> de Jean-Philippe Rameau ——> Direction musicale
William Christie ——> Mise en scène et chorégraphie
José Montalvo et Dominique Hervieu ————————>
Scénographie et conception vidéo José Montalvo
—> Topi Lehtipuu, Stéphanie d'Oustrac, Sandrine Piau,
François Piolino, João Fernandes, René Schirrer
Orchestre et Chœur des Arts Florissants / Danseurs
du Centre chorégraphique national de Créteil et du
Val-de-Marne / Compagnie Montalvo-Hervieu ———>
————> Coproduction du Théâtre du Châtelet-Paris
et du Barbican Centre-Londres ——————————>
16, 17, 19 et 20 octobre à 19 h 30 / 22 octobre à 16 h
Réservation: 01 40 28 28 40 /chatelet-theatre.com

l'opéra
hip-hop

Candide

Opéra de Leonard Bernstein —> —> Direction musicale
John Axelrod —> —> Mise en scène —> Robert Carsen
Lambert Wilson, William Burden, David Adam Moore,
Anna Christy, Joni Bern, Kim Criswell, John Daszak
Ensemble orchestral de Paris —> —> —> —> —> —> —>
—> —> —> —> —> Avec le soutien du Crédit Agricole
—> —> 11, 13, 15, 19, 23, 26, 28, 31 décembre à 19 h 30
le 17 à 17 h —> —> —> —> —> —> —> —> —> —> —>
Réservation: 01 40 28 28 40 / chatelet-theatre.com

Broadway
à Paris

The poster series for Châtelet's 2006 – 07 season revisits Apeloig's experimental font, Octobre, first developed in 1994 (page 84). The assignment was to promote shows that had not yet been curated, providing an opportunity to create unity within the series and a global visual identity.

Each employs bright or deep eye-catching colors and is punctuated by playful black and white notes. The weighty performance titles – *Les Paladins, Candide, Jazz* – contrast with the negative space above them and the fluid airiness of the texts below. The typeface was expanded to include capital letters, numbers, and arrows. The chunky woodblock forms of the Octobre letters contrast starkly with the rounded Akkurat letters used in the logo.

The first posters of the series are filled with heavy letters and signs that build up blocks of information on solid color backgrounds. Arrows and other punctuation direct the eye, while the letters form a geometric, architectural vocabulary. Together, these simple elements convey the visceral volume, force, and movement of music.

Posters
Les Paladins
Candide
Jazz
Châtelet, Théâtre musical de Paris
150 × 100 cm (59 × 39⅜ in.)
Screen print
Printer: Lézard Graphique
Typeface: Octobre
2006 – 07

Poster 1 (left)

le premier
opéra africain
création

Musique **Zé Manel Fortes**
Livret **Koulsy Lamko**

Direction artistique **Wasis Diop**
Mise en scène **Jean-Pierre Leurs**
Lumière **Jacques Rouveyrollis**
Décors et costumes **Oumou Sy**

Bintou Wéré

un opéra

25, 26 et 27 octobre 2007 à 20 h

du Sahel

châ
-te-
let

THÉÂTRE
MUSICAL
DE PARIS

Poster 2 (right)

Concert
exceptionnel

Vendredi
30 Mai 2008
à 21 h

Roy Hargrove

et RH Factor

invitent

MC Solaar

et Ron Carter

T. 01 40 28 28 40 / chatelet-theatre.com

châ
-te-
let

THÉÂTRE
MUSICAL
DE PARIS

The 2007 – 08 season at the Châtelet featured opera, classical concerts, jazz recitals, and dance. Each performance reflected a different world culture, and the poster series communicated those differences through inventive type and typography, while giving the overall series a unifying identity. The custom lettering, with its clean sans serif lines, is derived from the Akkurat typeface.

In the poster promoting the West African opera *Bintou Wéré: Un opéra du Sahel* (Bintou Were: A Sahel Opera), the letterforms attach to and sit beneath a series of levels – stacked, broken lines of varying density. The design for *Padmâvatî*, an opera composed by Albert Roussel, references India through its strong color and bold type, which hangs from broken horizontal bars and is reminiscent of Hindu script. The arrangement of the text throughout the series has a musicality that harmonizes with the subject matter, supplying tonal variation, rhythm, and dramatic emphasis.

Apeloig won the 2009 overall award from the International Society of Typographic Designers (ISTD) for this campaign.

Posters
Bintou Wéré
Roy Hargrove et RH Factor invitent
MC Solaar et Ron Carter
Châtelet, Théâtre musical de Paris
150 × 100 cm (59 × 39⅜ in.)
Screen print
Printer: Serica
Typefaces: Akkurat,
Akkurat Bollywood
2007 – 08

Poster
Padmâvatî
Châtelet, Théâtre musical de Paris
This poster is a later version than the one produced for the client.
150 × 100 cm (59 × 39⅜ in.)
Screen print
Printer: Serica
Typefaces: Akkurat,
Akkurat Bollywood
2007 – 08

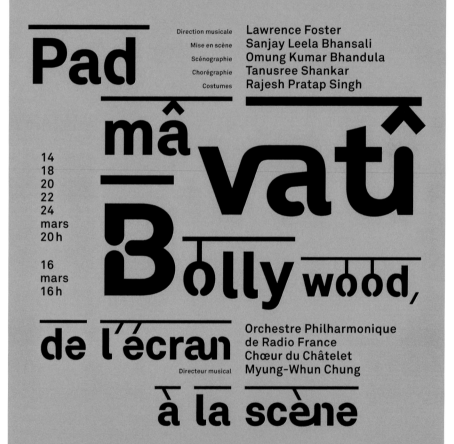

Kodo Dadan

The 2011–12 season at Châtelet featured Kodo, a Japanese troupe of "samurai percussionists" that reinterprets and preserves the traditional Japanese art form of *taiko*. The promotional poster is dominated by a circular shape containing a *mitsudomoe*, three whirling comma-like forms that serve as the Kodo logo. A scattering of lines ricochets across its surface, representing drumsticks. A soft yellow is used to define the central image, while the drumsticks are printed a light brown. In the four corners of the poster, white tangram or origami-shaped letters spell out "KODO." The background is solid black, establishing a deep contrast between light and dark that evokes the intensity of the percussionists live performances.

Street Scene

In 2013, Châtelet presented the 1946 American opera *Street Scene* by Kurt Weill. The story depicts life in a Lower East Side tenement between one evening and the following afternoon. Through expressive lettering, Apeloig's poster turns the title into a New York City stoop, the ubiquitous stage and front-row seat for urban theater. A low-tech approach was used to create it: paper stencils of each letter in the words "street" and "scene" were made and folded twice. These were then assembled and stacked, their cumulative folds creating a flight of steps lit as if by a single streetlight and seen from a receding angle. The folded planes also resemble parts of a building's façade: bricks, pediments, lintels, and arches. The negative spaces and shapes become doors, windows, crawl spaces, alleys, and crevices.

The irregularities of the handmade letters catch the light less predictably than would smooth surfaces, and other marks of process – creases and occasional stray lines – create movement and tension. The harsh, unforgiving nature of the urban landscape is evoked through strongly contrasting black and white, light and shadow.

Poster
Kodo Dadan
Châtelet, Théâtre musical de Paris
150 × 100 cm (59 × 39⅜ in.)
Screen print
Printer: Lézard Graphique
Typeface: Akkurat
2012

Poster
Street Scene
Châtelet, Théâtre musical de Paris
150 × 100 cm (59 × 39⅜ in.)
Screen print
Printer: Lézard Graphique
Typefaces: Champion Gothic, Akkurat
2013

Tambours
japonais
15 –18 février
2012

châ
THÉÂTRE
-te-
MUSICAL
let
DE PARIS

KODO

DADAN

Direction artistique
Tamasaburo
Bando

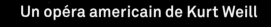

Un opéra americain de Kurt Weill

Livret
Elmer Rice

Lyrics
Langston Hughes
& Elmer Rice

En anglais, surtitré

Direction musicale
Tim Murray

Mise en scène
John Fulljames

Orchestre
Pasdeloup

Chœur
du Châtelet

25 – 31 janvier
2013

chatelet-theatre.com
01 40 28 28 40

Co-Production The Opera
Group / Young Vic Theatre,
coproduit originellement
avec le Watford Palace
Theatre. Présenté en
accord avec The European
American Music Corporation,
agent pour The Kurt Weill
Foundation for Music,
Inc., The Rice Estate and
The Hughes Estate

châ
THÉÂTRE
-te-
MUSICAL
let
DE PARIS

Program 2012–13

Châtelet's 2012–13 program is a 252-page special edition that celebrates the theater's 150th anniversary. It has a pocket-size, flip-book format, and its cover design references two of the season's major productions: John Adams's opera *I Was Looking at the Ceiling and Then I Saw the Sky*, and Stephen Sondheim's musical *Sunday in the Park with George*. Adams's two-act composition tells the story of his experience of the 1994 Northridge Earthquake in Los Angeles. Like the eerie atmospheric conditions that precede natural disasters, the metallic blue cover of the program takes on different hues in different light conditions. In addition, parallel rows of silver foiled dots are stamped into the medium-weight paper cover, with full flaps, creating an inverse Braille-like texture and suggesting a starry night or a close-up detail of a halftone image. These dots refer to Sondheim's subject: Georges Seurat and the creation of his painting *A Sunday Afternoon on the Island of La Grande Jatte – 1884*, which used his new pointillist technique.

A lightweight paper is used for the interior pages, which feels sensual and fluid in the hand. White rectangles structure the informational text and the section and production titles; headers and artists' names are set in small red lettering. Both contrast with the pages' soft gray backgrounds. Carrying the pointillist theme throughout, the booklet's sixteen sections are introduced by abstract images treated with a large dot screen-printed light blue or red. A selection of toned (slightly blue), full-bleed black-and-white reproductions – ranging from production and film stills to engravings and images of theatrical ephemera – brings Châtelet, now and in the past, fully to life, as does the final chapter. The 150th anniversary booklet, with its rich content, is not just a program; it is a keepsake.

Program
Saison 2012–13
Châtelet, Théâtre musical de Paris
9 × 14.1 cm (3½ × 5½ in.)
Printer: Stipa/PLJ Édition communication
Typeface: Akkurat
2012

SUNDAY IN THE PARK WITH GEORGE

Stephen Sondheim

les 15, 16, 17,
19, 20, 23, 24
et 25 avril
2013
à 20 h
—
le 21 avril
à 16 h

Tarifs p. 142
Plan A

Gabriel Davioud, architecte des théâtres de la place du Châtelet

Dès 1856, Haussmann charge Gabriel Davioud (alors architecte en chef des Promenades et des Plantations de Paris) de l'édification de ces bâtiments. Il s'agit, selon ses vœux, de « faire des nouveaux théâtres des monuments dignes de la capitale de la France ; les construire solidement et les décorer richement ; leur donner des accès larges et faciles ; des salles vastes, bien éclairées, bien aérées, pour que le public y circule aisément, y séjourne commodément ; enfin, mettre à profit les progrès des industries modernes, pour rendre ces théâtres attrayants et confortables » (Mémoires, tome 2). En octobre 1859, la Ville acquiert les terrains de la place du Châtelet sur lesquels seront bâtis les nouveaux édifices.

Architecture

Dans son projet initial, Davioud imagine, selon les souhaits du Préfet, deux théâtres symétriques aux façades semblables. Pour des questions de rentabilité, les façades latérales des théâtres doivent abriter des appartements loués à des particuliers et les espaces du rez-de-chaussée sont destinés à recevoir différents commerces (boutiques, cafés, restaurants…). Haussmann contrôle pas à pas le projet de Davioud : une façade polychrome initialement prévue est finalement remplacée par une façade en pierre, dans le style de la Renaissance italienne. L'apparence sobre et géométrique des deux édifices ne manque pas de susciter les critiques de certains contemporains qui reprochent à l'architecte son manque d'imagination et le caractère peu spectaculaire des théâtres de la nouvelle place.

LE CHÂTELET TRAVERSE L'HISTOIRE 1862 – 2012…

Le scandale de L'Après-midi d'un faune

Pour la saison 1912, en dehors de Thamar sur une musique de Balakirev, Diaghilev s'est adressé à des compositeurs français : Maurice Ravel pour Daphnis et Chloé, Reynaldo Hahn pour Le Dieu bleu (sur un argument de Cocteau) et Claude Debussy pour l'utilisation de sa musique du Prélude à l'après-midi d'un faune. Avec L'Après-midi d'un faune, Nijinski crée sa première chorégraphie, signant une œuvre d'une modernité et d'une audace choquantes pour une grande partie du public. Le succès est à la mesure du scandale : le lendemain, le Châtelet joue à guichets fermés.

1917 : Parade ou l'esprit nouveau

« Une insulte au bon goût et au bon sens ! » : Parade provoqua une véritable tempête le soir de la première, le 18 mai 1917. L'argument de Cocteau pour ce ballet chorégraphié par le jeune Léonide Massine jouait sur l'illusion du théâtre dans le théâtre. Picasso, à qui Diaghilev avait fait appel pour les décors, peignit un gigantesque rideau de scène, où se mêlaient réalité et fantastique. La discordance entre cette toile et la teneur du ballet, censé se dérouler sur un boulevard parisien, ainsi que les personnages étranges des Managers choquèrent le public. Quant à la musique d'Erik Satie, qui signait ici sa première œuvre de scène, « sa simplicité neuve, savante, linéaire » (Cocteau) ne fut guère goûtée, si ce n'est par les pairs du compositeur.

Théâtre national de Toulouse

The Théâtre national de Toulouse (TNT; National Theater of Toulouse) is a place where audiences can experience voices, gestures, and words from around the world. The program ranges from classical repertory to the avant-garde, as well as from dance and poetry to puppetry and circus. Apeloig began working with TNT in 2009 to redesign its marketing materials and to integrate a new, more direct style of communication in line with the theater's existing identity.

For the quarterly programs, bold photos, dynamic scaling, and cropping of the word "regard(s)" (look/gazes) build a distinct visual identity.

The 2012–13 poster breaks away from this, using a strictly typographic approach. Apeloig's original and experimental typography creates an allegory for the stage: form and color are fused, with the illusory use of primary hues against a black background creating a pictorial space. The composition consists of seven lines of text, shifting from left to right and swinging horizontally. The overlapping letters create areas of white that recall the sweep of theatrical lights and oscillate between rigid construction and deconstruction. Combined with the vivid palette, the letters' boisterous contact and intimacy reflect the joy of the season's festivities. The names of the artists and performers are incorporated into the block letters as if small, internal sparks of life.

Programs
Saison 2011–12
Théâtre national de Toulouse
Midi-Pyrénées
30 × 16 cm (11¾ × 6¼ in.)
Typeface: Akzidenz Grotesk Next
2011

Poster
Théâtre national de Toulouse
Midi-Pyrénées
Saison 2012–13
175 × 118.5 cm (68⅞ × 46⅝ in.)
Screen print
Printer: Lézard Graphique
Typefaces: original creation,
Akzidenz Grotesk Next
2012
See page 290

Publications

bilan et
perspectives
pour 89

89

les arts
p /a
s
t i
q u
e
s

Ministère de la Culture, de la Communication,
des Grands Travaux
et du Bicentenaire

Contacts presse

Ministère de la Culture,
de la Communication,
des Grands Travaux,
et du Bicentenaire

Bilan et perspectives
Les arts plastiques '89

This press kit was designed for the press confer-ence Bilan et perspectives '89, les arts plastiques (Assessment and Perspectives '89: The Visual Arts), which the French Ministry of Culture and Commu-nication called to announce its policy on visual arts. Its cover is one of the first designs Apeloig ever created on a computer, and its free-form curves, abstract shapes, and use of randomness illustrate the extraordinary capacity of software to inspire and elevate design. Attracted at the time to the practical, theoretical approach of Wolfgang Weingart, Apeloig's work with April Greiman in Los Angeles in 1987 and 1988 exposed him to the new possibilities afforded by technology, and to the idea of using randomness creatively. Early mistakes and unplanned, unexpected effects opened up new directions and ideas.

The cover employs a unique die cut on the inside flaps and features a complex typographic com-position. It seems eclectic – even unfinished – with scattered, layered letters suggesting a work in progress. The type floats freely, although a remarkable balance exists between empty spaces and grouped letters, which are linked visually by undulating shapes in the background. The use of silver Chromolux paper contrasts with the gray and soft yellow palette, while the darker gray matte areas evoke the texture of a crumpled newspaper, providing a sense of volume. These inventive design choices reveal Apeloig's idealistic desire to invent a new design language and to optimize a brand-new tool that would transform design.

Press release
**Bilan et perspectives '89,
les arts plastiques
Ministère de la Culture et de la Communication**
31 × 22.5 cm (12¼ × 8⅞ in.)
Open: 47 × 68 cm (18½ × 26¾ in.)
Screen print
Printer: Silium
Typeface: Univers
1989
See page 369

Comme
un coursier indompté

The limited-edition fine-art book *Comme un coursier indompté* (Like an Indomitable Racehorse) commemorates the bicentennial of the French Revolution. It contains forty-eight essays written by philosophers, politicians, thinkers, and writers – from Abbé Grégoire to François-Vincent Toussaint to Diderot – during the Age of Enlightenment (c.1650 – 1780), along with eight original lithographs by contemporary artists, including Pierre Alechinsky, François Rouan, Jean-Charles Blais, and Jean Messagier. Housed inside a large boxed case, the work was printed in an edition of two hundred and co-published by the Imprimerie nationale (National Printers) and the Centre national des arts plastiques (National Center of Visual Arts).

The phrase "comme un coursier indompté" comes from Jean-Jacques Rousseau's 1755 *Discourse on the Origin of Inequality*. The cover of the case features a spiral design suggesting the evolution of democracy through a series of progressive but disruptive movements. The curving swirls reflect early computer-based experiments with Bézier curves, and the image, carefully drawn, uses outlines to create a definite structure.

The design uses white and silver inks printed on black imitation leather. A shiny varnish has been selectively applied, creating a rich array of blacks. The title words are cut onto a horizontal base and move through the composition, beginning at the back of the case and continuing to the front. This work illustrates the freedom that computing afforded by this time and is a tribute to the Modernism of typography and its progressive ambitions.

Slipcase
Comme un coursier indompté
Imprimerie nationale
Centre national des arts plastiques
45 × 74 cm (17¾ × 29⅛ in.)
Screen print
Printer: Fourier
Typeface: Garamond
1989
See page 370

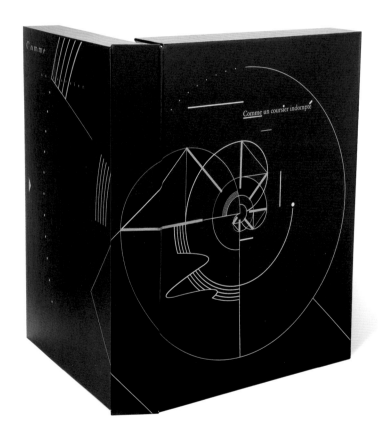

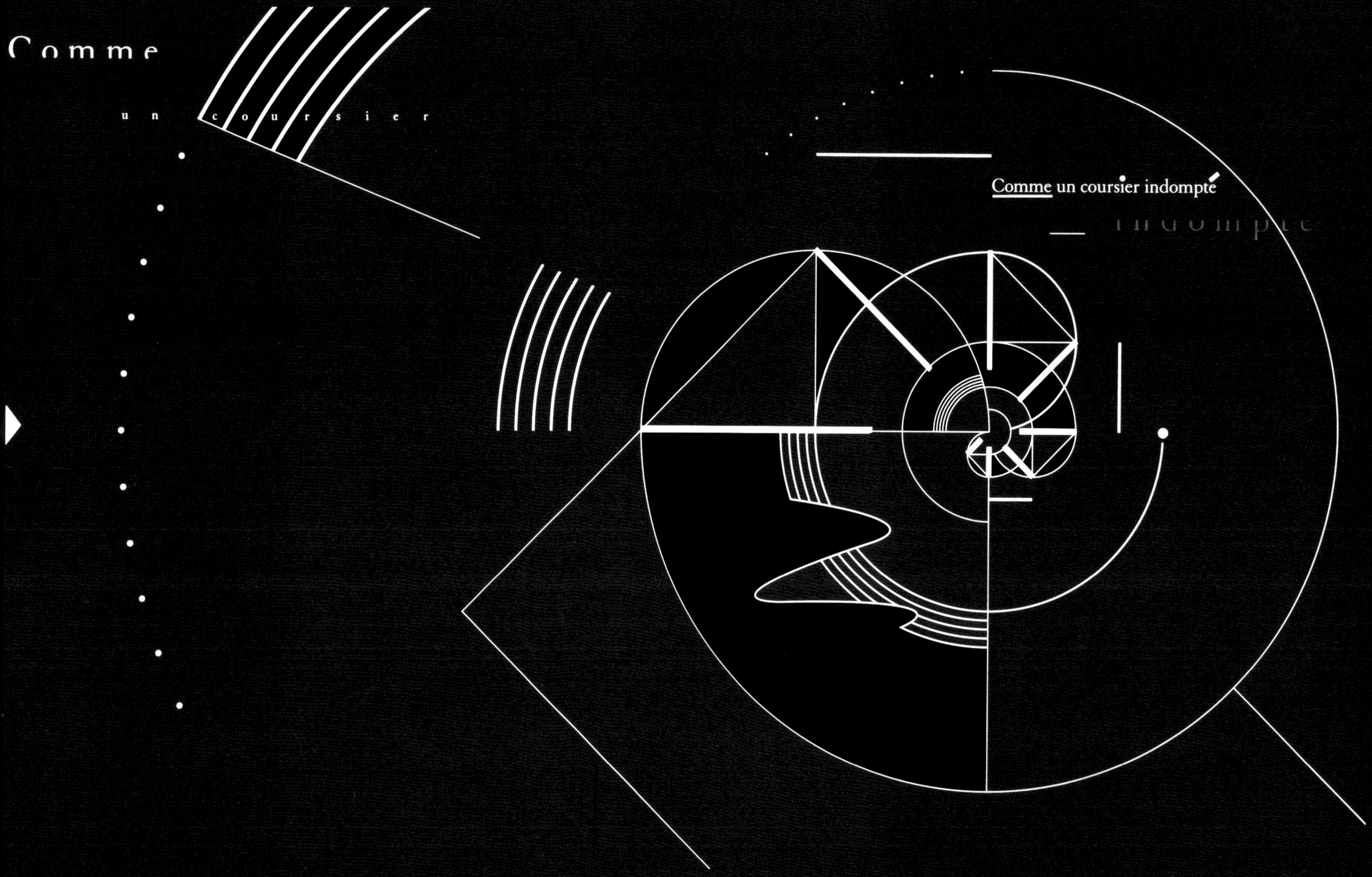

Comme

un coursier

Comme un coursier indompté

indompté

Collection
Acteurs de l'Histoire

Collection Acteurs de l'Histoire (Actors of History Collection), published by the Imprimerie nationale, is a series of historical texts by France's founding fathers commented by prominent contemporary historians. The series was produced in both soft-cover and hardcover editions, and the design mixes nineteenth-century Bodoni type with fluid Bézier curves. At the top of each cover, these undulating curves suggest the pages of an open book, while random lines create a sense of movement and point to the solid block of color that surrounds the author's name. The freedom of these lines challenges and contrasts with the traditional font.

This design features the free-form geometric lines that frequently appear in Apeloig's work of the early 1990s. It combines his traditional French training with the experimental approach he discovered and embraced in California.

Book
Perdiguier, Mémoires d'un compagnon
Collection Acteurs de l'Histoire
22 × 16.2 cm (8⅝ × 6⅜ in.)
Full leather binding
Printer: Imprimerie nationale
Typeface: Bodoni
1992

Book
Renan, Qu'est-ce qu'une Nation?
Collection Acteurs de l'Histoire
22 × 16.2 cm (8⅝ × 6⅜ in.)
Printer: Imprimerie nationale
Typeface: Bodoni
1996

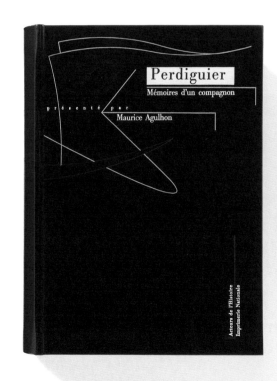

Bicentenaire
de l'Assemblée nationale

In 1990, the Assemblée nationale (National Assembly) commemorated their bicentennial by organizing an international competition for a sculpture to be permanently installed in the historical Court of Honor in the Palais Bourbon. The subtle complexity and sobriety of Walter De Maria's sculpture proved the perfect match for the site.

De Maria's minimalist granite sphere on a classical limestone pedestal pays homage to universal human rights. The bicentennial dates are engraved on either side of the pedestal, inside which the artist has concealed a gilt-bronze heart. The nearly ten-foot-tall sculpture is surrounded by a semicircular limestone railing, upon which eleven bronze plaques, engraved with the preamble and seventeen articles of the Declaration of the Rights of Man and of the Citizen, are embedded.

The gray cover of the catalog has a granite-like pattern and a reproduction of De Maria's hand-drawn aerial view of the installation, printed in white. Thick black bands on the sides and top of the booklet create structure and frame the drawing. A fine line printed in gold foil at the top center of the composition refers to the hidden heart.

Exhibition catalog
Une sculpture de Walter De Maria
Bicentenaire de l'Assemblée nationale
31.5 × 24.7 cm (12³⁄₈ × 9³⁄₄ in.), 40 pages
Offset and hot foil
Printer: Union
Typeface: Univers
1990

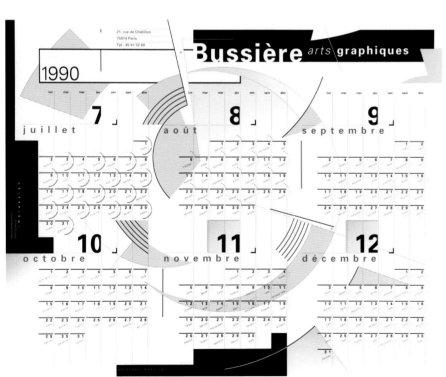

Bussière arts graphiques

Bussière is a French company that specializes in the graphic arts, including photoengraving, letterpress, phototypesetting, and digital work. Every year, the company commissions a new design for its corporate desk calendar. The 1990 design uses the Univers font and follows a grid, with a series of small curves identifying each month. One abstract line snakes around the printing surface, representing the advancing passage of time. Many steps were involved in the creation of this calendar. Numerous sketches were drawn by hand on tracing paper, then layered one on top of another to create a random, organic design, which was then translated via computer-aided design (CAD).

The design for each month remains thematically tied to the overall graphic construction. Lines circle in various directions around type elements – company name, month, and number. The cumulative effect is of a refined cut-and-paste job, in which different elements, glued and overlapping, yield fragmented, improvised shapes.

Desk calendar
Bussière arts graphiques Paris
39 × 49 cm (15⅜ × 19¼ in.)
Printer: Bussière
Typeface: Univers
1990
See page 368

Jardin des Modes

Jardin des Modes was founded in 1922 by Lucien Vogel, the charismatic founder of *La Gazette du bon ton*, French *Vogue* and *Vu*, and publisher of the first *Babar* albums. During the 1960s, art director Jean Widmer brought a strong sense of modernism to the publication with the help of his talented team of Swiss compatriots. In 1979, he was succeeded by Milton Glaser who enlarged the format, designed a new logo and layout, and transformed the magazine into a revolutionary design vehicle. All subjects were now covered equally – from fashion to furniture to graphic design to contemporary art – and infused with a fresh vision and new ideas. *Jardin des Modes* was a touchstone for anyone interested in design during the 1980s and 1990s.

In 1992, editor-in-chief Alice Morgaine offered Philippe Apeloig the position of art director. While respecting Milton Glaser's format and identity he made the layout more flexible, in particular, updating the typography, redefining and re-cutting it. His collaboration with the magazine came to a sudden end with his appointment as a resident of the Villa Medici in Rome. That same year, the special issue commemorating the magazine's seventy-fifth anniversary was accompanied by an exhibition at the Musée des Arts Décoratifs in Paris.

Working with current events poses unique challenges, but tight deadlines inspire innovation. This was reflected in the layouts and covers, which featured commissioned images by leading photographers, as well as collages of popular icons and symbols.

Magazine
Jardin des Modes, Paris
N°. 165, December 1992
N°. 166, February 1993
37.1 × 27.1 cm (14⅝ × 10⅝ in.)
Typefaces: Gill Sans, Goudy Oldstyle
1993

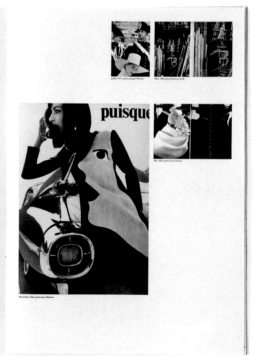

The Cooper Union
School of Art, New York

In the winter of 1998 and 1999, Philippe Apeloig moved to the United States, dividing his time between New York City and Providence, where he was teaching at the Rhode Island School of Design (RISD). He subsequently became a fulltime professor at The Cooper Union in New York, where he also acted as curator of the Herb Lubalin Study Center of Design and Typography from 2000 to 2003. During this time, Apeloig curated exhibitions, including "Jean Widmer: A Devotion to Modernism" and organized "Massin in Continuo: A Dictionary."

Apeloig developed an advanced design critique class titled GraphiCooper, which revolved around lectures by noted designers. The students researched each guest speaker's work, then designed posters inspired by his or her individual approach. Following each lecture, the speakers would critique the students' works. The highly attended GraphiCooper series, to which the public was also invited, featured Ruedi Baur, Fang Chen, Milton Glaser, Alain Le Quernec, Uwe Loesch, Luba Lukova, Bruno Monguzzi, Lars Müller, Melchior Imboden, Paula Scher, Leonardo Sonnoli, David Tartakover, Niklaus Troxler, Wolfgang Weingart, and many others. Each semester, Apeloig designed the program that announced the guest-speakers, enabling him to develop his graphic work in New York. The 2009 invitation for the Annual Student Exhibition and the programs for the conferences both used typography as the principal element of their layout.

Leaflet
Annual Student Exhibition
The Cooper Union School of Art,
New York
12.4 × 80 cm (4⅞ × 31½ in.)
Typeface: Akzidenz Grotesk
2001

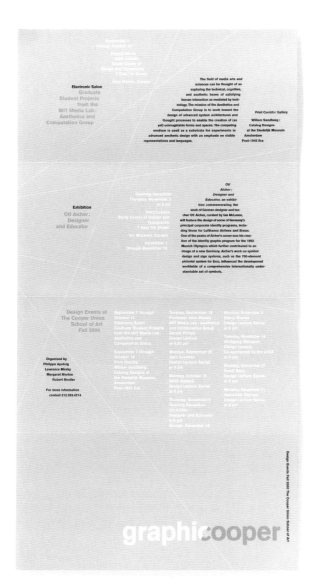

Leaflet
**GraphiCooper Fall 2000
The Cooper Union School of Art,
New York**
40.8 × 21.5 cm (16 × 8½ in.)
Typeface: Akzidenz Grotesk
2001

Leaflet
**GraphiCooper Fall 2001
The Cooper Union School of Art,
New York**
21.5 × 10 cm (8½ × 3⅞ in.)
Typeface: Frutiger
2001

Jean Widmer
A Devotion to Modernism

In 2003, the Herb Lubalin Study Center of Design and Typography at New York's Cooper Union School of Art presented the exhibition "Jean Widmer: A Devotion to Modernism." The Swiss-born, Paris-based designer and his international style and approach had had a huge influence on French graphic design in the 1960s and 1970s. Widmer is most famous for his timeless abstract logo for the Centre Georges Pompidou in Paris.

Apeloig curated the retrospective exhibition on the designer and created the accompanying brochure and catalog. He used Widmer's pictographic highway signage system to draw attention to the exhibition and to enliven a long window-lined corridor facing Manhattan's Fourth Avenue that runs nearly the length of the building. The signage system was also used as a motif for the catalog cover. The symbols were given a UV varnish, creating a Braille-like embossed texture on the front and back covers. The catalog and signage were created in Centre Georges Pompidou CGP, a typeface designed by Adrian Frutiger with the collaboration of Hans-Jürg Hunziker. Jean Widmer had also used it for a radical visual identity proposal for the Center's foundation in 1977.

Exhibition catalog
Jean Widmer: A Devotion to Modernism
The Herb Lubalin Study Center
of Design and Typography, New York
24 × 16.7 cm (9½ × 6⅝ in.), 96 pages
Typeface: Centre Georges Pompidou CGP
2003

· Could you describe the close relationship existing between the Swiss designers who had left their homeland?

+++ There were from fifty to sixty Swiss art professionals who had settled in Paris—photographers, designers, graphic artists and painters. I ran into several of my fellow students from my years at the Zurich School of Applied Arts, including Paris Apart, Adrian Frutiger, Peter and Sonia Knapp, Evert Endt and, later on, Ursula and Ernst Hiestand. The latter were there for a training course, and we teamed up for the Centre Georges Pompidou competition. We shared the same method of working, the same artistic approach. Obviously, our vision was radically modernist. The French public, especially on the art scene, fell in love with the new design philosophy. In retrospect, I realize that our Bauhaus-style education landed us in key positions in record time. We breathed new life into a profession that was qualified at the time as "commercial artist." This period (which saw the decorative arts, as we know them, draw to an end) was marked by major differences between varying modernist approaches, with numerous Swiss graphic designers swarming into the land. All the French agencies dreamt of adding a Swiss designer to their staff. The market expanded, became enormous and, I can now admit, the Swiss began replacing the French, a state of affairs that also explains why I was invited to teach in France. In Switzerland, you get to design a little announcement for the press; in France, a whole poster.

· Was leaving Switzerland a manner of rebelling for you?

+++ No, because I hadn't been planning to leave Switzerland. But the French had something to teach me, to offer me, and I just kept going from one project to the next. Without even realizing it, I got caught up in the system. The history of the period was also a factor. Paris got a hold of me and literally swallowed me up.

· Do you return to Switzerland regularly? What has become of the place where you grew up?

+++ I did return there regularly as long as my parents were alive. Nowadays, I go back occasionally to see the rest of my family. I have a brother and sister who live near Zurich. Our house was sold in the meantime. And the garden... well, it's been replaced by a villa and no longer has the least to do with the vegetable garden I once knew. My cousins have all gone off as well. All that is left for me is a visit to the cemetery.

· You discovered New York in 1959. Didn't you ever consider setting up residence there and enjoying an American career like Raymond Loewy did?

+++ To begin with, I turned down a post in London. Had I known, I would have hit the books again and learned English. That would have enabled me to stake out a new career across the Channel. At the time, however, I was working for the fashion magazine Jardin des Modes, where I had just begun to impose my sharply defined view of visual communication. I nevertheless asked for three months' leave to visit New York, threatening to quit my job in case of refusal.

Since I had already acquired a high-level status as their artistic director, they gave me my three months. Looking back, I think I might have done better not to have accepted them, as I certainly would have stayed on in New York. But there you have it: What we become reflects our choices.

My first discovery of the New World bowled me over. It was the golden age of dress design, as displayed in the department stores (Bloomingdale's, Saks, Orbachs) and spread across the pages of the fashion magazines. Then, too, I was as avidly interested in the city's architecture as everybody else, stunned by its handsome skyscrapers and captivated by its infernal tempo. The revolutionary spatial organization of the Guggenheim impressed me: I was fascinated by the spiral's monumental dimensions and the totally harmonious relationship it drew between form, function and space. New York never sleeps: I was sucked into the whirlwind of the city, and still today my eyes light up when I remember all the new things to be taken in at a glance. Modernism asserted itself in New York in an overwhelmingly rational manner. Each person, taken individually, found him- or herself swept into the present, with a unique immigrant history behind each figure. Clearly, a futurist society was being developed here. To live in New York was to accept the idea of modifying one's person, as an ongoing, open-ended creative process. Manhattan boasted the greatest designer names of the day: I met Alexey Brodovitch (and even attended his photography courses), Henry Wolf of Harper's Bazaar, Herb Lubalin, and Liberman (with whom I worked for several days). New York was the place to be for anyone enamored of novelty; indeed, the city's irresistible charm derived in the main from its endless range of the hitherto neither seen nor done. I even dared to entrust a New York gallery with some lithographs from my student days at the Beaux Arts in Paris. Dream on!

32 · 33

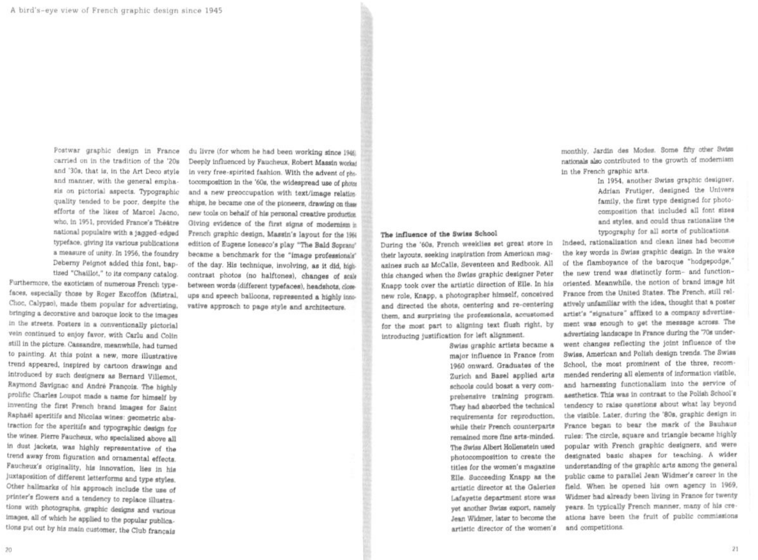

A bird's-eye view of French graphic design since 1945

Postwar graphic design in France carried on in the tradition of the '20s and '30s, that is, in the Art Deco style and manner, with the general emphasis on pictorial aspects. Typographic quality tended to be poor, despite the efforts of the likes of Marcel Jacno, who, in 1951, provided France's Théâtre national populaire with a jagged-edged typeface, giving its various publications a measure of unity. In 1956, the foundry Deberny Peignot added this font, baptized "Chaillot," to its company catalog. Furthermore, the exoticism of numerous French typefaces, especially those by Roger Excoffon (Mistral, Choc, Calypso), made them popular for advertising, bringing a decorative and baroque look to the images in the streets. Posters in a conventionally pictorial vein continued to enjoy favor, with Carlu and Colin still in the picture. Cassandre, meanwhile, had turned to painting. At this point a new, more illustrative trend appeared, inspired by cartoon drawings and introduced by such designers as Bernard Villemot, Raymond Savignac and André François. The highly prolific Charles Loupot made a name for himself by inventing the first French brand images for Saint Raphaël aperitifs and Nicolas wines: geometric abstraction for the aperitifs and typographic design for the wines. Pierre Faucheux, who specialized above all in dust jackets, was highly representative of the trend away from figuration and ornamental effects. Faucheux's originality, his innovation, lies in his juxtaposition of different letterforms and type styles. Other hallmarks of his approach include the use of printer's flowers and a tendency to replace illustrations with photographs, graphic designs and various images, all of which he applied to the popular publications put out by his main customer, the Club français

du livre (for whom he had been working since 1946). Deeply influenced by Faucheux, Robert Massin worked in very free-spirited fashion. With the advent of photocomposition in the '60s, the widespread use of photography took over the artistic direction of Elle. In his new role, Knapp, a photographer himself, conceived and directed the shots, centering and re-centering them, and surprising the professionals, accustomed for the most part to aligning text flush right, by introducing justification for left alignment.

Swiss graphic artists became a major influence in France from 1960 onward. Graduates of the Zurich and Basel applied arts schools could boast a very comprehensive training program. They had absorbed the technical requirements for reproduction, while their French counterparts remained more fine arts-minded. The Swiss Albert Hollenstein used photocomposition to create the titles for the women's magazine Elle. Succeeding Knapp as the artistic director at the Galeries Lafayette department store was yet another Swiss export, namely Jean Widmer, later to become the artistic director of the women's

The influence of the Swiss School

During the '60s, French weeklies set great store in their layouts, seeking inspiration from American magazines such as McCalls, Seventeen and Redbook. All this changed when the Swiss graphic designer Peter Knapp took over the artistic direction of Elle. In his new role, Knapp, a photographer himself, conceived and directed the shots, centering and re-centering them, and surprising the professionals, accustomed for the most part to aligning text flush right, by introducing justification for left alignment.

monthly, Jardin des Modes. Some fifty other Swiss nationals also contributed to the growth of modernism in the French graphic arts.

In 1954, another Swiss graphic designer, Adrian Frutiger, designed the Univers family, the first type designed for photocomposition that included all font sizes and styles, and could thus rationalize the typography for all sorts of publications. Indeed, rationalization and clean lines had become the key words in Swiss graphic design. In the wake of the flamboyance of the baroque "hodgepodge," the new trend was distinctly form- and function-oriented. Meanwhile, the notion of brand image hit France from the United States. The French, still relatively unfamiliar with the idea, thought that a poster artist's "signature" affixed to a company advertisement was enough to get the message across. The advertising landscape in France during the '70s underwent changes reflecting the joint influence of the Swiss, American and Polish design trends. The Swiss School, the most prominent of the three, recommended rendering all elements of information visible, by harnessing functionalism into the service of aesthetics. This was in contrast to the Polish School's tendency to raise questions about what lay beyond the visible. Later, during the '80s, graphic design in France began to bear the mark of the Bauhaus rules: The circle, square and triangle became highly popular with French graphic designers, and were designated basic shapes for teaching. A wider understanding of the graphic arts among the general public came to parallel Jean Widmer's career in the field. When he opened his own agency in 1969, Widmer had already been living in France for twenty years. In typically French manner, many of his creations have been the fruit of public commissions and competitions.

20 · 21

· How did you experience the development of technology, the transition from traditional methods to computers?

+++ Working with computers is great and has now become indispensable. I am thrilled to see computers making a place for themselves in our profession, for they change our behavioral patterns and create totally new situations. Layouts have become handsomer and truer to the printed end product. Students finish off their projects better. Everyone works faster and with greater precision. Computers have ushered in incredibly sophisticated technological progress benefiting one and all, and encouraging infinitely varied manipulations. This excellent shake-up is sweeping away generations of training in favor of the apparently boundless possibilities of image processing.

Nevertheless, as the head of an agency, it is my job to tackle problems that machines are unable to solve. The creative process—thinking up and developing concepts—takes place during the preliminary stage of sketches and explanations that lead to the actual project definition. Only then do I share my ideas with my fellow team members. Carrying them out and downloading them onto a computer is done by a computer graphics artist, whom I assist for the finalisation. I am always open to technical progress, but were I to work on a computer myself, I think I might feel trapped, might get caught up in the speed with which everything is produced, no matter how carefully I would think everything out beforehand. Basically, after all, computers are merely tools for doing a better job. Of course, it would be frustrating for

me if I were to stop working as part of a team someday. Then I would certainly change my professional habits and learn the basics of image processing, in order to continue to realize my ideas on my own. For the time being, however, I see no need to sit down in front of a computer.

· The standardization of graphic design owes much to the fact that designers, whether in Paris, London, New York or Tokyo, all use the same tools (computers and software). Seen from this angle, could one say that computers stifle creativity?

+++ I've noticed that young graphic designers tend to work things out directly by computer. They rush to their keyboard and, eyes riveted to the screen, strike out at the keys almost mechanically. Less consideration is granted nowadays to the art of sketching ideas, formerly the gauge of an artist's talent. Yet, it is the designing phase that takes up the most time and, at that point, computers have nothing much to offer. A graphic designer who has first carefully thought out a concept will have an easier time translating it onto paper. To my mind, resorting to computers for the initial designing of ideas is detrimental to inventiveness: All you get is an overabundance of preexisting images and stylistic effects. Computers are best suited to putting the finishing touches on designs, which requires mastering, above all, production and reproduction techniques. Research and creativity are intrinsic to the power of imagination, one of humanity's most important cultural assets.

· At what point do you make the switch from pencil to computer?

+++ I never let go of my pencil.

· Do you have any personal projects as an auteurist graphic designer?

+++ I still put out limited editions of signed silkscreens, abstract geometric compositions that I send to my clients for New Year's to thank them. And every year I get kind thanks from collectors. My prints are not done to commission or for communication purposes: They are an artistic endeavor in a deliberately subjective vein.

· Would you like having work of such a personal nature published?

+++ A book of my sketches? Why not? It would reveal the hidden side of my work. Publishing my drawings would be a way of explaining my approach, of helping people understand what is involved—for instance, all the hesitations, the shuttling back and forth, that go into a poster project. I start a number of things that end up dissatisfying me. The public would see how it is my concept-related research that remains at the core of this complex and at times somewhat muddled manner of proceeding. How adding just one more detail to a composition can turn the whole thing into something different.

84 · 85

303
Arts, recherches et créations

303, Arts, recherches et créations, La revue des Pays de la Loire (303: The Arts, Research and Creation: The Loire Regional Review) is published every three months and focuses on research, the creative process, and art. Within the Loire region – one of twenty-six in France – are five distinct areas, each with its own postal code: Mayenne (53), Sarthe (72), Loire-Atlantique (44), Maine-et-Loire (49), and Vendée (85). When all five codes are added together, the total is 303. This number, a palindrome that reads the same in either direction, is the journal's logo, which Apeloig designed in 2006. The numbers are stacked to create a vertical sculptural form. A thick line cuts the zero in two, creating a precisely geometric logo. When folded in half, the top mirrors the bottom with perfect alignment.

For a special issue dedicated to the novelist Julien Gracq, whose writing is emblematic of the region and whose novels take place there, a full-bleed portrait of the writer was filtered through a large dot screen (a solution to remedy the poor quality of the original image) and paired with a die-cut logo. For an issue dedicated to Alfred Jarry, the design played with one of the playwright's favorite shapes – spirals – using them as eyes for Père Ubu (Father Ubu), Jarry's grotesque caricature of modern man. For the cover of *Né à Nantes comme tout le monde* (Born in Nantes, Like Everybody), an issue dedicated to the work of artists from Nantes since 1980, a special typeface derived from the graphic identity of the well-known Petit Beurre biscuit company was used, with black letters against a silver background.

Invitation card
303, Arts, recherches et créations, Nantes
21 × 10.5 cm (8¼ × 4⅛ in.)
Typeface: The Sans
2006

Stationary
303, Arts, recherches et créations, Nantes
Typeface: The Sans
2006

Magazines
Julien Gracq
Alfred Jarry
La folle Journée
Né à Nantes comme tout le monde
303, Arts, recherches et créations, Nantes
30 × 22.5 cm (11¾ × 8⅞ in.)
Printer: Le Govic
Typeface: The Sans
2006 – 09
See page 310

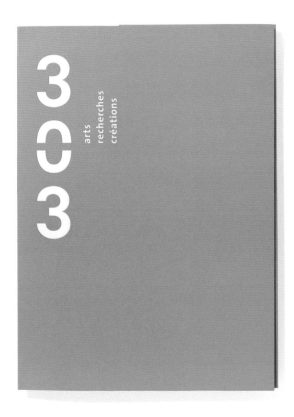

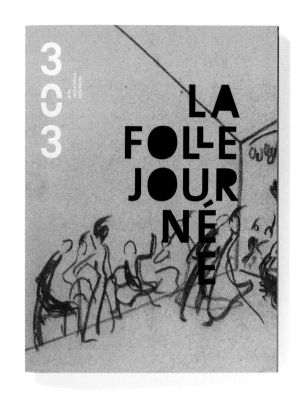

9ᵉ Semaine
de la langue française
et de la francophonie

The French Ministry of Culture and Communication organizes an annual week celebrating "la langue française" (the French language) and "la francophonie" (French-speaking cultures throughout the world). The event's purpose is to honor the essential link between francophone cultures and it promotes an understanding and appreciation of the breadth and depth of the French-speaking world through various programs. The visual identity features ten words borrowed from francophone authors. The word "farfadet" (sprite or elf) is borrowed from George Sand in recognition of her 2004 bicentennial, while the other nine words represent the voices of contemporary French-speaking authors working outside of France.

The mosaic of text projects the idea of diversity – of culture and language – spread over a vast geographical area. Each letter of each word wanders inside a differently colored rectangle, creating a mosaic and pattern that recalls African textiles and ceramics. There are no capital letters; all words are equal and deliberately modest. The Gravur Condensed font, a rounded typeface designed by Cornel Windlin and Gilles Gavillet between 1996 and 2001, contrasts with the grid's geometry and freedom of expression.

Brochure
9ᵉ Semaine de la langue française et de la francophonie
French Ministry of Culture and Communication
17 × 12 cm (6¾ × 4¾ in.)
Typeface: Gravur Condensed
2004

Collection
Exquis d'écrivains

In the title of this book series, the word "exquis" means exquisite, delicious, or delightful; "d'écrivains" means literary authors. Published by NiL Éditions, this ensemble of short contemporary works is about gourmet experiences inspired by language. Through fictional dreams and anecdotes, each writer offers his or her own vision and experience. Together they pay homage to the richness of the French language and the ability of words to capture the pleasure of eating and gastronomy.

The covers' textured backgrounds are based on reproductions of tea towels, napkins, and tablecloths. In each, a white plate frames the author's name and the book's title at the upper left of the composition. The shadow cast by the plate increases the three-dimensionality of the image. The center is reserved for a smaller white circle framing the collection title and the name of the publisher. This design brings quotidian elements into the higher realms of the literary and gastronomic arts, playfully mixing sophisti-cated typography – Galliard – with a vibrant color palette.

Book series
Collection Exquis d'écrivains
NiL Éditions, Paris
17.7 × 11 cm (7 × 4⅜ in.)
Typeface: Galliard
2005 – 10

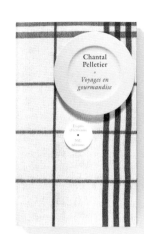

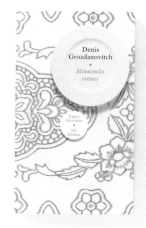

KERSTIN
THORVALL

LES ANNÉES
D'OMBRE

LE SERPENT À PLUMES

ROMAN

STURE
DAHLSTRÖM

LE GRAND
BLONDINO

LE SERPENT À PLUMES

ROMAN

AUGUSTE
CORTEAU

LE FILS
DE LA JOCONDE

LE SERPENT À PLUMES

ROMAN

ANTHONY
BURGESS

AU SUJET
DE JAMES JOYCE

LE SERPENT À PLUMES

ESSAI

CHRISTOPHE
LÉON

JOURNAL D'UN
ÉTUDIANT
JAPONAIS À PARIS

LE SERPENT À PLUMES

ROMAN

ALEXANDRE
TISMA

UNE NOUVELLE
QUE JE N'AI PAS
ÉCRITE

LE SERPENT À PLUMES

NOUVELLES

GEORGE
ORWELL

UNE FILLE
DE PASTEUR

LE SERPENT À PLUMES

ROMAN

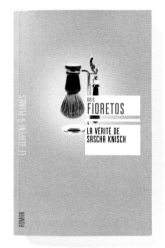

ARIS
FIORETOS

LA VÉRITÉ DE
SASCHA KNISCH

LE SERPENT À PLUMES

ROMAN

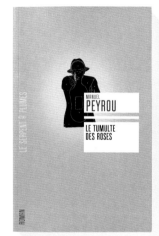

SYLVAIN
PRUDHOMME

LES MATINÉES
D'HERCULE

LE SERPENT À PLUMES

ROMAN

MANUEL
PEYROU

LE TUMULTE
DES ROSES

LE SERPENT À PLUMES

ROMAN

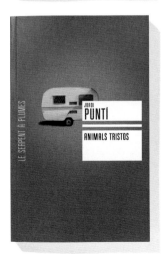

JORDI
PUNTÍ

ANIMALS TRISTOS

LE SERPENT À PLUMES

ROMAN

OTTO
DE KAT

TOUS LES BATEAUX

LE SERPENT À PLUMES

ROMAN

KERSTIN
THORVALL

LA RAGE
D'ÊTRE LIBRE

LE SERPENT À PLUMES

ROMAN

JORGE
EDWARDS

LE BON À RIEN DE
LA FAMILLE

LE SERPENT À PLUMES

ROMAN

JORDI
PUNTÍ

PEAU DE TATOU

LE SERPENT À PLUMES

NOUVELLES

Éditions
Le Serpent à Plumes

First launched as a literary review, Le Serpent à Plumes is now a well-known publisher, specializing in foreign fiction, crime dramas, music, and cinema. In 2007, the logo was redesigned and the signature typeface streamlined. The alphabet was completed in two weights, heavy and thin, to increase its versatility. The dynamic, low-cost book design uses a scanned linen texture in various colors for the background and retouched stock photographs to customize each title.

Each cover features one simple object – a fridge, an alarm clock, scissors, a sailboat – illuminated in a halo of light. Layered over the image are white boxes framing the title and the author's name and separated by a thin white rectangle. This multi-level composition invites the eye to shift continually between the title and the image. The spacing of the white rectangles mirrors the spacing of "Le Serpent à Plumes," which is printed vertically to the left. The author's name is printed in the same color as the inside cover. These details enhance the design identity that unifies all Serpent à Plumes products.

The yearly catalog is printed on smooth semi-thick paper that has the same finely woven linen texture as the book covers. The catalog unfolds, accordion-style, into ten parts. As each piece is opened and scanned horizontally, the precise concepts – layout, composition, and spacing – that informed the series repeat, showcasing the uniform graphic identity of the extensive collection.

Book series
Éditions Le Serpent à Plumes
20.5 × 13 cm (8⅛ × 5⅛ in.)
Typeface: Serpent
2007 – 10

Brochures
Éditions Le Serpent à Plumes
15 × 9 cm (5⅞ × 3½ in.)
Typefaces: Serpent, Frutiger
2007 – 09

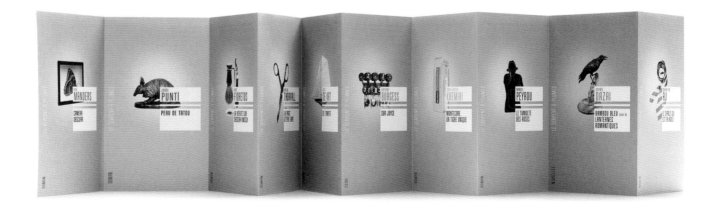

Collection
Pavillons poche

Designing a paperback collection of foreign literature for the publisher Éditions Robert Laffont, a player in a highly competitive market, has offered Apeloig the opportunity since 2005 to explore new ways of creating a popular book series. His approach, the result of long research, was to give independent photographers a chance to have their work reproduced on a book cover.

The typeface used on each cover is Foundry Sans, designed by David Quay and Freda Sack in 1991. The typography is all lowercase, a playful gesture that subverts expectations. Set inside a transparent band of color, the title floats in front of a photograph, just above the center of each cover. The colored band tints a portion of the image underneath, its hue varying with each book. The band also repeats on the spine, creating an eye-catching uniformity on the bookshelf. The covers are treated with a laminated varnish that reflects light, causing the colored bands to stand out even more.

Book series
**Collection Pavillons poche
Éditions Robert Laffont**
18.2 × 12.2 cm (7 ⅛ × 4 ⅞ in.)
Typeface: Foundry Sans
2005 – 13

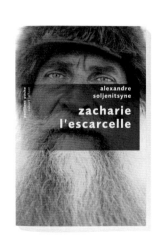

geoff
nicholson

comment
j'ai raté
mes vacances

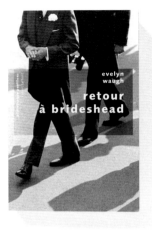

evelyn waugh

retour
à brideshead

evelyn
waugh

le cher
disparu

graham
greene

tueur
à gages

tennessee
williams

le poulet
tueur et la folle
honteuse

jaan
kross

le fou
du tzar

nicholson
baker

la mezzanine

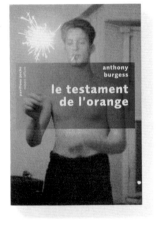

anthony
burgess

le testament
de l'orange

alexandre
soljenitsyne

le pavillon
des cancéreux

evelyn
waugh

scoop

margaret
atwood

œil-
de-chat

norman
mailer

les vrais durs
ne dansent pas

kent
haruf

colorado
blues

mikhaïl
boulgakov

la garde blanche

richard
yates

la fenêtre
panoramique

guillermo
martinez

la mort lente
de luciana b.

f. scott
fitzgerald

un diamant
gros comme
le ritz

alexandre
soljenitsyne

le premier
cercle

Book
**Freedom: A Photographic History
of the African American Struggle**
Phaidon
29 × 25 cm (11⅜ × 9⅞ in.), 512 pages
Typefaces: Champion Gothic, The Sans
2002

Freedom
A Photographic History
of the African American Struggle

Freedom: A Photographic History of the African American Struggle offers readers a monumental visual record of African American history from the early nineteenth century to the present day.

The jacket for the hardcover book uses an enlarged detail from a photograph by Ernest Withers of Civil Rights protesters. Withers documented the movement from its beginnings in the 1950s through to the 1960s. The photograph was printed darker than the original, with a large screen and grainy resolution to suggest the poor quality of newspaper printing. Inspired by handwritten words on a placard in one of his protest images, the title is rendered in sheer white for a slightly transparent effect and superimposed over the photograph. The white lettering against the darkened image creates a strong impact.

The typeface Champion Gothic, designed by Hoefler & Frere-Jones in 1990 and inspired by late nineteenth-century American woodtypes, is used for the table of contents and chapter headings. The thick font recalls newspaper headlines and underscores the historical content of the book.

Cave Art

The book *Cave Art* by world-renowned prehistorian Jean Clottes offers an introduction to the earliest known expressions of human creativity. It was conceived as a guided illustrated tour of the prehistoric caves of Europe and beyond and encompasses works of art created up to 35,000 years ago.

The cover, constructed from heavy cardboard, is tinted a solid brown; the title letters have been cut out, leaving only the outlines behind. The carved stencil-like letters allow readers to see the interior of the book, as if they were peering into a cave. (The use of stencils for handprints and other repeated symbols in cave paintings is well documented in this book.) The book is conceived as a journey into the world of prehistoric art, with the reader venturing first past images of rocky interiors, then going deep into the cave and encountering the art therein. All of the images bleed to the edges of the page. On the final page, one sees light filtering through as if from the cave's exit.

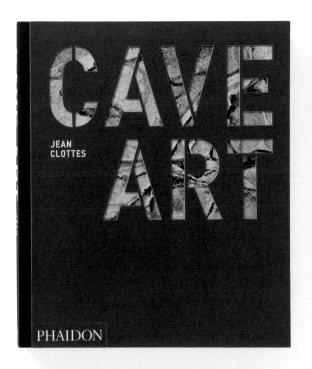

THE LASCAUX CAVE

Hall of the Bulls.
Painting on rock. Black pigment: manganese oxide.
Length of unicorn: 235 cm.
Lascaux Cave, Montignac, Dordogne, France.
Solutrean/Early Magdalenian.

Lascaux, the most famous painted cave in the world, was discovered in 1940 by four boys from a nearby village who followed their dog down a deep hole. Dubbed 'The Sistine Chapel of prehistory' by Abbé Breuil, Lascaux is world-renowned for the exceptional aesthetic quality of its paintings, which are large, numerous (915 animal figures have been documented) and deliberately spectacular. The entrance of the cave leads into the Hall of the Bulls, also called the Rotunda, a huge decorated chamber with a very impressive frieze of thirty-six animals circling the gallery. This frieze includes seventeen horses, eleven bovines (probably all aurochs), six stags, one bear and one fantastical animal known as the Unicorn. The Lascaux paintings were all made with mineral pigments such as manganese oxide, and therefore cannot be radiocarbon dated. For a long time, archaeologists attributed the Lascaux paintings solely to the Early Magdalenian period, based on an important habitation site found inside the cave that has been dated to around 17,000 BP. More recently, however, some artefacts from Lascaux have been dated to between 18,000 and 19,000 BP, indicating Solutrean origins.
The famous Unicorn, which faces to the right, can be seen at the far left of this photograph, following a horse. This strange animal is overlaid by three horses, with two red ones more or less discernable on its main body, and a black horse towards the front, whose head has spalled or flaked off from the cave wall. All these animals face towards the depths of the cave. The so-called Unicorn has nothing in common with the mythical animal of that name (not even its horn): its body is ungainly, with a distended belly, heavy legs, a short tail, a kind of hump on its back, and a square head with one eye. Half a dozen black ovals are scattered over its body. Mythical or not, this animal corresponds to no known species, despite some fanciful interpretations of it being a horse, bovine, feline or reindeer. It is an imaginary creature. A variety of different fantastical animals were painted throughout the Upper Palaeolithic and much later in rock art the world over.

Over to the right of the photograph, there are two large bulls facing each other. Located immediately to the left of the entrance to the Axial Gallery, these animals contribute a great deal to the impact of the art in this chamber. The bull on the left is unfinished, while the other is complete; at a length of 4.6 metres, it is one of the biggest animals painted during the Upper Palaeolithic. This most spectacular panel also includes several horses and stags with ornate antlers, as is often the case in Lascaux. The use of different colours (red, black, yellow, brown) for the animals is truly exceptional, as polychrome painting is unusual in Palaeolithic art. The remarkable research undertaken by Norbert Aujoulat has shown that the first animals to be painted in the cave were horses, followed by aurochs and then stags. Aujoulat's study of potential seasonal indicators, such as the heaviness and colouring of the animals' coats, was equally revealing. The artists apparently depicted horses as they appeared at the end of winter and in early spring, aurochs as in summer, and stags as in autumn, with the respective seasons corresponding to the mating periods of each animal. Thus, when considering the types of animals most commonly depicted in the cave, one of the main ideas conveyed by Lascaux is that of seasonal cycles, with a suggestion of fertility and renewal implicit.

Book
Cave Art
Phaidon
29 × 25 cm (11³⁄₈ × 9⁷⁄₈ in.), 324 pages
Typefaces: DIN Stencil, Vista Sans
2008

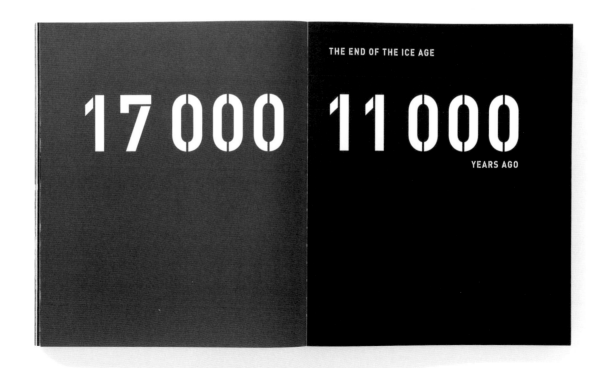

THE END OF THE ICE AGE

17 000 11 000

YEARS AGO

Japan Style

The book *Japan Style* examines Japanese culture and aesthetics. The hardback cover features a reproduction of a traditional Japanese stencil dating from the late nineteenth or early twentieth century. The starkly minimalist black-and-white image depicts cherry blossoms floating on sinuous currents of water.

Printed on tracing paper, the dust jacket offers a visual and tangible example of Japanese style. Its folded flaps create multiple layers of depth and transparency while separating the cover into four equally spaced rectangles. This precise division of space mirrors the perfect proportions revered by the Japanese. The two words of the title are stacked and printed in red capitals. As "Japan" and "Style" have the same number of characters, the type is arranged so that the letters in each word are aligned. Positioned mid-center on the cover, the precise, simple typography and alignment match the purity that defines Japanese style and spirit.

Book
Japan Style
Phaidon
27 × 20.5 cm (10⅝ × 8⅛ in.), 306 pages
Typeface: The Sans
2007

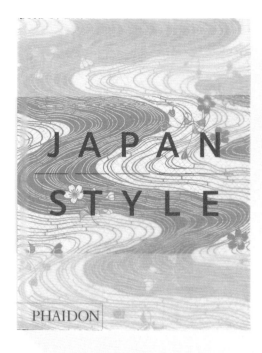

Yves Saint Laurent
Style

Apeloig first discovered Yves Saint Laurent's work when designing the catalog for a retrospective exhibition on the designer, organized by the Fondation Pierre Bergé – Yves Saint Laurent in 2008.

Saint Laurent disliked the word "fashion", preferring "style." In light of this preference, the latter is repeated on the cover three times, each iteration using less and less color to create an echo effect. The word "style" contains the initials *YSL*, a chance occurrence that is highlighted through its repetition. Some letters in the title are linked together, creating ligatures that reference sewing, the foundation of the couturier's trade. One can immediately see this between the capital *Y* and *V* in "Yves". The white composition of the cover is extremely pure and simple, almost bare. The impeccable harmony of the extra-light font reflects the elegance of Saint Laurent's *haute couture* and world. It matches the rigor of the designer, as well as the modern spirit of his collections. A strong, vibrant pink – one of the couturier's favorites – was chosen for the background of the English-language edition of the book, with the type in white. The French edition reverses this color scheme.

Book
Yves Saint Laurent Style
Éditions de La Martinière
27 × 22.5 cm (10⅝ × 8⅞ in.), 258 pages
Typefaces: Helvetica Neue Light, Frutiger
2009

Louvre

The concept for the book *Louvre* was to familiarize the public with the museum's collections. Only the six letters of "Louvre" invite the reader to dive into the book, and the museum's architectural history, wealth of treasures, and new initiatives. Enlarged details of paintings, sculptures, and *objets d'art* spill across the pages. The images are arranged in chronological order, providing the reader with an overview of the collections and contextualizing individual works within their historical periods.

The book was designed in a square format with a clear plastic slipcase that recalls the transparency of I. M. Pei's glass and metal pyramid, a groundbreaking addition to the museum that is also evoked in the book's black-and-white cover image and sketched geometrical grid.

Book
Louvre
Éditions de La Martinière
Musée du Louvre Éditions
21 × 21 cm (8¼ × 8¼ in.), 546 pages
Offset, gilt-edged, slipcase
Typeface: Foundry Sterling
2009

PEINTURES

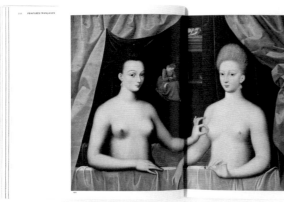

Musée du quai Branly

The cover of the book *Musée du quai Branly* pays tribute to Jean Nouvel's innovative design for the museum, which is devoted to the art of different civilizations around the world. The museum is also renowned for a vertical carpet of exotic plants that nearly swallows up one of its exterior walls. Patrick Blanc conceived this wall, while botanist and designer Gilles Clément designed the garden surrounding the main entrance. In reference to the use of vegetation as an architectural element, an image of ferns appears on the book's cover, spine, and title pages. Ferns first appeared in the fossil record millions of years ago. A primitive plant that is prolific today, used here they have multiple connotations: they reference the museum's mission (bridging the present and the past); they allude to its vertical green wall; and they also unify the book's design as a repeated graphic element.

The cover uses a matte material that contrasts with its glossy, embossed type. The type's palette is drawn from a row of colorful boxes that project from the museum's façade. Inside the book, the collection is shown to maximum advantage through copious photography: full-page spreads, bleeds, and enlargements of details. The non-Western focus of the collection is stressed typographically on the contents page, in which the names of the continents are broken up along its length, not by syllable but more arbitrarily. *Musée du quai Branly* offers readers a luscious, portable means to explore thousands of artworks, artifacts, and photographs from Africa, Asia, Oceania, and the Americas.

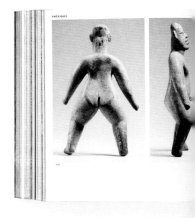

MUSÉE
DU QUAI
BRANLY

Book
Musée du quai Branly
Éditions de La Martinière
Éditions du Musée du quai Branly
21 × 21 cm (8¼ × 8¼ in.), 450 pages
Offset, screen printed on edges,
slipcase
Typeface: Foundry Sterling
2009

AMÉ
RI
QUES

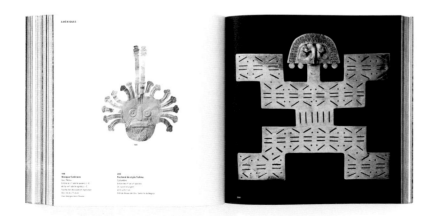

Yan Pei-Ming
Les Funérailles de Monna Lisa

As part of a program designed to bring contemporary art and artists into the Louvre, the Chinese-French painter Yan Pei-Ming was invited to create a site-specific work related to the museum's collections. Using a grisaille technique, he painted five large-scale works, which he titled *Les Funérailles de Monna Lisa* (The Funerals of Monna Lisa). The series was shown in the Salon Denon, not far from where the real Mona Lisa hangs in the Louvre.

The exhibition catalog was conceived in a landscape format to mirror the horizontal hanging of the paintings. The cover is designed with a bold modern type: Myriad Pro. The small dots placed above each *i* hint at the risks inherent in the Louvre's opening itself up to contemporary art. Like the small dot above the big blocky *i*, the contemporary artist risks looking small in comparison to Leonardo da Vinci, and yet his presence also gives da Vinci and his masterpiece new meaning. Bold type was used for the texts that introduce each chapter, alluding to Yan Pei-Ming's distinctively large brushstrokes. A flap was added to show how the paintings were hung in the gallery.

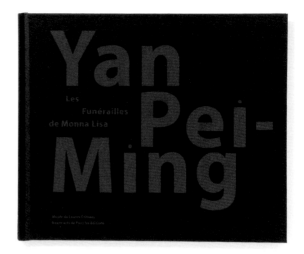

L'exécution, l'enterrement et les funérailles de Monna Lisa
Quand invitation lui a été faite d'élire une œuvre du Louvre afin de lui rendre hommage, le choix de *La Joconde* s'est très vite imposé à Yan Pei-Ming. Peintre du face à face, ce dernier, en effet, n'y est pas allé par quatre chemins, il a choisi le tableau qui incarnait, depuis son adolescence à Shanghai, la quintessence de la peinture occidentale, parce qu'elle était l'œuvre la plus reproduite : « C'était pour moi une évidence. C'est le sujet le plus célèbre du monde ». Ming décide néanmoins de ne pas copier *La Joconde*, de trop nombreux artistes, particulièrement en Chine, l'ayant copiée et recopiée *ad nauseam* …

Sommaire

Book
Yan Pei-Ming,
Les Funérailles de Monna Lisa
Musée du Louvre Éditions
Beaux-Arts de Paris les Éditions
24.5 × 30 cm (9⅝ × 11¾ in.), 100 pages
Typeface: Myriad
2009

Peinture morte

Copier, créer… D'après, selon, avec, contre …
Les relations des artistes contemporains
avec les maîtres anciens, sont nombreuses
et variées. Elles ont évolué au fil du temps
et des modes, de la copie traditionnelle
à la variation libre en passant par le pastiche,
la parodie, la paraphrase, l'hommage.
Après l'exposition des tableaux de Picasso
réalisés d'après *les Femmes d'Alger* de Delacroix,
il nous a semblé opportun de présenter la vision
contemporaine d'un peintre vivant sur le musée
du Louvre. Carte blanche a donc été donnée
à l'artiste franco-chinois Yan Pei-Ming pour produire
une œuvre nouvelle en relation avec une œuvre
du musée.

Pourquoi ce choix ? Parce que Yan Pei-Ming est un peintre, essentiellement peintre, attiré autant par l'image que par la picturalité. Peintre d'histoire et portraitiste, qui n'a pas peur de la monumentalité et n'est pas non plus inhibé, culpabilisé par le poids de l'histoire de l'art occidental. À l'ère de la mondialisation, et tenant compte de la visée universaliste du musée du Louvre, il est logique de faire appel à un peintre issu d'une double tradition orientale et occidentale. C'est sans doute ce grand écart, cette dialectique entre deux manières de peindre qui font la force, l'efficacité et la singularité de son style.

Très naturellement, Yan Pei-Ming a choisi de travailler sur le tableau le plus célèbre du monde qui signifie à lui seul le Louvre, *La Joconde*, la fameuse Monna Lisa, qu'il découvrit à Shanghai, en reproduction dans les manuels de peinture à l'huile. Peintre des archétypes et des clichés, après Mao, Bruce Lee, Jean XXIII, Marilyn, Obama, Yan Pei-Ming ne pouvait mieux tomber en affrontant cette icône mythique de la peinture occidentale.

Mais comment peindre aujourd'hui une image devenue quasi invisible par excès de visibilité ? Yan Pei-Ming a décidé de l'enterrer, mais de l'enterrer dignement, avec de somptueuses funérailles … Monna Lisa est donc accompagnée d'un portrait de son père mort et d'un autoportrait de l'artiste faisant le mort. S'agit-il, ici, d'enterrer l'icône médiatique pour revitaliser la peinture ?

Yan Pei-Ming mène depuis longtemps une réflexion sur l'homme, le cycle de la vie et la mort, la filiation du père au fils. *La Joconde* est par ailleurs un des rares portraits de femmes peints par Yan Pei-Ming. Elle est rendue, exceptionnellement, de façon réaliste, illusionniste, car Yan Pei-Ming voulait faire un beau portrait de femme et non le portrait de la peinture. Le paysage mystérieux qui se trouve derrière Monna Lisa est devenu immense. Deux tableaux horizontaux encadrent, comme un triptyque, le portrait central. Ils sont parsemés de crânes peints d'après des scans du crâne de l'artiste. « Peindre un paysage, c'est faire le portrait de l'homme », écrit François Cheng dans *Vide et plein, le langage pictural chinois*.

Vanités en grisaille qui disent pourtant le pouvoir organique de la peinture. Apparition et disparition des figures et des formes qui surgissent entre les coups de brosse, les superpositions de couches, les coulures de peinture, ces funérailles splendides conjuguent une double vision, celle fantomatique du modèle de Léonard et celle de la peinture en action de Yan Pei-Ming. Confrontation de deux temporalités, de deux espaces, l'un révélant l'autre et vice versa. D'un côté, l'art comme illusion, *cosa mentale*, de l'autre, l'expérience physique, l'énergie, qui avec impulsion et précision, donne vie et forme à la matière. Yan Pei-Ming inscrit ainsi au cœur du musée une nouvelle trinité : le père, le fils et la « sainte » *Joconde*, devenue sous l'assaut des pèlerins une véritable relique de la peinture occidentale et de la culture muséale.

Henri Loyrette

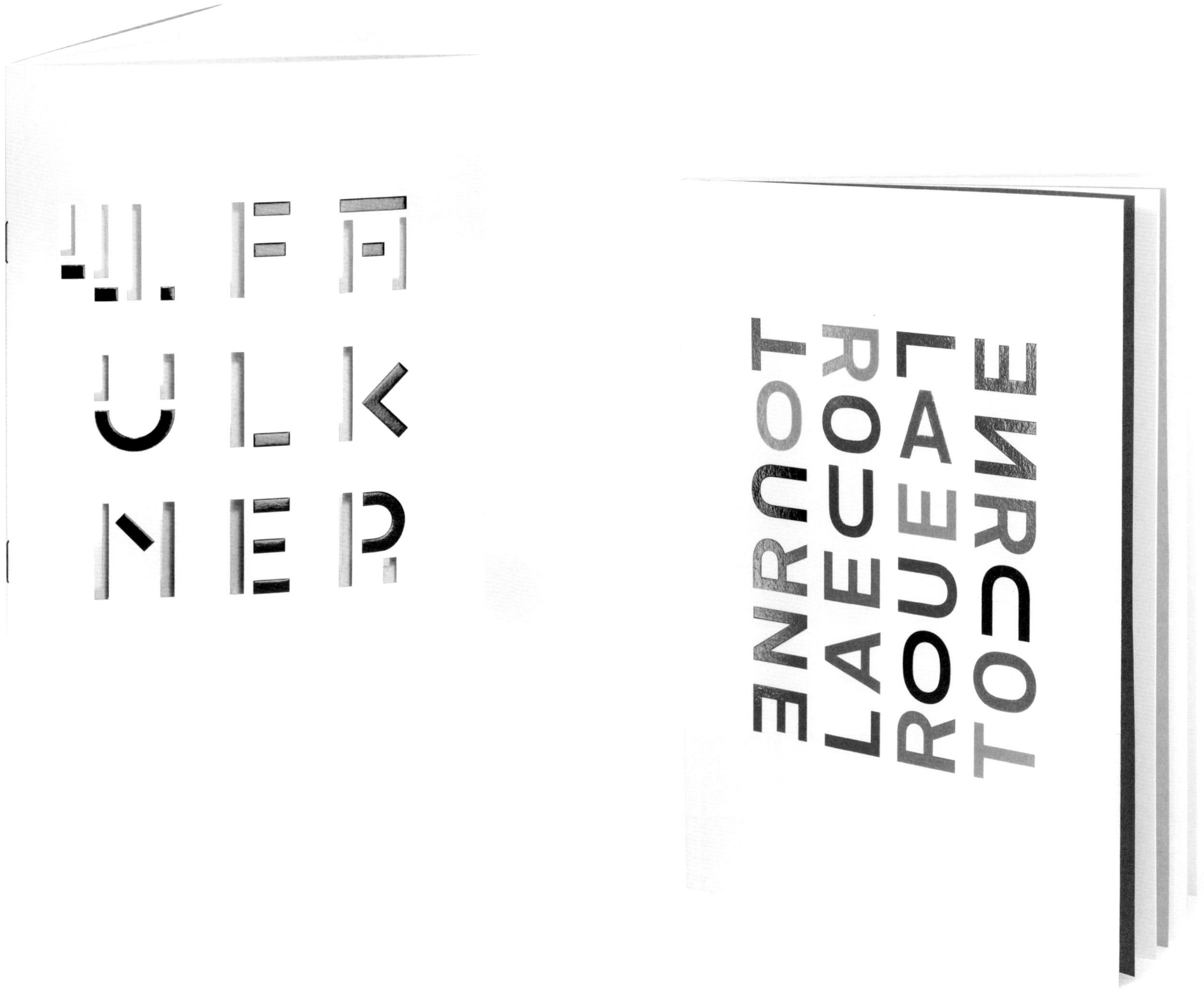

Jean de Gonet

W. Faulkner
La Belle Reliure parisienne et ses clones

Jean de Gonet is well known for his outstanding bookbinding. In 2009, he hand-bound nineteen French translations of books by the American author William Faulkner. Apeloig was asked to design a small sixteen-page catalog for the collection.

The minimalist white cover of the catalog has two folded flaps onto which the author's name is stenciled: the initial *W* and the eight letters spelling "Faulkner" set in a grid. The vertical parts of the letters are die cut, while the rest – diagonals, curves, horizontals – are embossed, printed in black, and varnished. The metallic silver paper used for the inside cover is visible through the cover's die-cut areas. The back of the cover has been silkscreened neon yellow and reflects from the silver, creating a multidimensional experience. The specialized binding uses black staples. This catalog is a unique object linking art forms: innovative writing, book-binding, and typography.

La roue tourne

La roue tourne (The Wheel Turns) is the title of the 2011 retrospective catalog that signaled Jean de Gonet's retirement from bookbinding. He organized an auction of his books. Detailed descriptions of twenty books paired with high-resolution images summarize a legacy of meticulous craftsmanship.

The phrase "la roue tourne" refers to the wheel of fortune and the role that chance plays in games, as well as life. On the cover, the title is repeated twice, with the multicolored sans serif letters turned upside down or rotated 90 degrees. The typographic arrangement is both fluid and fixed, as if the letters had spilled from a shaker. The design pays homage to de Gonet's open, artisanal approach to materials, shapes, orientation, new technologies, and chance.

Catalog
W. Faulkner
La Belle Reliure parisienne et ses clones
(Fine Parisian Bookbinding and its Clones)
19 volumes by Jean de Gonet
Jean de Gonet Artefacts
22 × 16.2 cm (8⅝ × 6⅜ in.), 16 pages
Printer: Jourdan
Screen print, die cut and embossed
with selective varnishing
Typeface: original creation
2008

Catalog
La roue tourne
Les livres reliés de Jean de Gonet
Jean de Gonet Artefacts
22 × 16.2 cm (8⅝ × 6⅜ in.), 88 pages
Printer: MM Artbook Printing & Repro
Typefaces: Akkurat, Augereau
2010

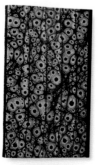

The New York Times Style Magazine

The New York Times publishes fifteen issues of its *T Magazine* per year, each devoted to a specific aspect of style. For each issue, an individual artist or designer is invited to respond to the content and commissioned to create unique artworks using the *Times*'s signature logo, an expanded black *T*.

T project

For the magazine's fall 2008 issue, dedicated to contemporary fashion in Russia, Apeloig designed a title page for the article "Constructivism Zone: Fashion in the Service of Revolution." Looking to Russian Constructivism for his inspiration, he deconstructed *The New York Times* logo and transposed it into a sort of montage with volume, using layers of Plexiglas elements that were photographed by Adam Savitch. Geometric forms by El Lissitzky, taken from his 1922 book *About Two Squares: In Six Constructions: A Suprematist Tale*, replaced bits of the down-stroke in the logo's gothic *T*. Instead, they were depicted in red inside a large white square so as to be reminiscent of Malevich's painting *White on White* (1918).

The square sits slightly on top of the *T*, hiding all but its edges. The two red diamonds' relation to this second layer is ambiguous: they both hover above and penetrate the white square. Drop shadows beneath the red shapes amplify their presence and also build narrative tension, causing the viewer to consider and complete the logo, by reading the partially obscured black curve of the *T*. A thin black vertical line bisecting the red diamonds exists independently, lending space and volume to the composition.

Magazine
T Magazine:
The New York Times Style Magazine
Autumn 2008

Animation
Website for T Magazine:
The New York Times Style Magazine
Length: 24"
2008

Faces

An animation for *T Magazine* graphically deconstructs the *T* into its various elements. These are then rearranged – without adding or subtracting anything from the existing logo – to create the features of glamorous-looking faces. The arrival of each new "persona" – as if on a red carpet – is met with applause and murmurs. The ovation that greets the *T*'s return to its iconic shape signals the end and indicates that, while *T Magazine* covers many important people, its signature logo reigns supreme.

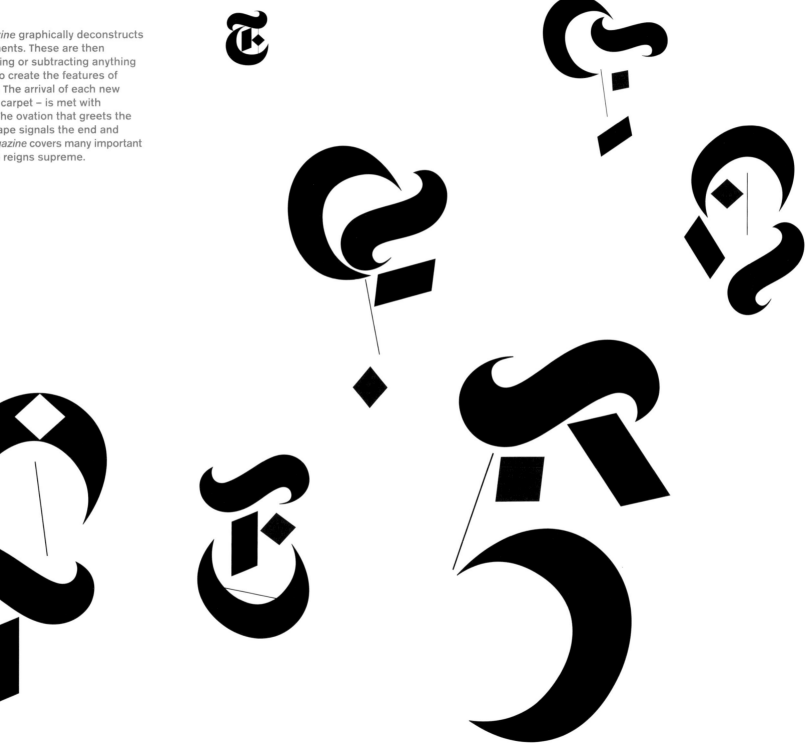

Mixt(e)

The slipcase design for the limited-edition issue of the fashion magazine *Mixt(e)* is built around the title's three consonants M, X, and T. The letters are cut into parts and pasted at the edges, forming counter shapes rendered in three different colors – blue, taupe, and black – that emphasize the negative space. The letters were printed with a transparent, glossy UV varnish to create slightly raised shapes. This work flirts with the idea of decorative applied arts and causes the viewer to wonder whether it is a work of experimental commercial design or a stand-alone artwork.

The designs of the introductory pages to the first five chapters respond to their titles: Creation, Aspiration, Inspiration, Respiration, and Generation. The original font was created by combining type elements, for example, /-\ to make a capital *A*, and |> to make a capital *P*. The letters are formed through the principles of repetition and assemblage. Letters of various sizes scatter across the page, evoking the sense of each word and highlighting the creative process, with each letter destined for further development.

This abstract architecture challenges conventional notions of font design by collaging the barest minimum of typographic elements into a formal system. The rhythmically bound, freely associated shapes become creative possibilities.

Magazine, slipcase
and interior pages
Mixt(e)
22 × 16.2 cm (8⅝ × 6⅜ in.)
Printer: CPI Aubin
Typeface: original creation
2011

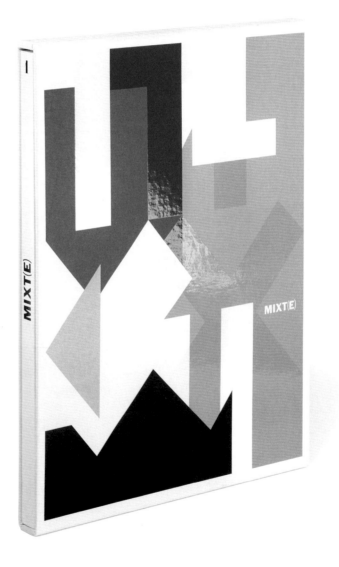

CréAtion

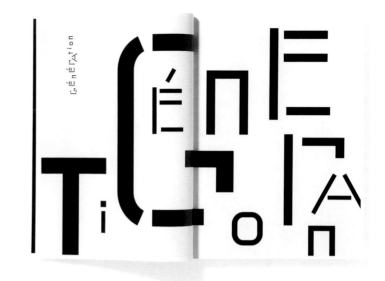

GénéraTion

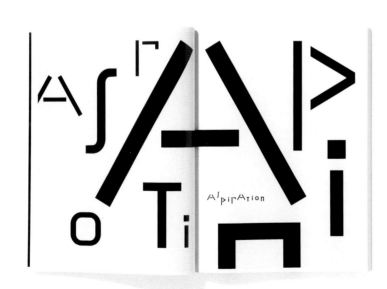

AspirAtion

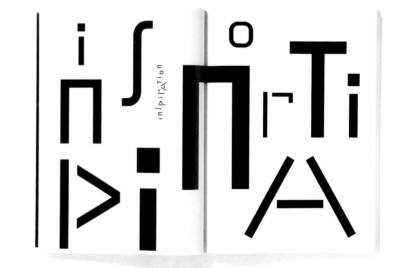

inSpirATion

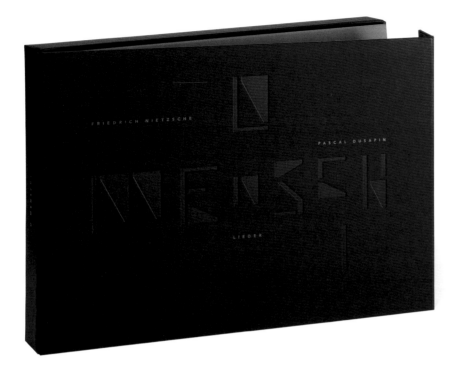

O Mensch!

The composer Pascal Dusapin's *O Mensch!* is a *Lieder* cycle based on the poems of Friedrich Nietzsche. The work was produced and presented at the Théâtre des Bouffes du Nord in 2011. To support the event, the fine-art printing studio Idem Paris produced a boxed limited edition of a facsimile of the original handwritten score. Apeloig was invited to design the portfolio and title page. His restrained typographic solution mixes lines with triangular shapes that nearly defy legibility but create a compelling aesthetic. The goal was to create, through harmony between typeface and content, the kind of mysterious, visceral response elicited by Dusapin's music.

Book
O Mensch!
Pascal Dusapin
Idem Paris
35.3 × 25 cm (13⅞ × 9⅞ in.)
Embossing and screen print
Impression: Idem
Typeface: original creation
2011

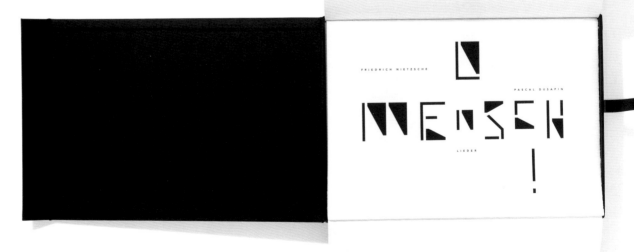

Collection Pierre Bergé

The Collection Pierre Bergé is a line of classical music made available to a wide public at an affordable price in packaging as sophisticated as the music inside. Consumers of the collection are treated to a musical journey – traversing musical forms ranging from opera to *Lieder* to chamber ensembles to symphonic music. The Collection Pierre Bergé is the only musical publishing house that brings together the great composers of the past along with living composers.

The new design identity for the Collection Pierre Bergé invents a linear typographic vocabulary that behaves consistently and aesthetically elevates the musical packaging of a realm – the classical arena – that has suffered a decline in recent years. The CD covers have identical layouts with a solid, bright background color, with the composer's name placed at the top in large black lettering, and the title of the musical work equally large below. The names of the artists, conductor, and venue are set in small, regularly sized type threaded throughout the composition. All of the large lettering is scaled to different heights, moving in a regular progression across the surface horizontally, but overlapping vertically. This creates an interlocking pattern that is simultaneously stable and fluid and resembles a melodic line. Reading it requires a sweeping circular scan across the entire visual field.

The font is spare, giving the background a lot of breathing room, and employs acute angles and generous curves. In a schematic fashion, the letters are interrupted by small breaks, or ligatures, creating visual noise and dissonance that reference directly the music. The series has a strong sense of materiality resulting from the use of bold color, a free structure, well-balanced proportions, even distribution and use of the entire surface, a feeling of lightness and ornamentation, and the object's own physicality. The CD disc comes in a solid color that correlates to the packaging's background color or lettering – blue, red, green – and is accompanied by a small illustrated booklet providing biographical and historical information about the composers and compositions.

CD covers
Collection Pierre Bergé
18.5 × 13.5 cm (7¼ × 5¼ in.)
Typefaces: original creation, Sero
2012

Gagosian Gallery

Jean Prouvé Architecture

The private-view invitation for the exhibition "Jean Prouvé Architecture" reworks a photograph of a building under construction, a typical prefabricated, modular structure from the postwar period. Details of the photograph are reproduced in yellow on both sides, in negative on the front and positive on the back, giving it an openly graphic quality. The text is arranged to match the forceful lines of the photograph.

**Brazil
Reinvention of the Modern**

The Gagosian Gallery in Paris presented an exhibition of Brazilian art from the late Modernist period, featuring works by artists associated with the Neoconcrete Movement of the late 1950s. The highly illustrated exhibition catalog is constructed of layered clear plastic squares, bound at the bottom left corner to create a fan. This innovative design recalls a 1971 book by Mira Schendel titled *Caderno Selos*, a loosely bound volume of six acrylic pages that could be rearranged by the viewer.

The title is printed in black on the round-cornered Plexiglas cover through which the book's title page, with the subtitle "Reinvention of the Modern," is visible, though somewhat out of focus thanks to the translucent cover. The reader is encouraged to play with this object-book, opening it out to find the works of each artist. As a whole, it echoes the geometric inspiration, sensuality, and subjectivity of Neoconcretism.

Invitation
Jean Prouvé Architecture
Gagosian Gallery, Paris
23.5 × 14.6 cm (9¼ × 5¾ in.)
Typeface: DTL Caspari
2010

Exhibition catalog
Brazil: Reinvention of the Modern
Gagosian Gallery, Paris
19 × 19 cm (7½ × 7½ in.), 82 pages
Printer: MM Artbook Printing & Repro
Typeface: Franklin Gothic
2012

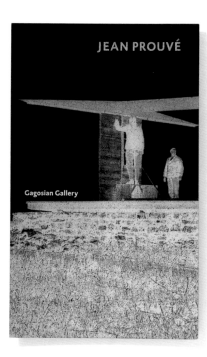
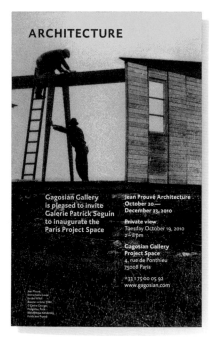

James Turrell

The design of the James Turrell exhibition catalog picks up on the artist's intensive exploration of light, color, and space using vibrant hues and a clean aesthetic. The font is Caspari, designed between 1990 and 1993 by Gerard Daniels for the Dutch Type Library. The book and slipcase are printed in two shades of blue, the artist's favorite color. The front of the slipcase is dark blue, with "James" printed in large light blue letters at the top; on the back, "Turrell" is set in dark blue against a light blue ground. The slight shine of the laminated slipcase contrasts with the matte material used for the cover. The inside of the slipcase is a bright, almost pulsating pink, which, juxtaposed with the blue, emulates the optical effects of Turrell's light installations.

Inside the book, images of artworks are arranged across the spread in contiguous groups of four and engage in a dialogue similar to that fostered by a gallery setting. Elsewhere, a full-spread photograph transports the reader into the artist's immersive universe. Throughout, using tangible physical form, the book's design conveys the radiance and wonder of Turrell's ephemeral works.

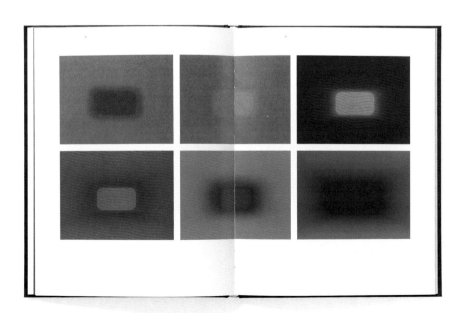

Exhibition catalog
James Turrell
Gagosian Gallery, London
31.8 × 25.5 cm (12½ × 10 in.), 88 pages
Printer: Shapco Printing
Typeface: DTL Caspari
2011

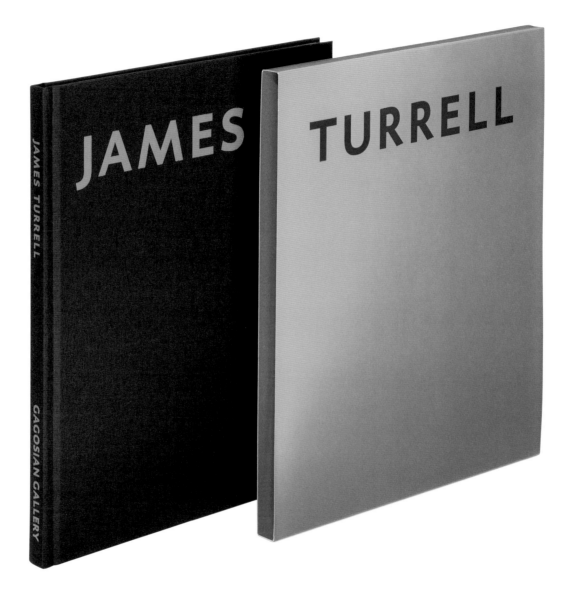

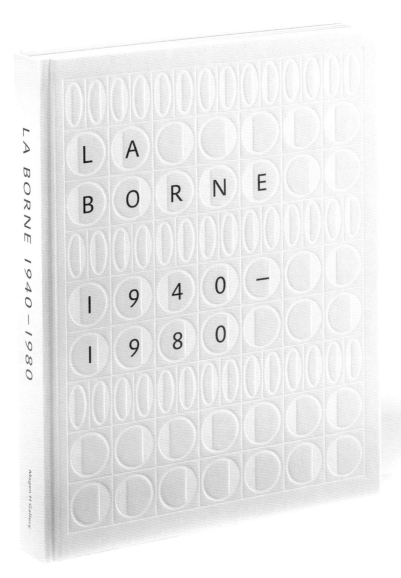

Magen H Gallery
La Borne 1940–1980

Magen H Gallery in New York specializes in sculpture, decorative arts, architecture, and ceramics, with an emphasis on postwar French designers. In conjunction with an exhibition of pottery from La Borne, France, spanning 1940 to 1980, the gallery produced a companion publication. Apeloig's design for the book uses an earthen palette of dark brown and cream. The cover's embossed pattern – white foil pressed into the cover's matte cream-colored paper – derives from a 1972 ceramic screen designed by Pierre Digan: a grid of oval and circular shapes. The title *La Borne 1940–1980* appears in dark brown type, all capitals. The subtitle, "A postwar movement of ceramic expression in France," appears in cream on a band of white Chromolux paper that wraps around the base of the book. A variant of Digan's pattern is also used on the endpapers, printed in gray on a dark blue ground.

The richly illustrated, 288-page book begins with a history of the village and the La Borne movement. Sepia-toned photographs appear on warm gray backgrounds, while the text and full-color plates appear on white. Numerous full-page spreads are devoted to details of the most intricate works. A third group of illustrations shows the sculptures inside collectors' homes. *La Borne 1940–1980* is bilingual: English text is set in black type at the top of the page, while a French text is printed below in sepia. The headline font is DTL Prokyon, designed by Erhard Kaiser; the body text is Miller. The blend of traditional and modern elements in the design captures the complexity of the La Borne movement: its deep traditions and radical modernity.

Exhibition catalog
La Borne, 1940–1980
Magen H Gallery, New York
24.5 × 20 cm (9⅝ × 7⅞ in.), 288 pages
Printer: MM Artbook Printing & Repro
Typefaces: DTL Prokyon, Miller Text
2012

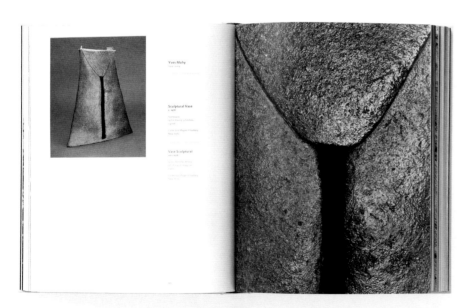

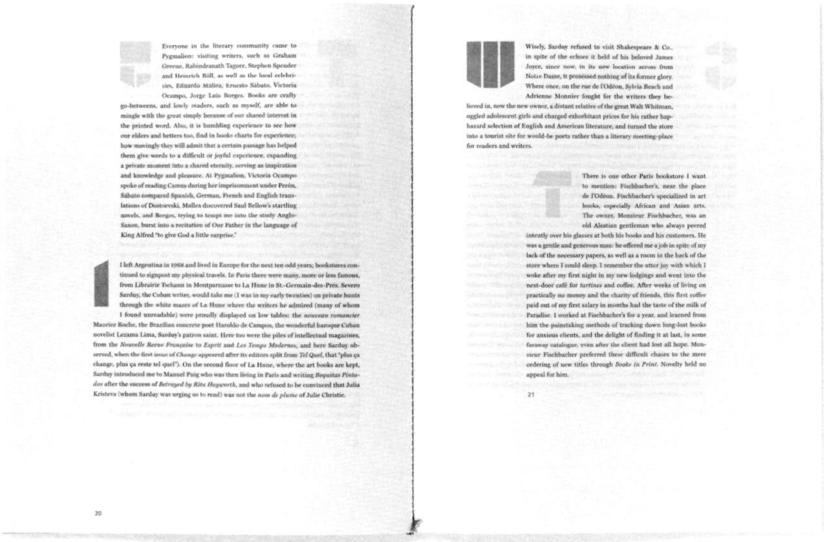

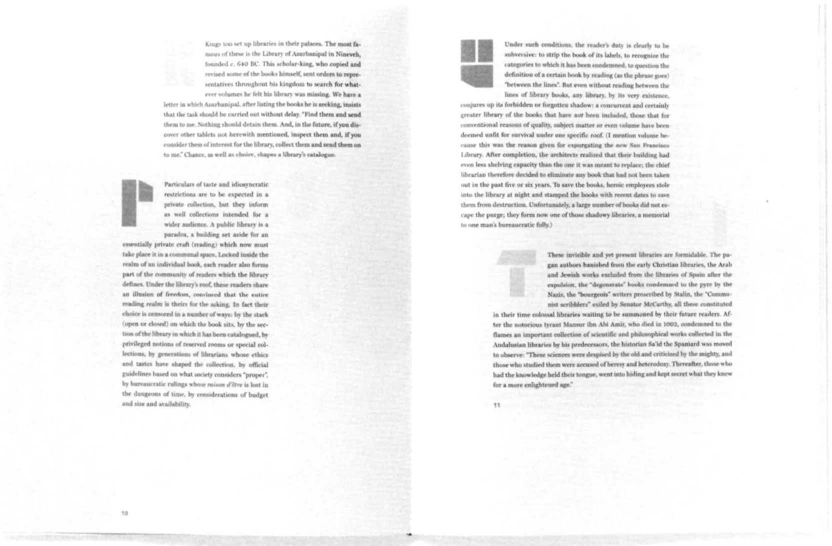

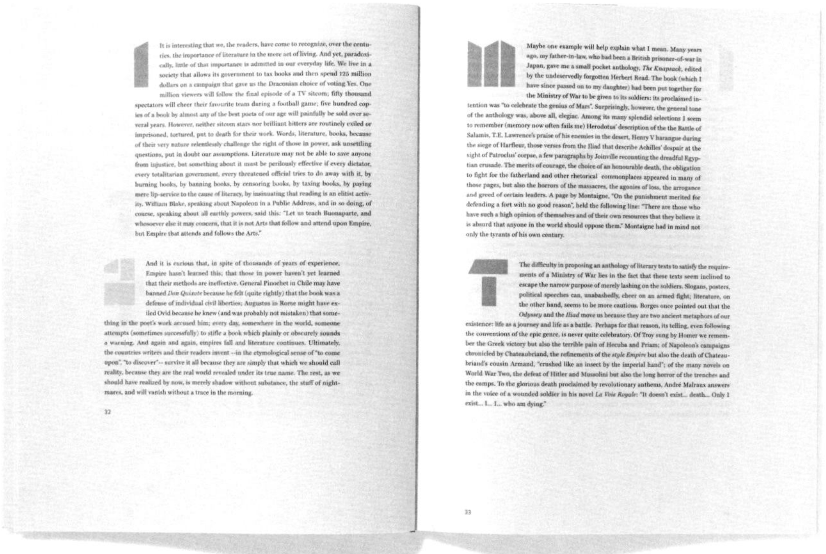

Book
Recto-Verso
Take 5
31 × 25 cm (12¼ × 9⅞ in.), 38 pages
Printer: Les Deux Ponts
Typefaces: original creation,
Miller Text, Syntax
2012

Take 5
Recto-Verso

Recto-Verso is a limited-edition book by the publisher
Take 5, with a binding inspired by a drawing by the
renowned Swiss binder Jean Luc Honegger. The book
is an investigation into the existence of books over
time and the role they play in society. A real dialogue
takes place between the photographs of the Turkish
video artist Ali Kazma and the text of Alberto Manguel,
the Argentine-born writer. Apeloig has turned his
graphic treatment of the essay and cards into a perceptual and spatial adventure that sensitizes the reader
to the unseen contributions of the skilled artists and
artisans behind each and every book.

The book contains eight large, original photographic
prints, a bound essay, and 176 cards illustrating
the varied realms of publishing: binding, books, book-
stores, libraries, manuscripts, paper, printing, restor-
ation, and tools. This juxtaposition of images originates
from Ali Kazma's idea of using several screens to
confront the gestures and realities of the different
professions.

The text traces the history of the book, stressing its
vital importance as a recipient of collective memory
and as a symbol of the social cohesion necessary
to any democracy. The book cover is made of three
overlapping flaps of different sizes, with the smallest
on top. As each flap is lifted, more and more of
the title is revealed. The succession of flaps reflects
the step-by-step evolution of the book. The title
is set in stencil letters built with a minimum of lines;
they use strong verticals and horizontals modified
by soft angles and are divided by heavy white
lines. Two shades of gray distinguish the words
"recto" and "verso."

The inside layout reflects the fluidity of the reading
process, with a textual arrangement well suited
to Manguel's personal reminiscences. The grid's
columns allow for paragraphs of different widths to
shift across the page. An indented drop capital marks
out each new paragraph, here modern and solid
but harking back to the ornate initial capitals used
by monastic scribes on illuminated manuscripts.
The page numbers, printed in red, are unconventionally
and dynamically placed close to the last line of text
on the left-hand page and near the bottom of the
right-hand page.

Posters and Typography

Henry Moore intime

In 1992, Paris's Galerie Didier Imbert featured an exhibition of British sculptor Henry Moore's small, intimate works, with the exhibition design by Christian Germanaz. Moore's monumental abstract works are displayed throughout the world and are instantly recognizable. Originally, the gallery wanted a photographic portrait of the artist for the poster, but Apeloig disagreed and likewise rejected the use of a Moore sculpture. His recommendation was to find a typographic solution. He made a visit to Moore's home and workspace in Much Hadham, England, found it inspiring, and had it photographed.

A photograph of Moore's house became the background of the design. It was printed as a bitmap image with heightened shadows and a grainy texture to suggest memory. A large-scale reproduction was installed on the doors leading into the gallery, inviting visitors to enter Moore's personal world. The Gill Sans typeface on the poster recalls the artist's British heritage and the solidity of his massive rounded forms. This theme is pushed further by converting the font to "ultrabold," which expands its volume, and using uppercase letters to build a sort of "letter sculpture" out of Moore's name. The oversized letters shine brightly against the shadowy backdrop, while individual characters are compressed to create wide curves and spaces that echo Moore's aesthetic. The fat *O* and sloping diagonals of the *M* and *R* evoke his reclining figures, while the diagonals in the *M* echo the house's sharply angular architecture in reverse.

Poster
Henry Moore intime
Galerie Didier Imbert, Paris
175 × 118.5 cm (68⅞ × 46⅝ in.)
Screen print
Typeface: Gill Sans
1992
See pages 360–63

**Henry Moore's family home,
Much Hadham, 1992**
Photograph
Prudence Cuming Associates Ltd

3 avril-24 juillet 1992

Didier Imbert
19 avenue Matignon
Paris

MOORE

HENRY MOORE INTIME

collection de l'artiste

Foire internationale du livre ancien

Since 1984, the Syndicat national de la Librairie Ancienne et Moderne (National Association of Antiquarian and Modern Booksellers) has organized an annual book fair in Paris, the Foire internationale du livre ancien (International Antiquarian Book Fair). Its 1991 festival poster embodies tradition and modernity, blending geometric and typographic motifs in a subtle, harmonious composition and using a palette that alludes to the materials and processes of publishing. Leather is suggested by the color brown, and parchment by the yellowish block containing the festival dates. The classical Garamond typeface connotes the world of literature. The irregular black rectangle – influenced by the Russian Constructivists, who were renowned for their superlative book design – acts in concert with page forms that shift and move in space. The containment of text inside thin rectangles and their visual arrangement, which is perpendicular to the horizontal composition, represent the spines of books either lying or standing on bookshelves.

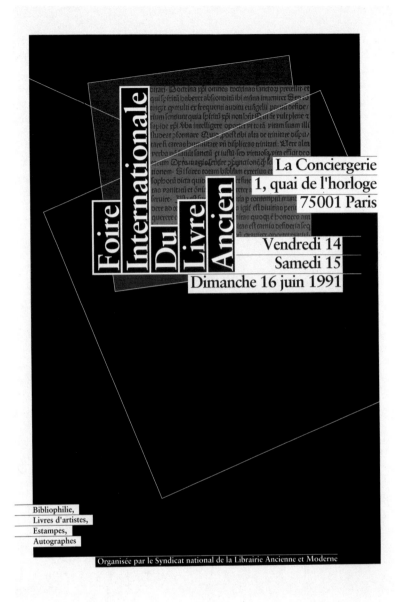

Poster
Foire internationale du livre ancien, Paris
175 × 118.5 cm (68⅞ × 46⅝ in.)
Screen print
Printer: Graphicaza
Typeface: Garamond
1991

Poster
Arc en rêve centre d'architecture, Bordeaux
175 × 118.5 cm (68⅞ × 46⅝ in.)
Screen print
Printer: Arts Graphiques de France
Typeface: Frutiger
1992
See pages 364–65

Arc en rêve
centre d'architecture

Arc en rêve centre d'architecture (Arc en rêve Architectural Center), a center for architecture whose name is a play on the French words for dream and rainbow, was founded in Bordeaux in 1981 to promote social awareness of architecture, urban planning, landscaping, and design, and to improve the quality of living spaces. In 1992, Arc en rêve wanted a promotional poster that would create a dialogue between design, construction, and corporate operations, as typified by Mies van der Rohe's Seagram Building (1954–58) in New York, which is a confluence of architectural and organizational intent that aspires to pure transparency and flexibility.

The poster composition delivered by Apeloig depicts a detail of an imaginary modular structure embodying these traits. Its architectural language is created through layered levels of transparency and nuanced color shifts from pale to dark gray. Together, shadow and light suggest a building under construction. The overall design, founded on a multiplication of bold and fine lines crossing at ninety-degree angles, is mathematically precise yet benefits from free, subjective layering. The use of multiple grids creates a *trompe l'oeil* effect that simulates both textures and objects. The lines increase in density, some of them escalating into solid black surfaces.

Set in Frutiger, the typography is integrated throughout, creating depth and a variable scale. Space and lettering are interlaced within a web of formal relations that is impossible to disentangle.

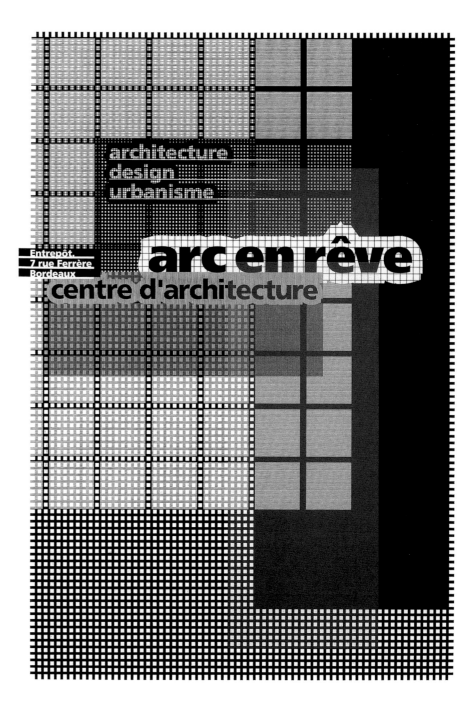

Approche

In 1995, the French Institute in Barcelona held an exhibition curated by Pierre Ponant titled "Approche" (literally, Approach), which featured the work of four young type designers: Pierre di Sciullo, M/M, Toffe, and Philippe Apeloig. The word "approche" also refers to the space between type elements, which designers call "kerning."

Instead of an exhibition catalog, each designer was invited to create a folded flyer in the form of a self-portrait. Apeloig repurposed a photo-booth picture from his childhood. He used classical Garamond for the cover, with the letter *g* at the end of his last name serving as spectacles for his five-year-old face.

Inside the folded flyer are the four modern typefaces that Apeloig designed during his residency at the French Academy of Art in Rome in 1993 and 1994. Using a grid system to abstract the shapes, the new fonts employ a primarily geometric motif.

In Carré, the letters are rationalized into nearly solid cubes with few openings or breakthroughs; the outline varies from very heavy to so fine that it almost disappear (page 165). In the most traditional of the typefaces, a condensed font called Cursive, the thickness of the letter is equal at every point and has minimal curves. It is drawn in two versions: one san serif, one serif.

The third, more experimental font, Aleph (page 164), is drawn from a basic calligraphic system influenced by the Banco font that Roger Excoffon designed in 1952. The lowercase letters are of equal thickness, with simple forms made of vertical strokes and slight curves. Its minimalist construction relies on expressive details to create nuance.

The fourth design, Octobre (used for the Octobre posters on page 84, and redesigned in 2006 for the Châtelet posters on page 96), is based on an agglomeration of pixel-like squares and a low-resolution, bitmap aesthetic – a throwback to the early days of computers. The letters are designed as solid bricks but with a pattern of missing parts that brings them close to the style of stencil letters.

Leaflet
Approche Philippe Apeloig
Institut français, Barcelona
22 × 17 cm (8⅝ × 6¾ in.)
Open: 44 × 34 cm (17⅜ × 13⅜ in.)
Typefaces: Garamond, Carré, Cursive, Aleph, Octobre, Linéale
1995
See page 358

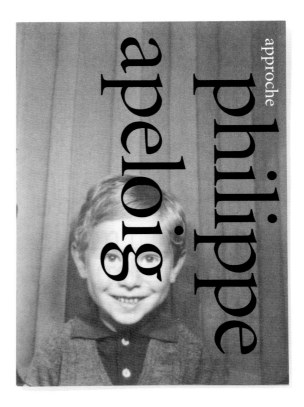

**Philippe Apeloig,
Exercices typographiques**

Mes recherches consistent à dessiner des caractères d'imprimerie utiles pour le texte en lecture continue, mais surtout à inventer des caractères de titrage dont la perfection de lisibilité n'est pas le principal critère et que j'aime utiliser pour mes créations d'affiche.

Ejercicios tipográficos

Su meta consiste en dibujar letras de molde que sirvan para el texto en lectura seguida, pero se dedica sobre todo a inventar letras para títulos que no sean precisamente fáciles de leer pero que él se complace en emplear para sus creaciones de carteles.

Je m'efforce de rationaliser le dessin des lettres capitales et de les comprimer dans une forme unique : le carré. En cherchant à les inscrire dans un carré, je n'ignore pas que la lisibilité des caractères est compromise. Je choisi une expression massive des lettres abandonnant les vides et les pleins, je les imagine comme des blocs de matière sans creux. Le volume des caractères est identique pour chacun d'entre eux mais des petites ouvertures rendent possibles la lecture de l'alphabet. Des contours d'épaisseurs différentes transforment les caractères, leur insufflent un dynamisme, et permettent d'aller jusqu'aux limites de l'effacement. Leur silhouette massive les rend lisibles surtout de loin, ce qui est idéal pour des conceptions graphiques de grand format.

Intento racionalizar el trazo de las mayúsculas y comprimirlas en una forma única : el cuadrado. Al intentar enmarcarlas en un cuadrado, soy plenamente consciente de que su lectura se ve comprometida. Opto por una expresión masiva de las letras abandonando huecos y llenos, las imagino como bloques de materia sin hueco alguno. Todos los caracteres tienen un volumen idéntico, pero algunas pequeñas aperturas permiten la lectura del alfabeto. Contornos de distinto grosor transforman las letras, les impregnan dinamismo y permiten incluso alcanzar el límite de la desaparición. Su línea compacta hace que se puedan leer sobretodo de lejos, lo cual resulta ideal para diseñar carteles de tamaño grande.

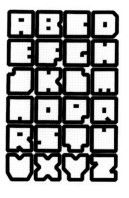
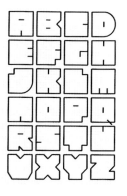

Un autre caractère est dessiné sur la base d'un tracé de plume rudimentaire comme des embryons de lettres pas encore développés.

L'aspect primitif de mes caractères et plus précisément ceux dits « pochoirs » (divisés en plusieurs blocs) renvoie aux premiers essais des dessins informatiques : absence de courbe et de diagonale. Leur dessin est « objectif » : tracé sec et minimal.

Otras letras se diseñarán sobre la base de un trazado de pluma rudimentaria como embriones de letras que aún no han tenido tiempo para desarrollarse.

El aspecto primitivo de mis caracteres y en particular los que llamo «plantillas» (divididos en varios bloques) recuerdan los dibujos de informática : sin curva o diagonal alguna. Su dibujo es «objetivo» : trazo seco y mínimo.

Je conçois également une « haute cursive » où l'épaisseur de la grasse est égale en tout point. Ce caractère bâton, décliné avec des serifs épais, peut être considéré comme un caractère de texte. Les longs jambages des bas-de-casse et la mise en valeur des blancs accentuent le contraste entre les lettres, cela de façon à pouvoir lire un texte ainsi composé même dans des corps de petites tailles. Dessinée avec un minimum de courbes, sur la base de formes géométriques simples légèrement étroitisées, cette nouvelle police m'a permis de m'interroger sur les questions fondamentales concernant la typographie, à savoir : la forme et l'esthétique, la fonction et l'utilisation.

Concibo así mismo una «alta cursiva» en que el grosor de la negrita es constante. Este tipo de letra palo, declinado con serifs grueso puede considerarse como un carácter de texto. Los palos largos de las cajas bajas y el realce de los blancos incrementan el contraste entre las letras, de forma a poder leer un texto compuesto de esta forma incluso en cuerpos reducidos. Dibujar con un mínimo de curvas a partir de formas geométricas sencillas, ligeramente estrechas, esta nueva fuente me ha permitido plantearme cuestiones fundamentales en cuanto a la tipografía, o sea : forma y estética, cometido y utilización.

La plupart des lecteurs lisent sans se soucier du type de caractère qu'ils sont en train de déchiffrer. La typographie appartient au monde du non-remarquable. Bousculer l'impartialité du lecteur sur le texte c'est transformer sa lecture et le contraindre à constater la présence des lettres et des signes en tant que forme. J'aime cette démarche qui l'invite à méditer plus encore le fond d'un texte. La typographie n'est pas seulement un mécanisme, le typographe doit s'efforcer de la rendre claire, évidente et pourquoi pas spectaculaire.

La mayoría de los lectores lee sin preocuparse por el tipo de letra que está descifrando. La tipografía pertenece al mundo de lo que no se nota. La tipografía zarandear la imparcialidad del lector sobre el texto consiste en transformar su lectura y obligarle a percatarse de la presencia de las letras y de los signos en tanto que formas. Me gusta esta forma de proceder que le invita a meditar más aún sobre el fondo de un texto. La tipografía no es sólo un mecanismo, el tipógrafo debe esforzarse para hacerla clara, evidente y por que no espectacular.

Posters in the Context
of French Culture

In 1998, after receiving the Gold Award from the
Tokyo Type Directors Club (TDC) for a series of posters
for the Octobre en Normandie festival (page 84) –
a project pivotal in his career – Apeloig was offered
an exhibition titled "Posters in the Context of French
Culture." The exhibition was shown at two galleries
owned by the Dai Nippon Printing Company in Japan.
One was the DDD Gallery in Osaka, the other the
GGG Gallery in Tokyo.

The poster and invitation card for the GGG show
represent the first use of Apeloig's calligraphy font,
Aleph. On the poster, the Latin letters are turned
ninety degrees, requiring vertical reading, as is the
case with Japanese writing. The invitation card
features letters resting on asymmetrical black and
gray rectangles constructed from layers of collaged
photographs.

Invitation
Philippe Apeloig:
Posters in the Context
of French Culture
GGG Ginza Graphic Gallery, Tokyo
21 × 14.8 cm (8 ¼ × 5 ⅞ in.)
Typeface: Aleph
1998
See pages 352 – 53

Poster
Philippe Apeloig:
Posters in the Context
of French Culture
GGG Ginza Graphic Gallery, Tokyo
103 × 72.8 cm (40 ½ × 28 ⅝ in.)
Typeface: Aleph
1998
See pages 352 – 53

PlayType

The Carré typeface was used for a poster promoting a 2005 exhibition of Apeloig's work at the University of the Arts in Philadelphia. When designing the font in 1993 and 1994, Apeloig approached each letterform as a toy to be played with and imagined the behavior of each one as mechanical and machine-like. The letters are stacked and deconstructed in an arrangement that recalls the computer game Tetris.

The letters *P*, *L*, and *A* take up the first line, requiring the eye to jump directly down to the *Y* on the second line to complete the word. This separation creates a substantial space in the center. The word "TYPE" is also playfully disjointed, with the *T* on the far left of the central space and the remaining letters below, on the third line. The letters function as spirited free objects, making the fragmented words seem poised for re-scrambling. The title is adapted from the 1967 movie *PlayTime* by French director Jacques Tati, which features hapless mortals contending with a sterile modern environment.

At the center of the poster, as if superimposed on the letters, is a transparent yellow rectangle. Its straight sharp edges reference the flat surfaces of print-making. The design's neon palette connects to the domain of gadgets and technology. PlayType rejects the traditional notion that type design should be about utility, readability, and comfort.

Poster
PlayType
University of the Arts, Philadelphia
175 × 118.5 cm (68⅞ × 46⅝ in.)
Screen print
Printer: 5ᵉ Couleur
Typeface: Carré
2005
See pages 314 – 15

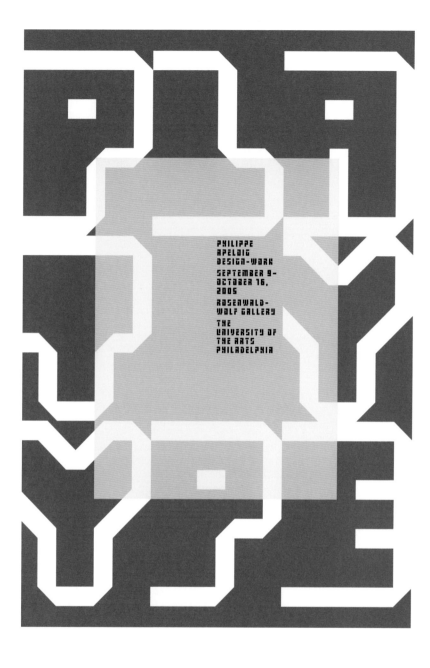

Affiches Philippe Apeloig

Apeloig has always found inspiration in art. Wall drawings by Sol LeWitt, three-dimensional geometric forms by Donald Judd, and Minimalist arrangements by Carl Andre are a few of the works that have challenged him and impacted his design. Minimalism has encouraged in him a certain sobriety, an interest in creating series, and exploring mathematical progression.

While utilizing such constraints, Apeloig strives for visual liveliness, a trace of illusionism, and at times an accidental quality. The design for a 2003 exhibition of his posters, "Affiches Philippe Apeloig," shown at La Médiatine in Brussels, and later at Galerija Avla NLB in Ljubljana, Slovenia, suggests an architectural plan viewed from above, perhaps one for a pyramid. Though perfectly flat, it implies depth.

The composition follows the principle of Russian nesting dolls. It also references the ephemeral nature of posters in public spaces – on the street a poster becomes the substrate for new posters of diverse styles and levels of expertise, layering memory upon memory, until the last poster covers all the rest. In Apeloig's design, continuous frames of cream and blue fit perfectly one inside another. Fingerlike cut letters at the top and bottom of each frame mediate mass and line, as well as structure and space throughout the composition: the words reach toward their mirror images, their geometric stretch setting up soft vibrations at the edges. The two-color contrasting palette has a reflective, historical feel.

The exhibition in Brussels was curated by the École Supérieure des Arts de l'Image "Le 75"; the Ljubljana presentation was curated by *Emzin Arts Magazine* and the Emzin Institute of Creative Production.

Poster
Affiches Philippe Apeloig
La Médiatine, Brussels
Galerija Avla NLB, Ljubljana
175 × 118.5 cm (68⅞ × 46⅝ in.)
Screen print
Printer: Dubois Imagerie
Typefaces: Champion Gothic, Fago Mono
2003

AFFICHES

PHILIPPE

APELOIG

la médiatine de stockel
45 chaussée de stockel
bruxelles

23 octobre
au 9 novembre
2003

ouvert
du jeudi au dimanche
12h—18h

APELOIG

PHILIPPE

AFFICHES

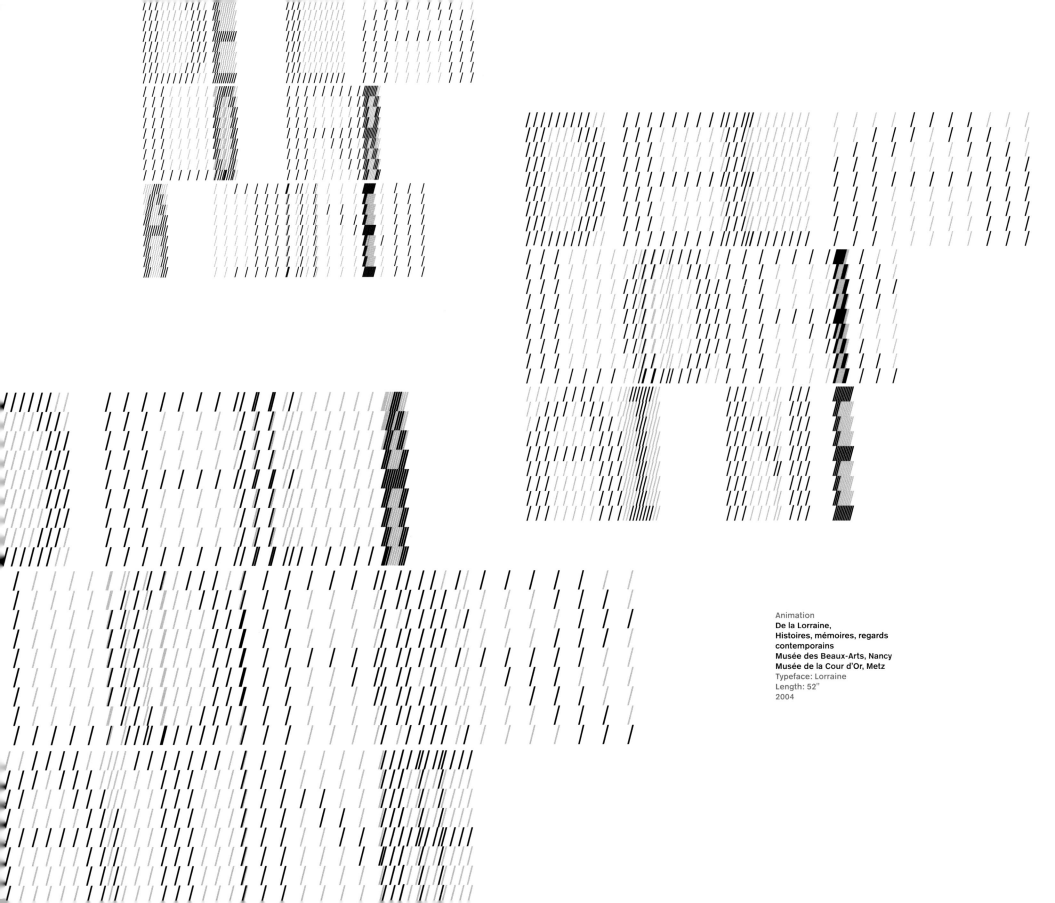

Animation
**De la Lorraine,
Histoires, mémoires, regards
contemporains
Musée des Beaux-Arts, Nancy
Musée de la Cour d'Or, Metz**
Typeface: Lorraine
Length: 52"
2004

De la Lorraine

The Lorraine, an important crossroads at the heart of Europe that borders Germany, Belgium, and Luxembourg, has spawned diverse art forms and craft traditions that draw on its abundant natural resources. The 2004 exhibition "De la Lorraine, Histoires, mémoires, regards contemporains" (Of the Lorraine: History, Memory, a Contemporary Look), presented a fresh vision of the northeastern region through the works of contemporary artists, writers, and historians. After the exhibition had been mounted, Apeloig developed an entire alphabet as a purely experimental, personal project inspired by the region's textiles.

Each letter is composed of tens of embroidered stitches. The top half of the poster features the inverted words "De la Lorraine," which are repeated, right side up, on the bottom half. The letters sit inside individual color blocks organized into a grid. The combination of the regular grid, the vivid red and yellow (from the Lorraine coat of arms), and the dynamic letters – fashioned from so many slashing stitches – creates a dynamic rhythm that draws the eye across the page. The typeface looks contemporary and is versatile despite its simple structure: the same letters can appear differently depending on their width. An animated version provides another depiction of the subject, with the letters shrinking or growing in rhythm to the music.

Poster
De la Lorraine,
Histoires, mémoires, regards
contemporains
Musée des Beaux-Arts, Nancy
Musée de la Cour d'Or, Metz
This poster is a later version than the one produced for the client.
175 × 118.5 cm (68⅞ × 46⅝ in.)
Screen print
Printer: 5ᵉ Couleur
Typefaces: Lorraine, Foundry Monoline
2004
See pages 324 – 25

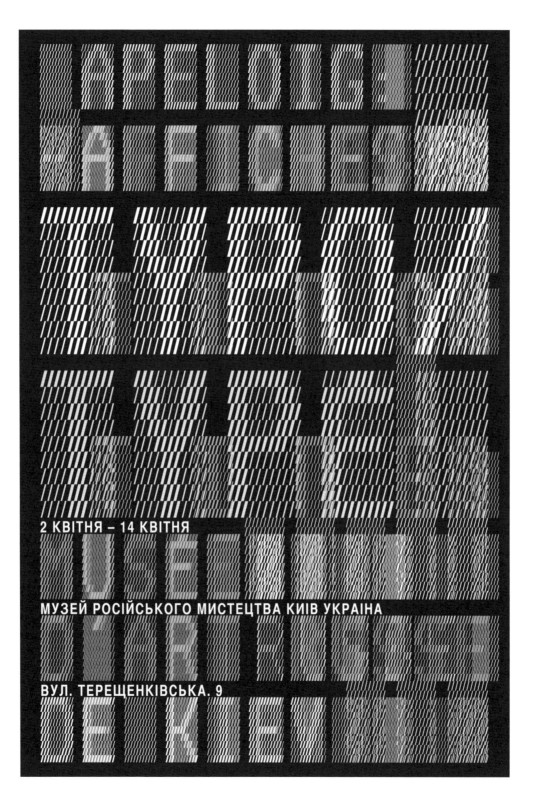

2 КВІТНЯ – 14 КВІТНЯ

МУЗЕЙ РОСІЙСЬКОГО МИСТЕЦТВА КИЇВ УКРАЇНА

ВУЛ. ТЕРЕЩЕНКІВСЬКА. 9

Typo/Typé

The posters for the 2005 exhibition "Typo/Typé" on Apeloig's work, which was held at the Carré Sainte-Anne in Montpellier, France, and at Kiev's Museum of Russian Art, showcase the designer's original Lorraine typeface. Designed for the 2004 exhibition "De la Lorraine," it was inspired by the textile production of the Lorraine region, as well as by the nineteenth-century photographic motion studies of Eadweard Muybridge and Étienne-Jules Marey. Lorraine is an organic typeface composed of layer upon layer of transparent colors that create complex vibrating patterns and systems in unlimited combinations, implying time and movement.

While both exhibition posters are similar in composition and typography, the Montpellier version (page 32) is sketchy and rough, mixing cool and hot shades on a white background, with blues overlapping reds. The Kiev poster uses similar shades of blue, but adds other colors to create a blended, painterly quality.

The centers of both posters hold the exhibition title "Typo/Typé," a bit of rhyming wordplay with layers of symbolism that echo the constructed letterforms. "Typo" (type) represents the designer's passion, while "Typé" (of a recognizable type) refers to his own lineage. For Apeloig, design and typography hold unlimited rhythmic potential that can be harnessed to create meaningful art. His imaginative strategies are intended to transform the design profession, pushing it toward pure artistic expression.

Poster
Typo/Typé
Carré Sainte-Anne, Montpellier
Museum of Russian Art, Kiev
175 × 118.5 cm (68⅞ × 46⅝ in.)
Screen print
Printer: 5ᵉ Couleur
Typeface: Lorraine
2005

Invitation
Typo/Typé
Carré Sainte-Anne, Montpellier
21 × 15 cm (8¼ × 5⅞ in.)
Typefaces: Lorraine,
Franklin Gothic
2005

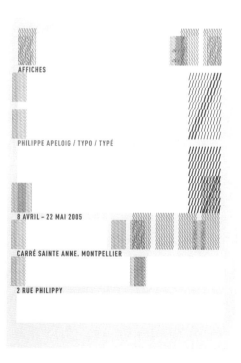

Vivo in Typo

The 2008 exhibition "Vivo in Typo, Affiches et alphabet animé" (Vivo in Typo: Posters and the Animated Alphabet) featured large-scale posters and motion graphics by Apeloig and was held at the Espace Topographie de l'art (Gallery for the Topography of Art) in Paris. Thirty-two unframed, two-sided posters floated in the raw industrial space, suspended by cables. The minimal installation utilized the full height of the ceilings. The vivid contrast between the refined prints and their unfinished surroundings brought the delicacy of the paper and the silkscreened surfaces into relief. On one side of each suspended piece were completed poster designs, while on the other were experiments in type design: large-scale letterforms rendered black on white and white on black, with each character printed twice. The overall impression throughout the lively installation was one of transparency, depth, and movement. The idea of juxtaposing single letter designs with complete polished designs came from a small booklet Apeloig had designed in 2007 for the twentieth anniversary exhibition of the Type Directors Club in Tokyo.

Slogan-like, the title "Vivo in Typo" reaches out from the exhibition's promotional poster through bold color and interwoven form. The poster design and typography use dashes, crosses, and points, with woven strands of thread creating lumps, ridges, fragments, and dots. A feeling of transparency, depth, and movement is evoked. The letters are alive within the complex layering of the visual field – pulsating, shivering, pushing forward, falling back. Some parts of the same character appear to be on different planes.

In a separate gallery, a video of motion-graphic work displayed Apeloig's experimentation with typefaces and animation. The exhibition was mounted again in 2009 at the Design Center of the University of Quebec in Montreal, Canada.

Exhibition catalog
Vivo in Typo
Philippe Apeloig Affiches
Espace Topographie de l'art, Paris
15.8 × 11.3 cm (6¼ × 4½ in.)
Printer: LM Graphie
Typeface: Akkurat
2008

Poster
Vivo in Typo
Philippe Apeloig,
Affiches et alphabet animé
Espace Topographie de l'art, Paris
175 × 118.5 cm (68⅞ × 46⅝ in.)
Screen print
Printer: Sérica
Typefaces: original creation, Akkurat
2008

Philippe Apeloig
Affiches
et alphabet animé
12 avril - 25 mai
2008
Espace Topographie
de l'art
15 rue de Thorigny
Paris 3ᵉ

Exhibition
Vivo in Typo
Philippe Apeloig,
Affiches et alphabet animé
Espace Topographie de l'art, Paris
2008

Booklet
Selected letters
Philippe Apeloig
Dai Nippon Printing
15.8 × 11.3 cm (6¼ × 4½ in.)
2007

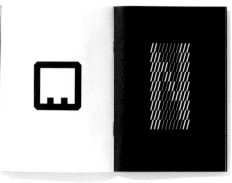
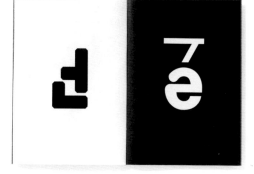
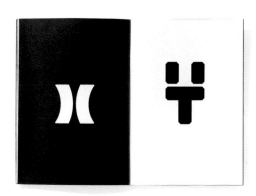
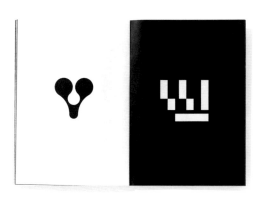

Fête du livre, Aix-en-Provence

Every year since 1981, Aix-en-Provence has hosted an annual festival of foreign literature called the Fête du livre (Festival of the Book). Organized around a specific theme, culture, or writer, the literary festival presents three days of intense debate, film screenings, exhibitions, staged readings, and other thought-provoking experiences. The event draws a diverse, cultured audience of avid readers and writers of international stature. Debates sparked by the headliners and their works are often political, exploring the pressing social and political issues faced by their countries of origin. Apeloig has created the posters for the Fête du livre since 1997.

L'Afrique du Sud au présent

"L'Afrique du Sud au présent" (South Africa Today) was the theme of the 1997 Fête du livre. Apartheid was abolished in South Africa in the early 1990s after a long, violent struggle. Apeloig began designing the 1997 poster by playing with type, attempting to visually capture the anger and frustration engendered by apartheid. But it was American artists such as Ellsworth Kelly and Frank Stella who finally inspired the finished poster. Consisting of five columns of alternating, irregularly geometric black and white stripes, the painting evokes both natural and manmade associations – from bamboo to zebras to prison bars to books on a shelf.

The poster is divided into two equal parts: the top black, the bottom ivory. These solid color blocks (representing the South African population) meet in the center, where an irregular series of light brown stripes stitches them into a "mixed zone." The long, narrow type, which matches the length of the stripes, is based on a typeface by Walter Käch, a calligraphy teacher at the Kunstgewerbeschule (School of Arts and Crafts) in Zurich. The letters are tangled among the stripes, passing in front of and behind them, as if hand sewn or an animal darting through tall grass.

Poster
L'Afrique du Sud au présent
Fête du livre, Aix-en-Provence
175 × 118.5 cm (68⅞ × 46⅝ in.)
Screen print
Printer: Sud Marquage
Typeface: based on a character by Walter Käch
1997
See pages 348 – 49

Fête du Livre

l'Afrique du Sud au présent

8-12 octobre 1997 Cité du Livre
Aix-en-Provence

Lire la Caraïbe
Haïti, Cuba

The flickering rays of light and deep shadows in this poster evoke the humidity of a Caribbean night and were inspired by the work of the American photographer Alex Webb, who had an exhibition in Aix-en-Provence that same year.

Words crisscross diagonally over an image of an open book, like the syncopated rhythms of Caribbean music. A complex collage of tattered palm fronds forms the letters. The heavy type was printed on transparent film and then projected to create permutations and distortions that add nuance. The frayed lettering seems to fly off the rifled pages. Like the nomadic spirit of many of the featured writers, the text is in constant motion, dynamically evolving and exploding in a cacophony of meaning.

Poster
Lire la Caraïbe, Haïti, Cuba
Fête du livre, Aix-en-Provence
175 × 118.5 cm (68⅞ × 46⅝ in.)
Screen print
Printer: 5ᵉ Couleur
Typeface: Akzidenz Grotesk
1998
See pages 340 – 41

Alex Webb (born in 1952)
Bombardopolis, Haiti, 1986
Photograph

The Roth Explosion

The American writer Philip Roth was the focus
of the 1999 Fête du livre. On the poster, Roth's face,
shown close up, stares straight out at the viewer
in a portrait composed from the titles of his novels,
repeated in a mass of small letters. This laborious
process of typographic modeling echoes Philip Roth's
prolific output, his obsessive nature, and his own
experience of psychoanalysis. The title is treated in
a similar fashion.

Poster
The Roth Explosion
Fête du livre, Aix-en-Provence
175 × 118.5 cm (68⅞ × 46⅝ in.)
Screen print
Printer: Arts Graphiques de France
Typeface: Univers
1999
See pages 332–35

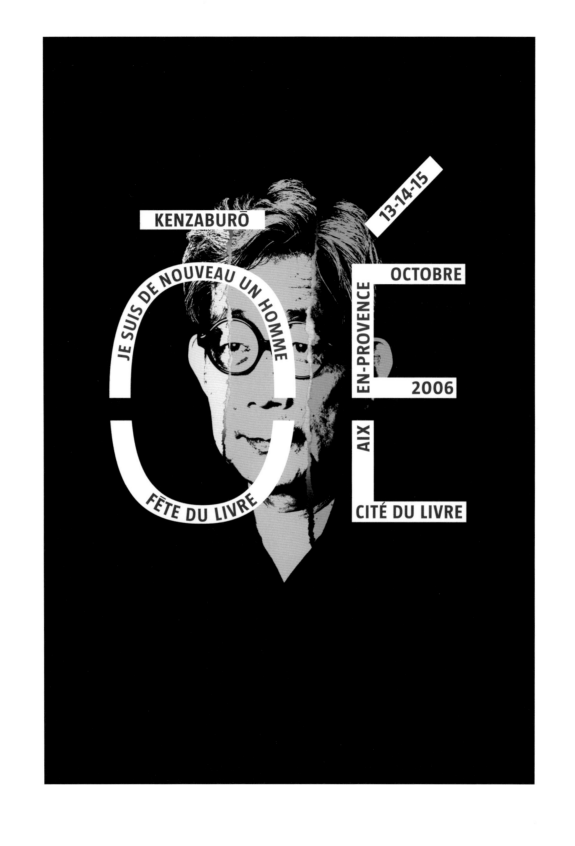

KENZABURŌ

JE SUIS DE NOUVEAU UN HOMME

FÊTE DU LIVRE

Œ

13-14-15

OCTOBRE

EN-PROVENCE

2006

AIX

CITÉ DU LIVRE

Kenzaburō Ōé
Je suis de nouveau un homme

In 1995, Japanese author Kenzaburō Ōé, an outspoken pacifist, boycotted the Fête du livre to protest against the decision of the French President, Jacques Chirac, to run a series of nuclear tests underground in the Mururoa Atoll in French Polynesia. It took ten years of negotiations before Ōé, the 1994 Nobel Prize winner, agreed to be the guest of honor at the 2006 festival. The event was titled "Je suis de nouveau un homme" (I am a man once again) and paid tribute to Ōé's writing and his political involvement.

Ōé was deeply affected by the Hiroshima bombing and has criticized both his own country for the atrocities it committed during World War II, and the United States for its occupation of Japan. His work was also influenced by the birth of his handicapped first son, an experience that gave him new perspectives on life and literature.

The festival poster features a photograph of the writer pieced together from three torn sections. The tears in the paper reflect Ōé's deep anxieties and anguish. From left to right, the pale green of the background grows darker, like the progression of a bruise. In front of the portrait are his initials, *Ō* and *É* (with an accent in the French), in large white type. Cut like stencils, they have been forced into their simplest elements. With their layered arrangement, interrupted pictographic shapes, and accent marks, the letters take on the appearance of Japanese characters. The informational text for the festival sits in smaller red type inside the large letters, adapting to both their curves and diagonal, vertical, and horizontal lines. The typography is bold and straightforward, while subtly and powerfully contrasting scale and graphic weight.

As a visual unit, the *ŌÉ* initials form a striking geometrical abstraction that defines and dominates the festival identity. It is a versatile design that Apeloig played with throughout the 2006 promotional materials by making the letters extremely weighty at times and topped by thin delicate accents, or by changing the scale and position of the logo in relation to other compositional elements.

Poster
Kenzaburō Ōé
Je suis de nouveau un homme
Fête du livre, Aix-en-Provence
175 × 118.5 cm (68⅞ × 46⅝ in.)
Screen print
Printer: 5ᵉ Couleur
Typeface: Taz
2006
See pages 312–13

Wole Soyinka
La maison et le monde

Nigerian-born poet, novelist, and dramatist Wole Soyinka received the Nobel Prize for Literature in 1986. In 2007, he was invited to Aix-en-Provence as the Fête du livre's guest of honor. An outspoken human rights activist, he has been imprisoned by repressive regimes, placed on trial on trumped-up charges, undergone periods of political exile, and had a death sentence placed on his head. His voice articulates a modern identity for Africa through its manmade and natural challenges and its successes in art and politics.

His personal journey mirrors the relationship between the home and the world, which was the 2007 festival title and theme, "La maison et le monde." After completing university, Soyinka left Africa to pursue a career in theater in England, where he wrote his first mature plays and experienced tremendous success. He returned to Nigeria at age twenty-six with a Rockefeller Research Fellowship and has been writing, lecturing, and advocating for a new, reborn Nigeria ever since. Like the fabrics woven by Soyinka's master-weaver Yoruba ancestors, whose stories are so often portrayed in his works, his portrait and the poster were designed using layers and strips of paper. The portrait was laser-printed twice, with two different tints of orange, then cut into narrow bands that were woven by hand, thus creating not only the motion and look of traditional weaving but also a three-dimensional object. The writer's portrait emerged through these colored layers. The final result was drawn from different scanned and slightly retouched drafts.

The poster's typography follows the same logic, as each word appears woven into the interlaced paper. The final design preserves the border made by the two papers, celebrating the labor-intensive weaving that is part of Soyinka's cultural heritage.

Poster
Wole Soyinka,
La maison et le monde
Fête du livre, Aix-en-Provence
175 × 118.5 cm (68⅞ × 46⅝ in.)
Screen print
Printer: Sérica
Typeface: Taz
2007
See pages 304 – 07

Yoruba textile, Nigeria, *c.* 1900
Musée du quai Branly, Paris

184|185

FÊTE DU
LIVRE
L'ASIE DES
ÉCRITURES
CROISÉES
UN VRAI
ROMAN
15-18 OCT.
2009 CITÉ
DU LIVRE
AIX-EN-PROVENCE

L'Asie des écritures croisées
Un vrai roman

While Japanese literature has been translated for Western readers for years, much other Asian literature has not. Although there has recently been a marked increase in access to contemporary Chinese literature in translation, very few novels from Korea, Vietnam, or Thailand – areas of substantial literary output – have been translated into French. The 2009 Fête du livre explored the rapidly shifting political, economic, and social landscapes of these and other countries through their literature. The festival title, "L'Asie des écritures croisées. Un vrai roman" (An Asia of Intersecting Writing: A Real Novel), captured the feeling that literature acts as a crossroads, an idea that pervades the featured works. Many of the writers explore themes of migration, racism, rootlessness, displacement, the search for identity, and cultural diversity.

The 2009 poster represents urban population density, a fact of life in cities such as Taipei, Seoul, Bangkok, and Hong Kong. Among the world's most heavily populated areas, these cities teem with people and can be difficult to navigate. Inspired by several photographs that captured the claustophobic atmosphere, a typographic composition was designed to represent the façades of skyscrapers. A loose grid of black and white pixel-shaped boxes creates the backdrop for the text, which is placed inside larger colored rectangles. The pixels peek through these larger "windows," inside which the letters stand and lean, evoking a feeling of voyeurism in the viewer.

Resembling a page of Chinese ideograms, the composition references both traditional and contemporary subjects. A cloud of pollution spreads throughout the design, creating a visceral spatial experience. Rich pinks, spanning dark to bright hues, represent textile dyes, cherry blossoms, peonies, and Asian spices. The colors also call to mind the cheap plastic toys and household goods mass-produced in Asia and then shipped around the world. With such diverse associations, the palette captures the myriad influences on these writers' works, from the natural to the traditional to the contemporary.

Poster
L'Asie des écritures croisées,
Un vrai roman
Fête du livre, Aix-en-Provence
175 × 118.5 cm (68⅞ × 46⅝ in.)
Screen print
Printer: Sérica
Typeface: Taz
2009
See pages 298–99

Paolo Pellegrin (born in 1964)
Hong Kong, 2010
Photograph

Bruits du monde

The theme of the 2012 Fête du livre was "Bruits du monde" (Noises of the World). Featured writers included Peter Esterházy of Hungary, Juan Goytisolo of Spain, David Grossman of Israel, Yan Lianke of China, and Antoine Volodine of France. Aware of harsh political realities and of the violence and absurdity of much conflict, each writer maintains an independent stance, speaking out against repressive regimes and preserving space for intimacy. Their works challenge the prevailing order and share visions of alternative realities.

The festival's poster captures the diversity of human perspectives and experiences. The background is a blue expanse across which an archipelago of black lowercase characters spells out "Bruits du monde." The letters are misaligned and smeared, with some rotated ninety degrees. Heavily inked fingerprints have been impressed upon them; whether they represent an act of maiming or of staunching a wound it is difficult to tell. The ink stains open up paths across the page, some of which cross over – undefined paths, like the shadows of tremulous, awkward gestures. As they draw away from the precision of the letters, they call to mind movement and spontaneity. The spare aesthetic, quality of space, and attenuated marks recall Asian calligraphy and painting, and speak eloquently of vulnerability and exposure. Apeloig has created an abstract composition infused with feeling that evokes boundaries subject to invasion and all kinds of bombardment – ideological, political, journalistic, militaristic, and interpersonal.

Poster
Bruits du monde
Fête du livre, Aix-en-Provence
175 × 118.5 cm (68⅞ × 46⅝ in.)
Screen print
Printer: Lézard Graphique
Typeface: Taz
2012

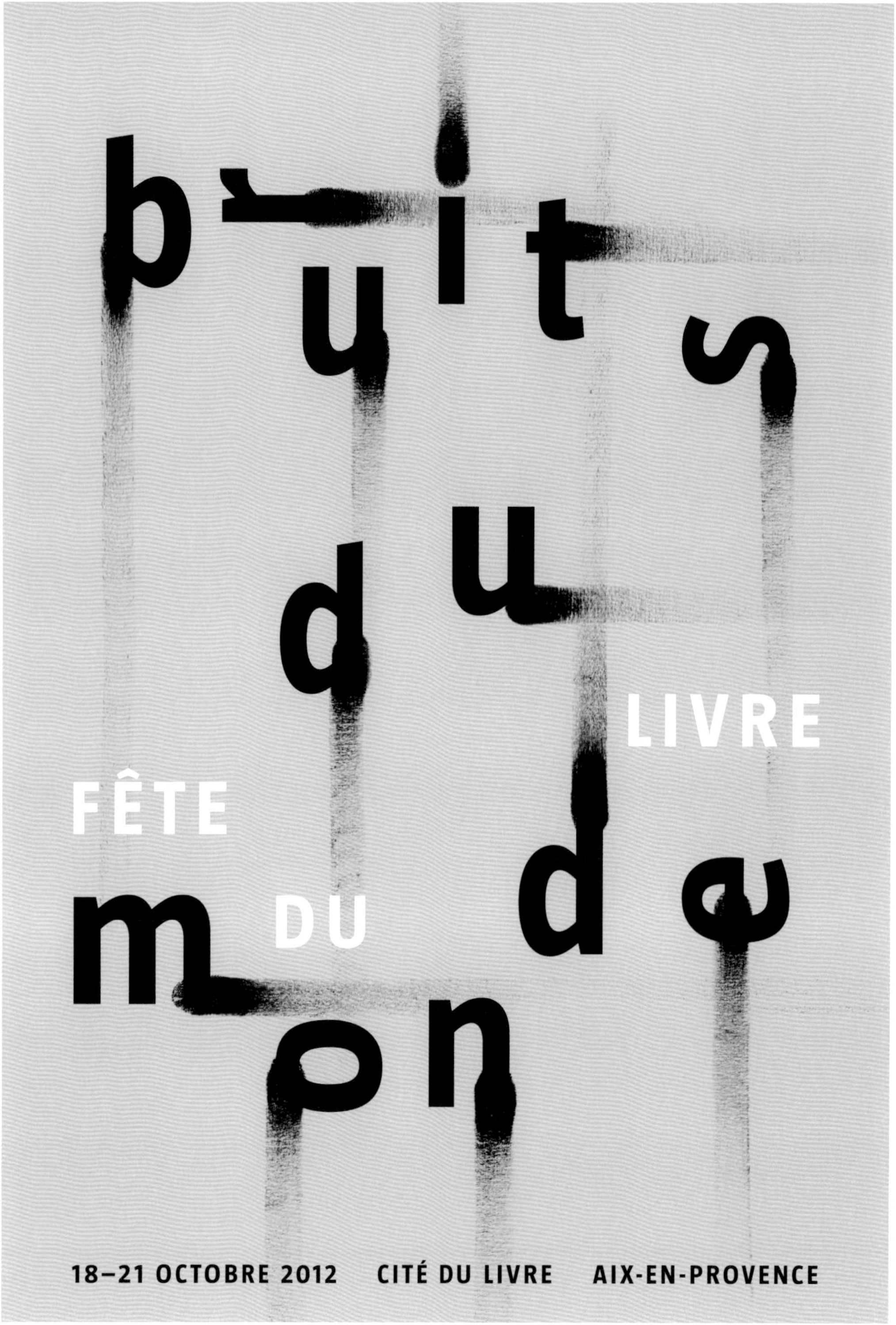

bruits
du
monde

FÊTE DU LIVRE

18–21 OCTOBRE 2012   CITÉ DU LIVRE   AIX-EN-PROVENCE

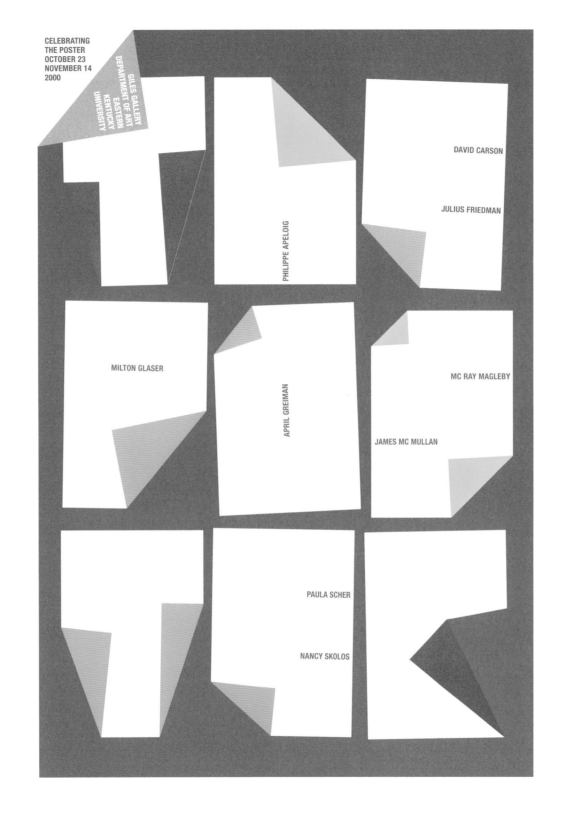

CELEBRATING
THE POSTER
OCTOBER 23
NOVEMBER 14
2000

GILES GALLERY
DEPARTMENT OF ART
EASTERN
KENTUCKY
UNIVERSITY

DAVID CARSON

JULIUS FRIEDMAN

PHILIPPE APELOIG

MILTON GLASER

APRIL GREIMAN

MC RAY MAGLEBY

JAMES MC MULLAN

PAULA SCHER

NANCY SKOLOS

The Poster

"The Poster: Celebrating the Poster" was a group exhibition of internationally renowned designers held at Eastern Kentucky University's Fred Parker Giles Gallery in 2000. The exhibition poster illustrates how abstract typography and a reductive formal language can create narrative simply and powerfully. It portrays a grid of nine rectangular forms in a gray environment. The front of each is white. The corners are folded, revealing the backs – colored fuchsia, yellow, green, blue – and defining letters through these angled edges and the suggestion of curves. While not instantly legible, the blocky letters and words gradually come into view to spell out "The Poster."

Only seemingly simplistic, the design's *trompe l'oeil* effect is richly layered in literal and metaphorical associations. The forms can represent either folded sheets of paper, tabulae rasae, open windows, or metaphysical portals. The lettering is built on a strict mathematical grid without sitting straight within its visual field. Each letter tilts and shakes, creating a sort of delirium that awakens the reader's eye. The dynamic movement and vivid palette affirm the vitality of life and of the poster itself, an ephemeral object destined to be discarded or replaced.

The names of the participating designers are placed in small type inside each letter, allowing the poster to be read on multiple levels at once. The colored fragments and tiny type elements are both connected to and in tension with each other. Echoing the letters' folds, the upper left-hand corner of the poster appears to be folded over revealing the exhibition's title, dates, and location.

Poster
The Poster: Celebrating the Poster
Eastern Kentucky University, Richmond
175 × 118.5 cm (68⅞ × 46⅝ in.)
Screen print
Printer: Arts Graphiques de France
Typeface: Franklin Gothic
2000

Bateaux sur l'eau, rivières et canaux

The Armada de Rouen is a popular event held in Rouen, one of Normandy's main cities on the river Seine. During this annual celebration, the world's finest sailboats converge upon the city's harbor and anchor. For the 2003 Armada, the public institution Voies navigables de France (Navigable Waterways of France) curated an exhibition of vintage sailboats, barges, and small-scale models of watercraft. The title of the exhibition, "Bateaux sur l'eau, rivières et canaux" (Boats on the Water, Rivers, and Canals), was inspired by a verse from an old children's counting rhyme.

The poster design relies on creative typography to convey the thematic content while playing with the spatial relationship between words and empty space. The monochrome blue background implies water and the type's elongated segments float through the poster, conjuring images of barges and their reflections in the water. The partially submerged words disappear like the hulls of boats beneath the surface, creating depth and volume. This treatment embodies the content and focus of the event. The font is Foundry Sans, designed by David Quay and Freda Sack in 1991.

The poster also draws inspiration from Japanese prints. Despite its flatness, it achieves the illusion of a distant horizon through its precise composition. It also references Monet's *Water Lilies,* with floating words as substitutes for water lilies. By creating an impression of slow motion, the design depicts an abstract landscape that is peaceful and still.

Poster
Bateaux sur l'eau, rivières et canaux
Armada de Rouen
Voies navigables de France
175 × 118.5 cm (68⅞ × 46⅝ in.)
Screen print
Printer: Dubois Imagerie
Typeface: The Foundry Sans
2003
See pages 326–27

Claude Monet (1840–1926)
Water Lilies, 1904
Oil on canvas
Musée d'Art Moderne André-Malraux,
Le Havre

bateaux

Armada Rouen 2003 Voies navigables de France

Exposition 28 juin – 5 juillet 2003

sur l'eau

rivières et

canaux

Le Havre
Patrimoine mondial
de l'humanité

Severely bombed during World War II, parts of the city of Le Havre, Normandy, were reduced to rubble. Between 1945 and 1964, the architect Auguste Perret led a team to rebuild the city. The effort resulted in pioneering new developments in architecture, technology, and urban planning, with Perret's contribution now viewed as one of the most complete realizations of Modernism in the twentieth century. In 2005, UNESCO designated Le Havre "patrimoine mondial de l'humanité" (World Heritage Site), acknowledging it to be of "outstanding importance to the common heritage of humanity."

The poster is, first and foremost, an homage to Perret. With a composition created from the superimposed façades of three of Le Havre's buildings and rendered in the three primary colors – yellow, blue, and red – the poster explores the relationship between the modular grid system (one of Perret's greatest innovations), architectural height and width, and the rhythms of patterns. Crosshatched balconies enliven the façades, representing the minimal ornamentation allowed by the architect's Modernist code. Layered over the window grid, the lettering of the subtitle is regulated and harmonized by the modular system, but because it occurs at the overlap between the three grids, it appears to be slightly jarred. At the top of the poster, the words "Le Havre" superimpose all three hues. The primary palette is a hallmark of both the Modernist and Constructivist vocabularies. The poster was designed for a competition won by another designer, but Apeloig so valued the result that he printed it in a limited edition for his portfolio.

Poster
Le Havre, Patrimoine mondial de l'humanité
175 × 118.5 cm (68⅞ × 46⅝ in.)
Screen print
Printer: Sérica
Typeface: Helvetica Neue
2006
See pages 308–309

Francis Fernez (born in 1928)
Block V6 with Block V4
in the background,
Le Havre, November 1950
Photograph
Archives Municipales, Le Havre

Lucien Hervé (1910–2007)
Seafront, Le Havre, 1956
Photograph

Type Directors Club
New York

The "Call for Entries" poster for the 2008 Type Directors Club of New York is composed of four vertical columns. The letters of "typography," the acronym *TDC*, and the number *54* (it was the fifty-fourth annual competition) are all divided and aligned within the grid. The font Akkurat was chosen for its extreme perfection and simple design, imbuing the poster with a refined sense of order.

The simple geometry and straightforward typography impose a poetic dimension on the functional and aesthetic requirements of the contest. The design is a sculptural solution governed by emotional relation- ships that are expressed through light and shadow, solids and voids, transparency and pure typography. Their interplay establishes a sober Modernist voca- bulary. By masking part of each letter and rendering it as a shadowed form, Apeloig manifests light as a graphic material, a metaphor for the emergence of young talent onto the honorific stage – recognized and illuminated.

The two-tone concept was used for other printed materials, such as the award card and cover for the annual catalog, *Typography 29*.

Invitation card
TDC 54 Call for Entries
Type Directors Club, New York
17.8 × 12.7 cm (7 × 5 in.)
Typeface: Akkurat
2007

Annual
Typography 29
Type Directors Club, New York
28 × 21 cm (11 × 8¼ in.), 376 pages
Typeface: Akkurat
2008

Poster
TDC 54, Call for Entries
Type Directors Club, New York
175 × 118.5 cm (68⅞ × 46⅝ in.)
Screen print
Printer: Sérica
Typeface: Akkurat
2007

TDC ANNUAL

TDC 54 · TDC! 2008

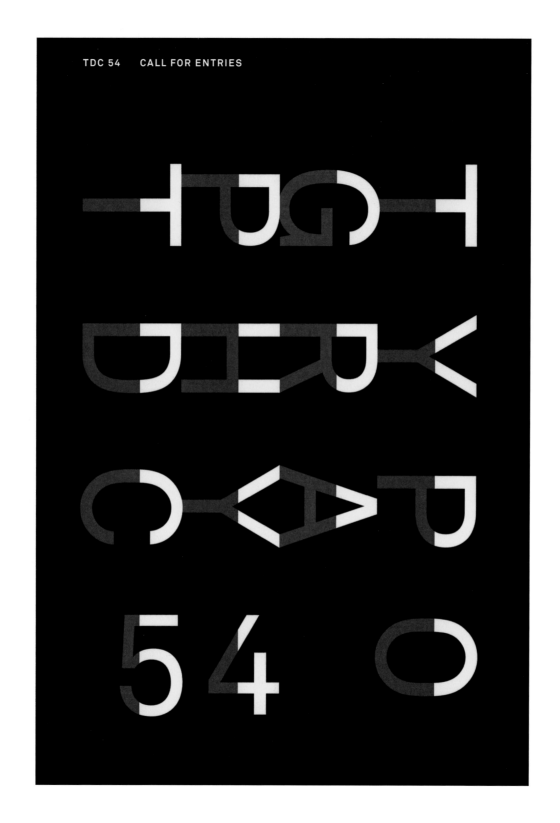

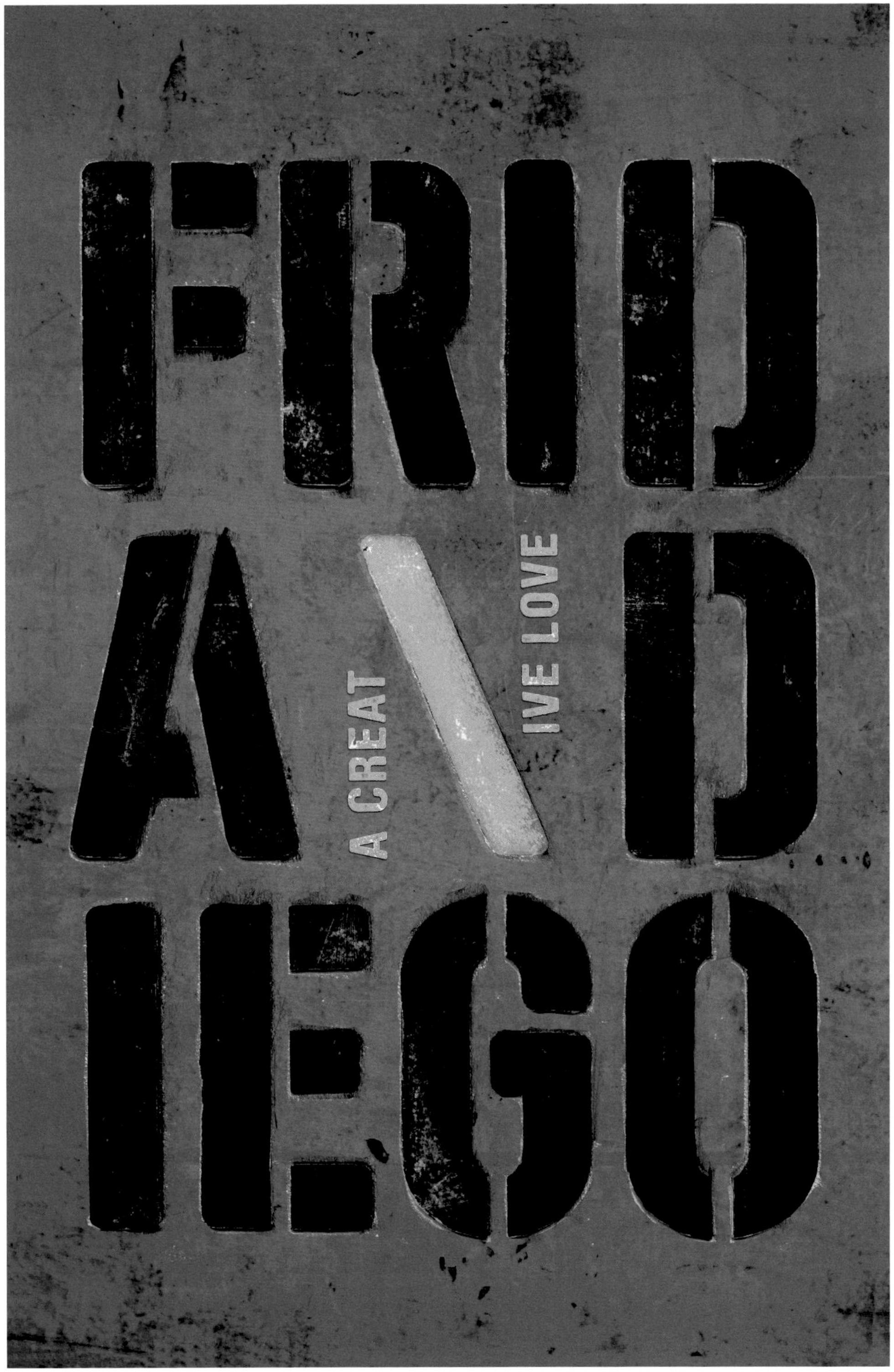

FRID
A\D
IEGO

A CREAT
IVE LOVE

Frida and Diego
A Creative Love

2007 marked the one hundredth anniversary of Frida Kahlo's birth and the fiftieth anniversary of Diego Rivera's death. These two great artists showed the world new ways of seeing and being – moving beyond the banalities of daily life to experience and depict both the passion and agony of the human condition. To celebrate their lives, at the initiative of the Mexican graphic designer Gabriela Rodríguez Valencia, one hundred posters designed by members of the AGI, Alliance Graphique Internationale, were exhibited in Mexico City in 2008.

Although several photographs were available, Apeloig took a text-based approach for his poster. The capital *A* at the end of "FRIDA" begins the word "AND," which is completed by the capital *D* of "DIEGO." Split in two on either side of the backward slash, the subtitle, "Creative Love," appears printed vertically in small type to form the two upward strokes of the *N* in "AND"; the backward slash positioned between them completes the letter.

The colors for the poster are inspired by Kahlo's emblematic blue house. Its lush blue is accented with the plush pink of its window frames, as seen in a 1954 Werner Bischof photograph. The lettering has been treated to look like a bold stencil with irregularities. Its rough look and the weathering effect applied to the background make the poster read like a section of decaying wall. The passion and tension inherent in Kahlo and Rivera's relationship are implied by the deep cuts used to construct the letters. The central pink slash alludes to their narcissism, serving as both mirror and divider.

Poster
Frida and Diego, A Creative Love
AGI, Alliance Graphique Internationale
175 × 118.5 cm (68⅞ × 46⅝ in.)
Screen print
Printer: Sérica
Typeface: based on Brauer Neue
2008
See pages 300 – 01

Werner Bischof (1916 – 1954)
Casa Azul, Frida Kahlo's family home,
Mexico City, 1954
Photograph

Alfred Nobel
Au service de l'innovation

In 2008 and 2009, entrepreneur Alfred Nobel was the subject of the touring exhibition "Alfred Nobel, au service de l'innovation" (originally titled "Alfred Nobel: Networks of Innovation" in English), which made a stop at the Palais de la découverte, a science museum in Paris. The exhibition was organized by the Nobel Museum in Stockholm and explored the man behind the world-famous prize. Nobel was a person of varied interests, reflected in the disciplines honored by his award: physics, chemistry, economics, literature, medicine, and peace. He can be seen as a central figure in the advancement of technology.

Apeloig's poster design is inspired by the computer chip and the diagrams used by engineers to correct or verify a circuit design. The letters are made up of large out-of-focus dots mixed with smaller dots in a grid. The lines of text are laid out in a series of stacks, with arrows providing directional flow. Within each word or character, the dots' density ranges from heavy, tightly packed dots to smaller, more widely spaced ones, which creates an undulating movement. The background photograph consists of overlapping, semitransparent orbs – enlargements of the dots that call to mind flashbulb explosions of inspiration. The design also recalls the aesthetic of the electronic news ticker, a constant flow of information and ideas.

Poster
Alfred Nobel
Au service de l'innovation
Palais de la découverte, Paris
This poster is a later version than the one produced for the client.
175 × 118.5 cm (68⅞ × 46⅝ in.)
Screen print
Printer: Sérica
Typeface: original creation
2008
See pages 302–03

Radical Jewish Culture
Scène musicale New York

In 2010, the Musée d'art et d'histoire du Judaïsme (Jewish Art and History Museum) presented "Radical Jewish Culture, Scène musicale New York," an exhibition about the work of the experimental New York music label of the same name, which represents a group of composers and musicians who invented a hybrid music bridging the traditional and the avant-garde. The ensemble's influences range from Jewish *klezmer* to Lou Reed's rock to Steve Reich's minimalism.

The idea for the poster design was to create a facsimile of a graffitied wall. People have spontaneously inked and scratched surfaces in public spaces since ancient times. While some of lower Manhattan's original signage has been preserved, on many buildings the faded silhouettes of old lettering have been covered by new graphics. These walls, doorways, and façades have become living testaments to the passage of time.

The poster uses a detail of a sketch by composer John Zorn that combines graffiti with the compositional process. The backdrop connotes the seedy but vibrant environs of the Lower East Side, conveying the energy of a city in flux and representing the neighborhood's physical and spiritual connections to the label's music. A very rounded open-stencil font was designed to reference experimental music. Reminiscent of neon signage, it assumes physical weight and dimension. The letters reside within a defined system but appear free and loose. Together, they create a strong rhythmic pattern. The names of the artists are positioned vertically throughout the title grid and set in small neon yellow capitals. A gritty aerosol effect is applied to the logo as if, like graffiti, it were also written into the city's fabric.

Poster
**Radical Jewish Culture
Scène musicale New York
Musée d'art et d'histoire
du Judaïsme, Paris**
175 × 118.5 cm (68⅞ × 46⅝ in.)
Screen print
Printer: Sérica
Typefaces: original creation, Vectora
2010
See pages 296 – 297

**Alex Jay (born in 1953)
Garden Cafeteria, Lower East Side,
Manhattan, New York, 2008**
Photograph

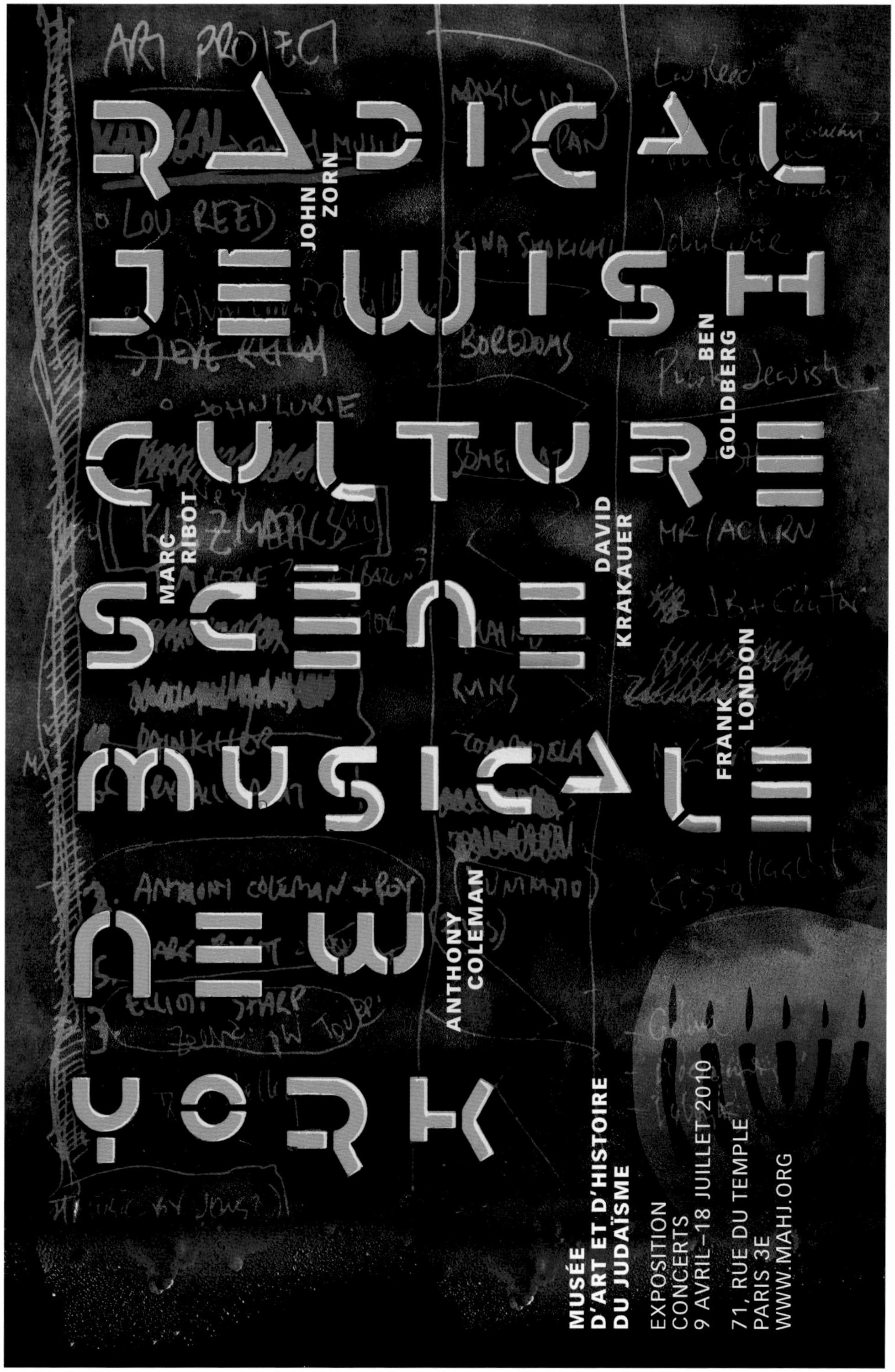

RADICAL JEWISH CULTURE SCENE MUSICALE NEW YORK

JOHN ZORN
BEN GOLDBERG
MARC RIBOT
DAVID KRAKAUER
FRANK LONDON
ANTHONY COLEMAN

MUSÉE D'ART ET D'HISTOIRE DU JUDAÏSME

EXPOSITION
CONCERTS
9 AVRIL–18 JUILLET 2010

71, RUE DU TEMPLE
PARIS 3E
WWW.MAHJ.ORG

Afrique contemporaine

Founded in 1962, *Afrique contemporaine* is a quarterly academic journal that focuses on the geopolitical challenges facing the African continent. The review is published by the Agence française de développement (AFD; French Agency for Development), a financial institution that implements French assistance to developing countries. In 2010, AFD commissioned Apeloig to design a new logo and promotional materials. For this opportunity he invented the typeface Ndebele, which draws on the South African Ndebele people's vibrant style of house painting. Apeloig's all uppercase font has rounded angles and a geometric motif; it consists of stylized forms that are representational but verge on abstraction. The open parts in the letter forms recall textiles and carvings, as well as pottery, vessels, figurines, and toys.

The Ndebele font evolved as a quasi-legible type. The fine vertical break in the middle of each letter is progressively enlarged in three stages to create more negative space. The gradual disappearance of a cohesive letter shape creates a complexity that flirts with the decorative arts. The result is a free-for-all optical phenomenon: while the central logo breaks apart at the center of the design, the deconstructed parts scramble to reassemble.

Journal
Afrique contemporaine
Agence française
de développement, Paris
24 × 16 cm (9½ × 6¼ in.)
Typefaces: Ndebele,
Akzidenz Grotesk, Miller Text
2010

Poster
Afrique contemporaine
Agence française
de développement, Paris
175 × 118.5 cm (68⅞ × 46⅝ in.)
Screen print
Printer: Sérica
Typefaces: Ndebele,
Akzidenz Grotesk Next
2010

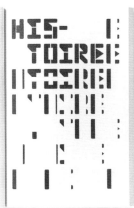

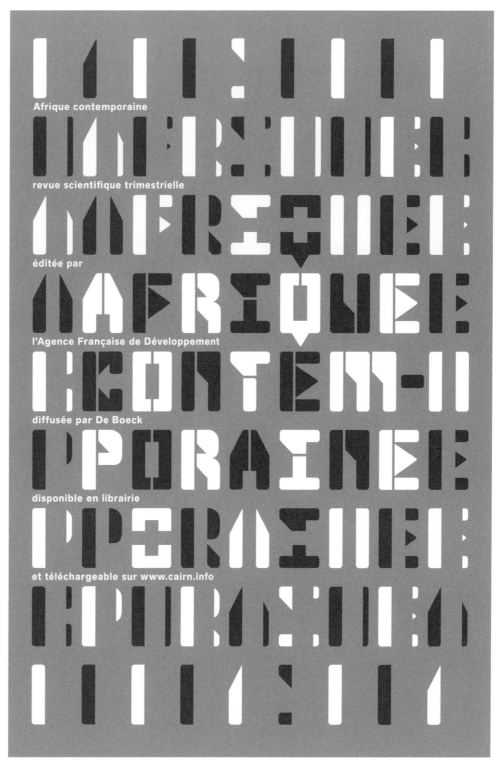

Afrique contemporaine

revue scientifique trimestrielle

éditée par

l'Agence Française de Développement

diffusée par De Boeck

disponible en librairie

et téléchargeable sur www.cairn.info

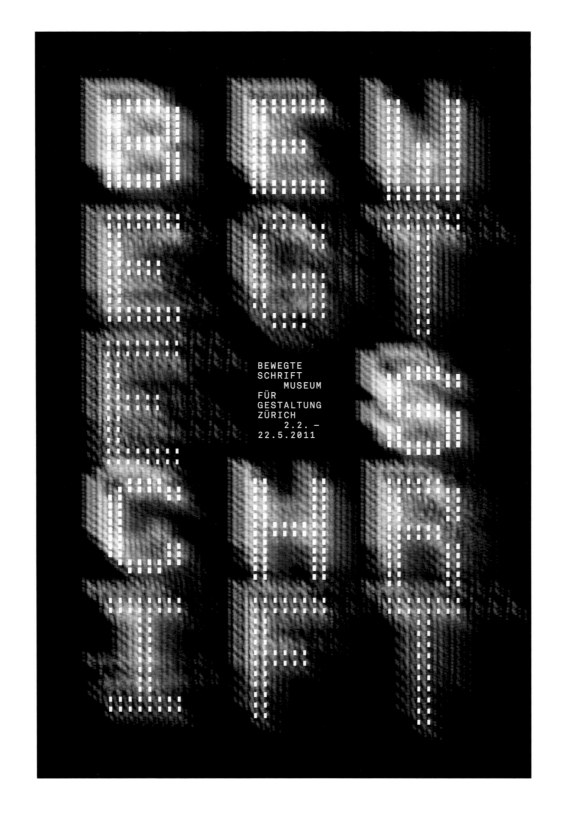

BEWEGTE
SCHRIFT
MUSEUM
FÜR
GESTALTUNG
ZÜRICH
2.2. –
22.5.2011

Bewegte Schrift

Technology has created a world in which we are constantly confronted with moving words and text. "Bewegte Schrift" (Moving Type), a 2011 exhibition at the Museum für Gestaltung (Museum of Design) in Zurich, explored how designers employ an array of tools to transform words into dynamic images, often syncing the rhythm of language to music and sound.

The optically vibrating poster involves the dissolution of the two title words, which, by chance, have an equal number of letters, allowing them to be placed in a grid. The letters consist of smaller grids of pointillist pixels that float like dust in the air, with multiple soft-focus layers that recede into the background and create depth. A blurred halo effect creates more movement. The design combines this three-dimensional illusion with horizontal directionality and, despite the fragmentation of the two words, remains legible. Each word's graphic weight dissipates as one reads left to right; starting out bold, they diminish to a whisper. The visual crowding and evanescent quality of the letters inspire a hallucinatory feeling.

A large-scale animated display based on the poster design appeared in Zurich's main train station during the run of the exhibition. This enormous pop-up advertisement in one of the city's busiest public spaces drew many visitors to the show.

Poster
Bewegte Schrift
Museum für Gestaltung, Zurich
128 × 90.5 cm (50⅜ × 35⅝ in.)
Screen print
Printer: Uldry
Typefaces: original creation, Akkurat Mono
2011
See pages 292–93

Video screen
Bewegte Schrift
Main train station, Zurich
2011

Wim Crouwel
A Graphic Odyssey

The exhibition "Wim Crouwel: A Graphic Odyssey" was presented at the Design Museum in London in 2011. In celebration of this event, Tony Brook, head of the British design studio Spin, and Unit Editions, his publishing venture with Adrian Shaughnessy, commissioned five designers and design studios on which Wim Crouwel has been an important influence to create a limited-edition series of posters. Each poster was to use the unique grid structure Crouwel had developed as a template for his significant "Vormgevers" poster, designed in 1968 for the Stedelijk Museum in Amsterdam.

For his poster, Apeloig used the gutter of the Crouwel grid to design extended letters with progressive height, creating a continuous undulation of form from one line to the next. There are irregularities within the rigorous design: missing letter parts and small white dots. The poster's edges are serrated so as to resemble a postage stamp. These visual blips focus the eye, complicate the spatial experience, and represent the designer's assertion of subjectivity within the authority of the grid.

Poster
Wim Crouwel: A Graphic Odyssey
Design Museum, London
95 × 64 cm (37³⁄₈ × 25¼ in.)
Screen print
Printer: Bob Eight Pop
Typeface: original creation
2011

Wim Crouwel (born in 1928)
Vormgevers, 1968
Poster
95 × 64 cm (37³⁄₈ × 25¼ in.)
Stedelijk Museum, Amsterdam

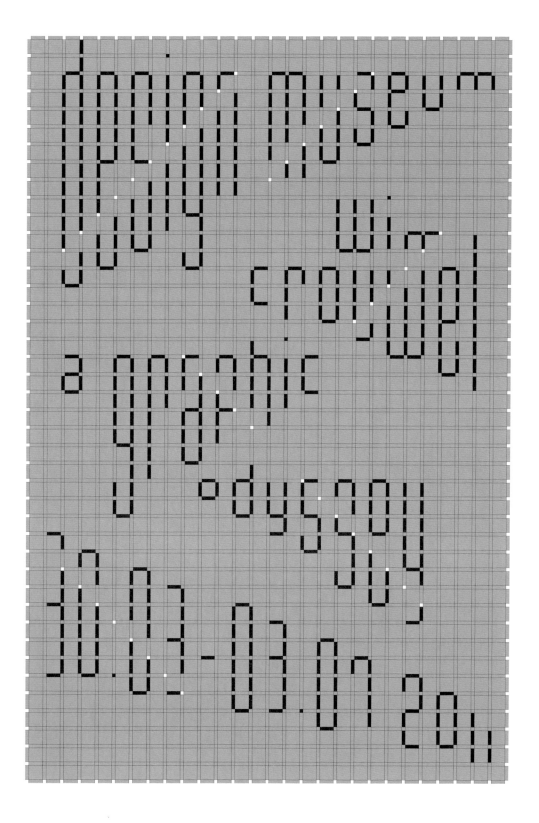

design museum
design
body   wim
crouwel
a graphic
odyssey
30.03–03.07 2011

Saut Hermès

Inaugurated in April 2010 by the luxury label Hermès (originally a saddler), the Saut Hermès (Hermès Jump), held at the Grand Palais in Paris, is an elite competition of world-class show jumping. Hermès commissioned Apeloig to design the poster for the 2013 event. Expressive typography dominates with each letter seemingly caught mid-jump. The characters exercise within a spatial void filled only with the signature color of Hermès: a pure orange. Form and meaning merge as the title text, set in white type and broken up into six lines, careens across the surface, neither centered nor aligned left or right. The letterforms vary in weight from bold to extra light, a subtle modulation that intensifies the energy of the composition. The capital *A*s are the most strenuous – real hurdlers – with legs set at oblique angles. The lines of text are interwoven with a spare drawing depicting a rider on a jumping horse. The duo is modeled out of short black lines and enters the picture plane from the left, moving forcefully to the right. The angling of the clean, tapered black strokes creates a sense of forward momentum and speed. The drawing is interwoven with the letters so that the two elements overlap and penetrate one another — an edgy equilibrium remains between them. The design overall is spontaneous and free, as befits this sporting event.

Invitation
Saut Hermès
au Grand Palais, Paris
23 × 17 cm (9 × 6¾ in.)
Open: 23 × 51 cm (9 × 20⅛ in.)
Typefaces: original creation, Avenir
2013

Poster
Saut Hermès
au Grand Palais, Paris
175 × 118.5 cm (68⅞ × 46⅝ in.)
Screen print
Printer: Lézard Graphique
Typefaces: original creation, Avenir
2013
See pages 284 – 85

SAUT
HERMÈS
AU
GRAND
PALAIS
PARIS

12/13/14 AVRIL 2013
JUMPING INTERNATIONAL CSI 5*

Logotypes and Visual Identities

Atelier Électronique

In the summer of 1983, Apeloig designed his first logo. It was for his parents' electronics repair company, Atelier Électronique. Influenced by his Total Design internship, Apeloig brought new geometric elements to the company's initials *AÉ*. The accent over the letter *É* takes the form of a parallelogram and its angles are repeated in the edges of the horizontal bars of the *A* and the *É*, setting up a rhythm. The same oblique angle is found in the slope of the letter *A*. The construction grid remains visible so that one can understand the logo's structure, and the dots at its intersections enable one to glimpse the path of the printed line.

École nationale supérieure des arts décoratifs

The École nationale supérieure des arts décoratifs is a public university of art and design under the supervision of the French Ministry of Culture. Its mission is to cultivate the development of creative artists through a scholarly curriculum combined with rigorous apprenticeships in the arts. In 1992, Apeloig was hired by Richard Peduzzi to teach graphic design and typography there and, a few years later, he designed the school's new logo. For this assignment, he was inspired by the black square, a universal symbol and shape associated with both art and process, and in particular Kazimir Malevich's 1915 painting *Black Square,* which reduced abstract painting to a previously unheard-of simplicity. The square represents a two-dimensional space and, by extension, the pixel, the smallest building block of digital images.

The school's name, positioned to the right of the square, forms the outline of a second undefined square, with delicate lines between each word. The placement of the article "des" inside the solid colored square, next to the transparent square, creates a mirrored world of light and shadow, yin and yang. The duality set up in Apeloig's logo highlights the equal emphasis given to theory and practice at Ensad, as well as its renowned open-mindedness. The design also highlights the acronym Ensad in red letters on the vertical axis. The brochures were designed in the same spirit, sometimes with variations on the visual identity and in a wider range of colors.

Logotype
Atelier Électronique, Choisy-le-Roi
1983
See page 373

Logotype
École nationale supérieure des arts décoratifs, Paris
1994

Ministère
de la Culture

Ensad
31 rue d'Ulm
75005 Paris

téléphone :
(1) 42 34 97 00
(1) 06 88 26 00

télécopie :
(1) 42 34 97 05

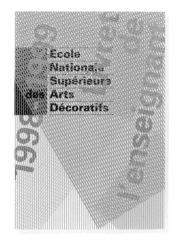

Letterhead
**École nationale supérieure
des arts décoratifs, Paris**
Typeface: Univers
1994

Brochures
**Entrée en première année
Rapport du concours
(Report on the first-year admissions exam)
1995 exam period
Entrée en première année
Rapport du concours
(Report on the first-year admissions exam)
1998 exam period
Admissions Information Year 1999 – 2000**
29.7 × 21 cm (11⅝ × 8¼ in.)
Typeface: Univers
1995 – 2000

Brochures
**Livret de l'élève 1998 – 1999
(Pupil's Handbook 1998 – 1999)
Livret de l'enseignant 1998 – 1999
(Teacher's Handbook 1998 – 1999)**
21 × 15 cm (8¼ × 5⅞ in.)
Typeface: Univers
1998

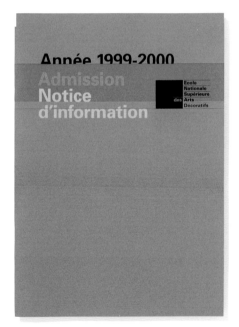

Visual Identity
Philippe Apeloig

Throughout his career, Apeloig has designed many different ranges of stationery. While some use a very pure approach with simple type, others are more experimental and employ unusual printing processes and papers. One range uses transparent paper to challenge both the visual and tactile senses. The address is printed on a white bar silkscreened onto the back of the letterhead. The design depends on light and invites touch, wavering between emptiness and opacity.

On first moving to New York, Apeloig created architecture-inspired stationery that functioned similar to a three-dimensional design. The paper is perforated with bold lines crossed by finer ones, as if cut by a blade, and type elements are set in a chaotic and seemingly unfinished state, creating a unique typographic shape that moves across the surface. The envelope is in a gray tone with white lines, the inverse of the white letterhead.

Philippe Apeloig
12 cité Griset
F-75011 Paris
tél. 01 43 55 34 29
fax 01 43 55 44 80
e-mail :
apeloig@
club-internet.fr

siret:
401 315 049 00015
code APE : 923 A

Stationery
Philippe Apeloig, Paris
Screen print
Typeface: Univers
1995

Stationery
Philippe Apeloig, New York
Typeface: Univers
1999

philippe apeloig
graphic designer
apartment 45 b
7-13 washington square north
new york ny 10003
e-mail: apeloigph@aol.com
tel-fax: (212) 982 3007

Greeting Cards

New Year's greeting cards have offered Apeloig the opportunity to create a series of free-style designs interwoven with typography that defy most expectations of holiday cards. Many use nearly illegible type.

For 1997, the four numerals of the New Year were created using bits of charcoal placed into a stencil and printed on translucent paper. Scanned at variable contrasts, they repeat down the length of the folded card, mutating as they progress. The numbers' shifting colors, density, and shape give the piece a filmstrip-like quality. The strength and roughness of the typography contrasts with the fragility of the paper.

The New Year's cards for 1998, 2001, and 2002 were created as three-fold posters, printed on lightweight paper.

The 1998 Constructivist design creates a sense of discovery through the random organization of the individual pages. The number is illustrated by geometric shapes that create a second visual layer, as the digits work with and against the grid created by the folds of the card. An illusion of transparency is produced by the play of the two printed colors, with silver overlapping black.

The 2001 card depicts a computer-generated, three-dimensional downpour using a cascade of *1*s. The volume of foreshortened and angled numerals is densest at the mid- to lower-right corner of the page, as if one were caught in a sudden shower and looking up. The mass thins out at the upper right corner, creating a sense of atmosphere and space.

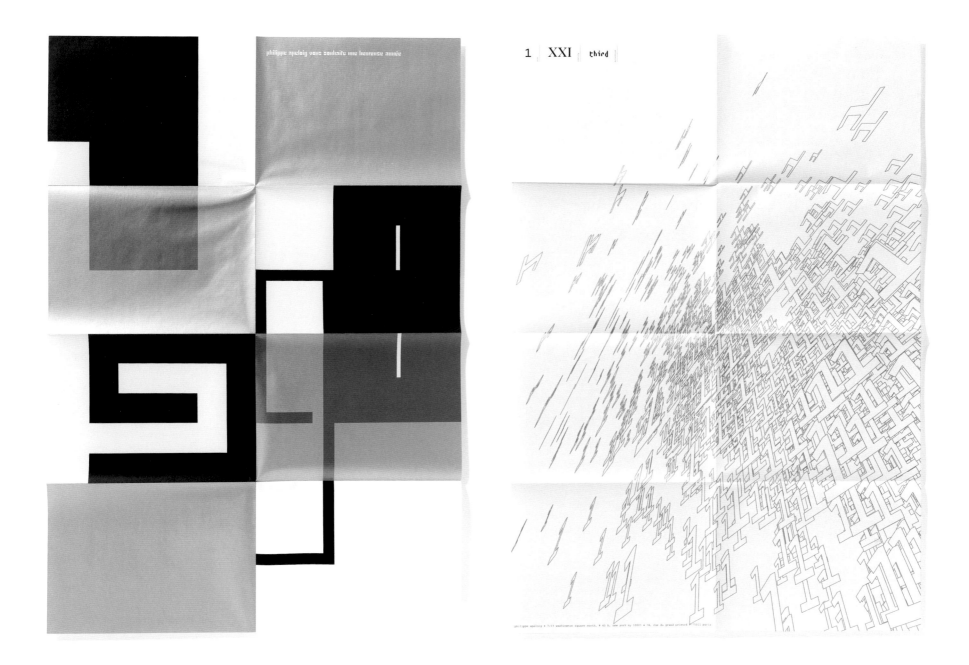

philippe apeloig vous souhaite une heureuse année

enivrez-vous...   c'est two.

philippe apeloig
18, rue du grand prieuré
f-75011 paris

7-13 washington square north
45b
new york ny 10003

The 2002 New Year's greeting card uses the symmetry of the number as the starting point for the design. On one side of the card, large heavy black type on a white background comes across boldly but the other side acts as a mirror in the reverse color scheme. The individual numbers are cut in half, expressing the sublime balance inherent in a numeric configuration that will not appear again until the next millennium.

The 2003 card is a paper sculpture that features a narrow ribbon folded to form a geometric 3, with "Happy New Year" printed in French on one side and in English on the other. The recipient unfolds and refolds the ribbon to read the message.

Folded poster
New Year's greeting card 2002
42 × 60 cm (16½ × 23⅝ in.)
Typefaces: Champion Gothic,
Letter Gothic
2001

Folded card
New Year's greeting card 2003
9.2 × 21 cm (3⅝ × 8¼ in.)
Open: 35 × 5 cm (13¾ × 2 in.)
Typeface: News Gothic
2002

The greeting card for the year 2004 represents Apeloig's first experimentation with a motion-graphic missive delivered via email. Inspired by dance, the animated piece choreographs the movement of four simple outlined squares. The abstract characters roll in from the left edge of the screen like ungainly wheels, with the last arriving, by surprise, from the right. Once aligned, they begin to open at their intersections. Slowly they become longer and taller, doubling, unfolding, and rotating to eventually form the desired number, 2004.

The 2007 card, also an animation, presents a mechanical ballet. First, one sees twenty-four small black squares. To a scratchy techno soundtrack, they turn into horizontal then vertical lines that swing, fold, and turn on their axes. As they fold over, they reveal color on their reverse sides. The lines explore their surroundings from their stationary bases – some remaining lines, some randomly turning into the number 7 – until they suddenly snap into formation, at which point they start moving in unison to create a colorful downward salute, then an upward swing into a grid of colorful 7s. As a finale, the lines straighten up and shrink back down into their starting configuration.

Animation
New Year's e-card 2004
Length: 16"
2003

Animation
New Year's e-card 2007
Length: 26"
2006

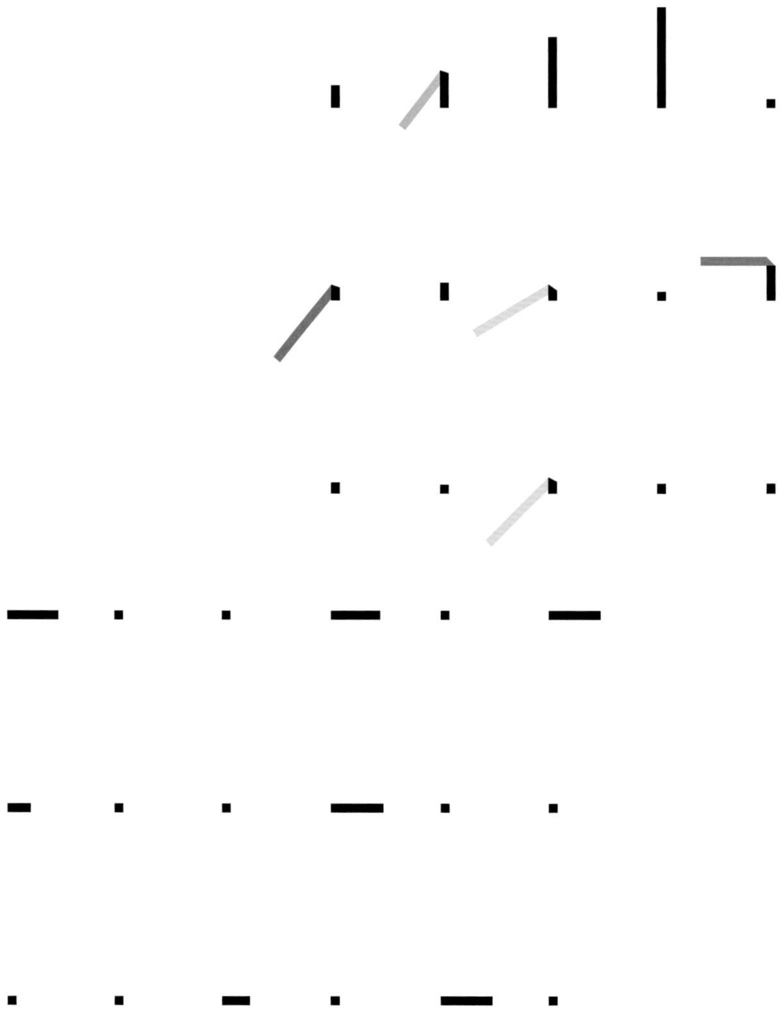

Carré d'Art

Designed by architect Norman Foster, the city of Nîmes's Carré d'Art opened in 1993. The building is a temple of glass and steel and houses a contemporary art museum, research center and library, temporary exhibition space, auditorium, and offices. It stands across the street from the Maison Carrée, a first-century BC Roman temple, to which it responds architecturally. The Carré d'Art's simple geometric forms and colonnade of slender pillars speak of its modernity.

The logo design and visual identity follow the building's architecture, forging a link between old and new references. The basis for the logo is a square, a shape that graphically represents the museum's form and plays an important role in the works of some of the artists on show, such as Jean-Pierre Raynaud and Wolfgang Laib. The vivid red of the square evokes the culture of Nîmes – from its blazing southern heat and tiled rooftops to the red capes used in bullfights popular throughout the region.

The graphic identity of the printed materials uses the font family Rotis, which Otl Aicher designed in 1988 working closely with Foster. In the logo, the first word, "Carré," is white and placed inside the square, while "d'Art," in black, is outside. This sets up contrasts that balance one another – positive/negative, wide/narrow, delicate/heavy – allowing for perfect legibility and personifying the encounter between cultural space and the public.

Stationary
Carré d'Art, Nîmes
Typeface: Rotis Semi Sans
1993
See pages 356 – 57

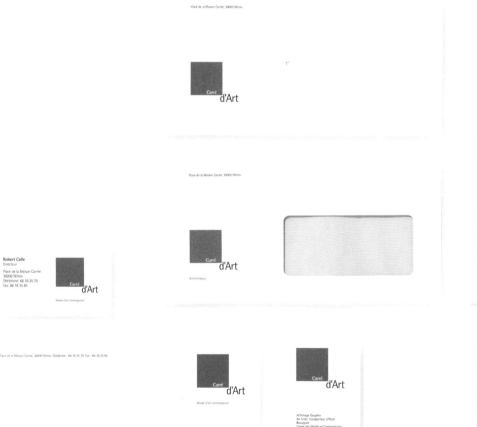

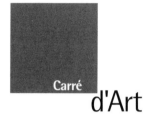

Carré d'Art

Musée d'art contemporain

Carré d'Art

1 | Yves Klein

une œuvre,
un commentaire

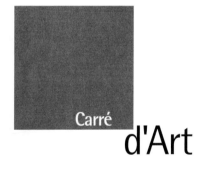

Carré d'Art

3 | Janvier–Mars '94

Carré d'Art

Carré d'Art

Musée d'art contemporain
Bibliothèque

A l'occasion de l'ouverture
de Carré d'Art

Jean Bousquet,
Député du Gard, Maire de Nîmes
serait heureux de vous accueillir
à une rencontre avec

Emmanuel Le Roy Ladurie,
directeur de la Bibliothèque
nationale

Germain Viatte,
directeur du Musée national
d'art moderne et
du Centre de création industrielle

Sir Norman Foster,
architecte

le jeudi 6 mai 1993 à 19h
au Théâtre de Nîmes
1, Place de la Calade

Entrée libre dans la mesure
des places disponibles
Renseignements : 66 76 35 35

Press release
Nîmes, Carré d'Art
30.5 × 22 cm (12 × 8⅝ in.)
Typeface: Rotis Semi Sans
1993

Brochure
Nîmes, Carré d'Art
26 × 24 cm (10½ × 9½ in.)
Typeface: Rotis Semi Sans
1993

Program
January – March '94
Nîmes, Carré d'Art
15.5 × 21 cm (6⅛ × 8¼ in.)
Typeface: Rotis Semi Sans
1994

Invitation card
Nîmes, Carré d'Art
15.5 × 21 cm (6⅛ × 8¼ in.)
Typeface: Rotis Semi Sans
1993

Direction des musées de France

The Direction des musées de France (National Museum Board of France, an arm of the Ministry of Culture and Communication) has administrative responsibility for thirty-four national museums and over 1,150 regional, local and associatively run museums. In need of a standardized, uniform system to identify every institution under its purview, the government agency launched a competition for a universal ideogram, which Apeloig won. The goal was to create a logo that would allow the public to instantly identify the museums on a map, in publications, and in situ as part of this network.

The design concept was developed around a lower-case *m*, set in Frutiger Condensed Black. The small *m* is friendlier and less intimidating than a capital *M* and so suited to making public sites of high culture seem more accessible. The *m* is placed inside an open rectangle delineated by dotted and dashed lines. The compositional arrangement resembles a gallery floor plan with diverse access points. Surrounded by open space, the *m* becomes the object on display – as if it were a drawing, painting, or sculpture. The logo embodies both functionality and modernity, and all manner of museum collections.

Logotype
Direction des musées de France, Paris
Typeface: Frutiger Condensed Black
2004
See pages 316 – 17

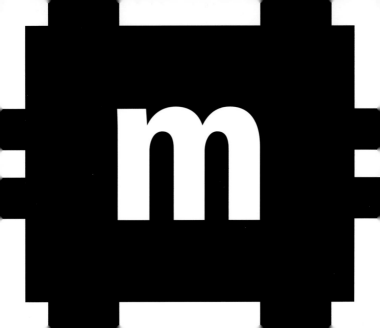

Institut national d'histoire de l'art

The mission of the Institut national d'histoire de l'art (INHA; National Institute of Art History), a public corporation set up in 2001, is to further scientific activity and international cooperation within the fields of art history, archaeology, and cultural heritage. INHA conducts research, disseminates knowledge, and organizes talks, seminars, and conferences. Each of the acronym's four letters is placed in an upright rectangle that functions as a frame and template. To the left, occupying the space of two invisible rectangles, sits the full name of the institute stacked in four lines. The unity of the four rectangles reflects the interdisciplinary work of INHA and symbolizes its serious, rational approach to research. The text is composed in Galliard, a contemporary adaptation of Robert Granjon's sixteenth-century typeface.

Cézanne Aix 2006

For the one hundredth anniversary of Paul Cézanne's death, the city of Aix-en-Provence organized a series of cultural events, the highlight of which was the "Cézanne in Provence" exhibition co-produced by Aix's newly renovated Musée Granet and the National Gallery of Art in Washington, DC.

The geometry underlying Cézanne's painting inspired the arrangement of the letters in an open square; it was also useful that the exhibition title had the perfect number of characters for this design. Although the name "Cézanne" is fragmented, both "Aix" and "2006" are intact. Set in the Fago Monospace font, the letters alternate between bold and normal weight so as to be suggestive of Cézanne's pictorial brushwork.

The logo was also rendered in color, alternating between three different hues in Cézanne's palette: a blue he used for skies, a green, and an orange.

Musée Girodet

The Girodet Museum, located in the Montargis region in north-central France, was founded in 1853 and named after local artist Anne-Louis Girodet-Trioson, who was a pupil of the Neoclassical painter Jacques-Louis David, and a forerunner of the Romantic movement in painting.

The logo designed for the museum uses a Didot font that was created during the artist's lifetime. The letter shape, characterized by slab-like serifs, is redolent of that period. The geometric Classicism of the letters is accentuated by hatching, highlighting the contrast between the downstrokes and the upstrokes that are specific to Didot. Reduced to an outline, the logo conveys a feeling of weightlessness and immateriality.

Logotype
Institut national d'histoire de l'art, Paris
Typeface: Galliard
2001

Logotype
Cézanne Aix 2006, Aix-en-Provence
Typeface: Fago Monospace
2005

Logotype
Musée Girodet, Montargis
Typefaces: Didot, Gravur Condensed
2005

Institut
national
d'histoire
de l'art

INHA

CÉZAN
CAIX NE
NE
X2006

musée GIRODET

Musée d'art et d'histoire du Judaïsme

The Musée d'art et d'histoire du Judaïsme (Museum of Jewish Art and History) opened in 1998 in the Marais, Paris's old Jewish quarter. For the museum's visual identity competition, Apeloig initially proposed a spiral within a star and a hand with seven fingers. The jury initially shied away from using the Star of David but encouraged the basic allegory of the design. Apeloig decided to employ four symbols of Jewish culture: the spiral, the Star of David, the hand, and the menorah. Though each image is recognizable on its own, their combination creates new layers of meaning, exploring the dual focus of art and history, and the complexities of religion.

The spiral refers not only to the concentric circles of the Kabbalah but also to a cross-section of the Torah scroll, and the origins and unfolding of life. In Apeloig's design, the spiral sits within the Star of David, unwinding outward and conveying the idea of integration and emancipation. The seven-fingered hand is drawn from Marc Chagall's *Self-Portrait with Seven Fingers* (1912) and a 1922 Constructivist collage by El Lissitzky, which features a handprint and Hebrew letters. At the jury's behest, the menorah, with its seven branches, became the primary symbol in the final design; Apeloig's version has uneven edges and a primitive appearance, alluding to the ancient origins of the Jewish people.

In conjunction with the museum's opening, the Swiss publisher Gabriele Capelli published *La Spirale, la main et la ménorah, Musée d'art et d'histoire du Judaïsme à Paris: l'identité visuelle* (The Spiral, the Hand and the Menorah: The Museum of Jewish Art and History in Paris: The Visual Identity), which illustrated the process behind the creation of this logo.

Logotypes
Early version
Final version
Musée d'art et d'histoire
du Judaïsme, Paris
1997
See pages 342–45

Book
La spirale, la main et la ménorah,
Musée d'art et d'histoire
du Judaïsme à Paris: l'identité visuelle
Gabriele Capelli Editore, Mendrisio
15.5 × 21 cm (6⅛ × 8¼ in.)
Printer: CGA & P Lugano
Typeface: Adobe Jenson
1997

Marc Chagall (1887 – 1985)
Self-Portrait with Seven Fingers, 1912
Oil on canvas
Stedelijk Museum, Amsterdam

El Lissitzky (1890 – 1941)
Illustration from Ilya Ehrenburg's
"Boat Ticket" *Six Stories with Easy Endings*, 1922
Indian ink and collage on paper
The Israel Museum, Jerusalem
The Boris and Lisa Aronson Collection
Purchased through a bequest
from Dvora Cohen, Afeka

Petit Palais
Musée des Beaux-Arts
de la Ville de Paris

The Petit Palais was built for the 1900 World Exposition in Paris and now houses the City of Paris's Museum of Fine Arts. In the first decade of the twenty-first century, it underwent extensive renovation.

Apeloig's strikingly simple 2004 logotype creates a double *P* – a small version inside a monumental one – from one continuous line. The empty space surrounding the letters creates visual unity and balance. The viewer reads the logo in a spiral fashion that mimics the visitor's journey through the museum, while the strong bottom serif lends stability to the whole.

The curve-within-a-curve motif echoes some of the museum's main architectural features: arched doors, a vast dome, and a circular interior courtyard. The flowing outline also evokes the building's Art Nouveau decorative details while adding a touch of Modernism.

Logotype
Petit Palais
Musée des Beaux-Arts
de la Ville de Paris
2004
See page 328

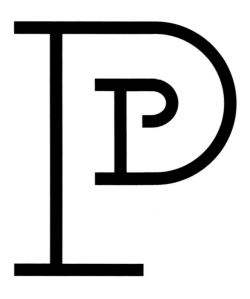

Palais de la découverte

Located in the west wing of the Grand Palais, the Palais de la découverte (Palace of Discovery) is a science center and museum showcasing scientific history and discovery. The initial logo designed by Apeloig in 1993 was based on a famous illustration of the Cartesian principle. The words are positioned like coordinates on a graph, evoking the field of mathematics, the foundation for all scientific research.

In 2010, the Palais de la découverte merged with La Cité des sciences et de l'industrie (The City of Science and Industry), another science museum, which is located in Paris's Parc de La Villette. The new logo needed to complement the identity of La Cité and its logo featuring a red square. The robust circle that evolved not only evokes the three-dimensional shapes of the planets spectacularly displayed in the Palais's main gallery, but also references the planetarium and famous Pi Room, which contains the first 707 digits of pi, which were first calculated in 1874.

The pure geometry of the circle is accentuated by the intersecting arrangement of the two words: "Palais" in large, thick letters and "découverte" in small capitals. The Akkurat font evokes the exactitude of science through the regularity of its design, and positions the logo in the here and now. The two words are placed perpendicular to each other to create two axes, preserving a connection with the original logo. The articles "de" and "la" are excluded.

Logotype
Palais de la découverte, Paris
Typeface: Foundry Old Style
1993

Logotype
Palais de la découverte, Paris
Typeface: Akkurat
2010

FRAC Bourgogne

The Fonds régionaux d'art contemporain (FRAC; Regional Collection of Contemporary Art) is a group of regional institutions that promote and collect contemporary art throughout France. The logo of FRAC Bourgogne is a modular piece featuring the simple, universal rectangle. Its body is black, with strips of white that interweave and overlap, keeping the actual edges of the rectangle hidden. A dynamic and mutable shape, the logo can grow larger or smaller, and move in and out of the page or screen frame. Each movement is a pulse in time, like the tick of a metronome. The graphic breathes and shifts shape, in the same way that contemporary art is never static and forever changing.

The individual letters are set in Gravur Condensed capitals, a font that suits any kind of art thanks to its standard appearance and regular weight. Each of the four letters in FRAC has a dash in front of it that implies motion and unifies the logo.

Stationary
FRAC Bourgogne
Typeface: Gravur Condensed
2002

Animation and logotype
FRAC Bourgogne
Typeface: Gravur Condensed
Length: 9"
2002

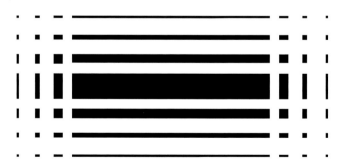

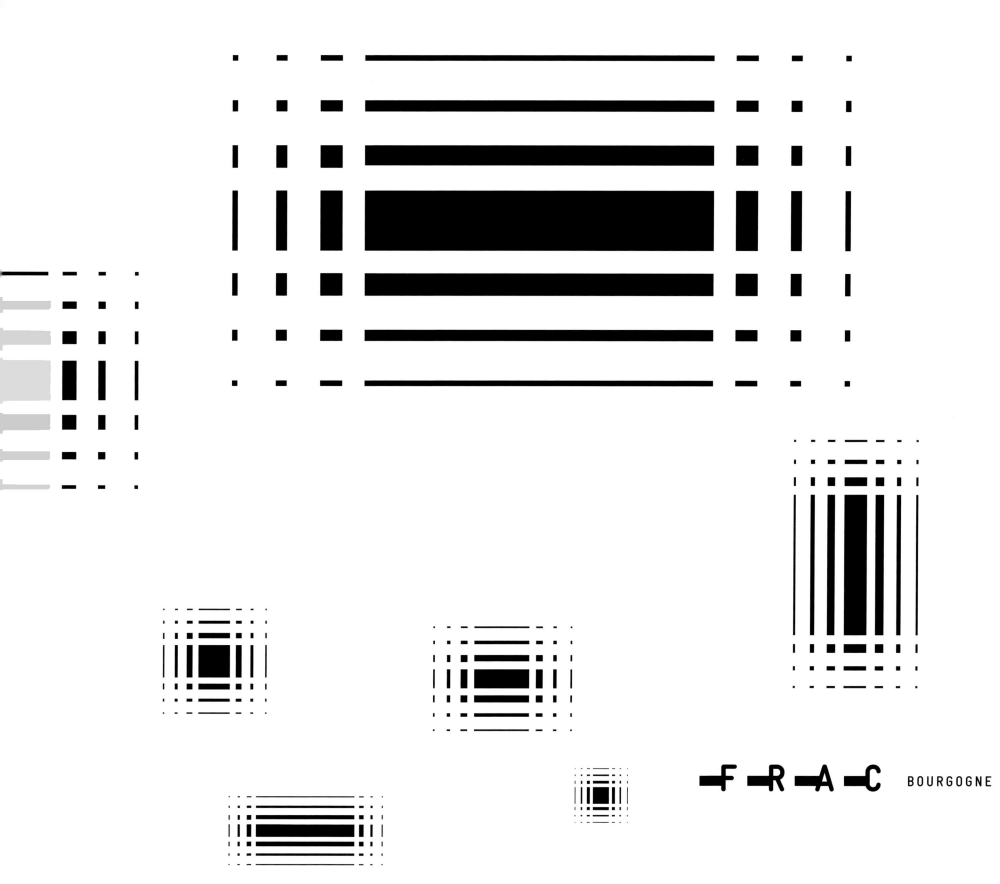

Istituto Universitario
di Architettura di Venezia

For its seventieth anniversary in 2004, the Istituto Universitario di Architettura di Venezia (IUAV; University Institute of Architecture, Venice) launched an international competition for a new logo that would convey its leading role in contemporary architecture, art, and design. Instead of an abstract symbol or figurative illustration based on existing motifs, Apeloig chose to play with the four letters of the institute's acronym. He found that the only thing these letters have in common is that, as capitals, they are symmetrical and can be read in a vertical column. The typographic solution he adopted breaks with the traditional horizontal layout of acronyms, relying upon the renown of the institution and its initials.

,

The font is Fago Mono, a monospace typeface designed by Ole Schäfer in 1999. This choice eliminates the problem of variable letter widths, as the I with its strong serif occupies as much width as the other letters, avoiding confusion with the numeral *1*. The logotype acts as a typographic totem, balancing abstract, symbolic forms one on top of the other. It was inspired by Brancusi's stacked modular sculpture, *Endless Column*. Each letter is centered inside a virtual square, bordered by perforated lines that allow the eye to roam freely without impeding readability. The dotted borders evoke the striped poles to which Venice's gondolas are moored, as well as horizon lines and meridians. The geometric parameters of the blocks strictly regulate size and spacing, as well as the proportion of the letters and negative space.

Formal versatility is one of the logo's most advantageous features. Each letter is perfectly symmetrical so that the logo reads the same even if flipped and is unaltered when mirrored or viewed through a transparent surface. Cropped on its vertical axis, with only half its letters showing, as if cut in two, it is still completely identifiable.

Logotype
**Istituto Universitario
di Architettura di Venezia**
Typeface: Fago Mono
2004
See pages 330–31

Constantin Brancusi (1876–1957)
View of the artist's studio, *c.* 1929
Gelatin silver print
Centre Pompidou, Paris

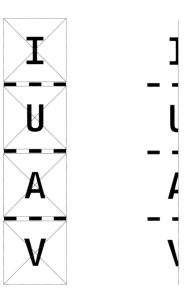

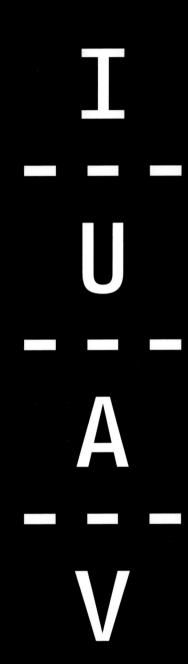

ANNÉE DU BRÉSIL EN FRANCE   MARS–DÉCEMBRE   2005

www.bresilbresils.org

Poster
BrésilBrésils
Association Française
d'Action Artistique
150 × 100 cm (59 × 39³/₈ in.)
Screen print
Printer: 5ᵉ Couleur
Typefaces: Futura,
Gravur Condensed
2005
See pages 318–19

Press release
BrésilBrésils
Association Française
d'Action Artistique
29.7 × 22 cm (11⁵/₈ × 8⁵/₈ in.)
Printer: AGIC
Typefaces: Futura,
Gravur Condensed
2005

BrésilBrésils
Année du Brésil en France

In 2005, France held BrésilBrésils, a yearlong festival celebrating Brazilian culture. The *s* at the end of the second "Brésil" evokes the country's multiculturalism and its wealth of folk traditions. The logo consists of stacked, vertically condensed capital letters. The vivid colors – blue, green, and yellow, as in the Brazilian flag – and the graphic design reference Brazilian Neoconcretism (1959–61), a movement that took inspiration from Concrete Art but broke with its rigor. Its principal exponents were Lygia Pape, Mira Schendel, and Hélio Oiticica. The title words are split into blocks of mirrored letters, like sound typography, and create a bouncing rhythm inspired by samba and bossa nova.

The letters' alignment and spacing create relief and the impression of depth, which also comes from the alternating positive/negative treatment of individual characters. The characters *B*, *E* and *I* merge to form hybrids. The logo and poster design hint at a culture in constant motion and flux – and at a festival honoring that extraordinary vitality.

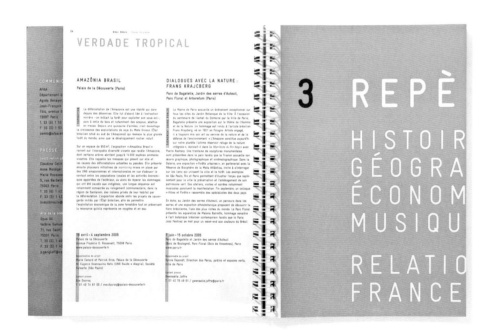

Jean-François Chougnet
Commissaire général

AFAA
Association française d'action artistique
1ᵉʳ avenue de Villars
75007 Paris

T +33 (0)1 40 03 74 72
F +33 (0)1 53 69 83 93
jf.chougnet@villette.com

Année du Brésil en France

AFAA
Association française d'action artistique
1ᵉʳ avenue de Villars
75007 Paris

T +33 (0)1 53 69 83 53
F +33 (0)1 53 69 83 93
bresil@afaa.asso.fr
www.bresil-bresils.org

Année du Brésil en France

Année du Brésil en France

AFAA
Association française
d'action artistique
1ᵉʳ avenue de Villars
75007 Paris

F +33 (0)1 53 69 83 53
F +33 (0)1 53 69 83 93
bresil@afaa.asso.fr
www.bresil-bresils.org

Stationary
BrésilBrésils
Association française d'action
artistique
Typefaces: Futura Condensed,
Gravur Condensed
2005

French Institute Alliance Française

The French Institute Alliance Française (FIAF) in New York City offers innovative programs in education and the arts that explore the evolving diversity and richness of French cultures. The "fi:af" logo was designed to make a clear visual connection between English and French, the two languages represented in the organization's name. The colon in the logo visually divides, as well as connects, the two symbols. The Minion typeface, designed in 1990 by Robert Slimbach and inspired by the beauty of late Renaissance fonts, brings a touch of French Classicism to this modern design. The two dots making up the colon use colors shared by both national flags – red and blue – but the logo and the corporate identity can use many other colors as well. The logo adapts readily in order to reflect the diversity of the francophone communities celebrated by FIAF, whether African, Haitian, or Lebanese, among others.

Apeloig's innovative two-dot column for the logo was the beginning of a more sophisticated and complex design that would permeate the organization's entire design identity and combine both old and new approaches to art. Apeloig was strongly influenced not only by Georges Seurat but also by Roy Lichtenstein and his famous Ben-Day dots, one of the basic elements of offset printing.

Apeloig extended this identity throughout FIAF's building on East Sixtieth Street: all seven floors received a wall panel with an emblematic image of France. The creation and modeling of each was a subtractive process that involved removing dots from the grid, leaving the desired icon shown in a form of mechanical Pointillism. Each illustration has an iconic color as well: blue for the Eiffel Tower, yellow for the Tour de France, and so on. These creations, which are treated like pictograms, establish a link between artistic references and vitalize the institute's programming, while also providing effective signage.

FIAF's quarterly programs expounding on themes such as French fashion or gastronomy provided Apeloig with the opportunity to create coherent graphics for the covers and inside pages.

He also developed an easily identifiable visual language for the publications he designed for the institute's French language school, the Language Center. The invitations he designed for the Trophée des Arts, an annual gala held to raise sponsorship, followed the same principles: a stylized image of the sun alludes to the Sun King and footlights.

Signage, wall panel
French Institute Alliance Française, New York
2005

Logotype
French Institute Alliance Française, New York
Typeface: Minion
2004

fi:af

Georges Seurat (1859 – 1891)
The Eiffel Tower, 1889
Oil on board
Fine Arts Museum, San Francisco

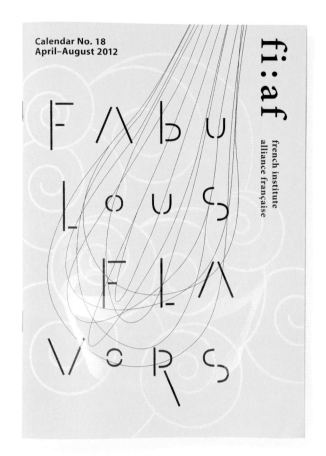

Brochures
Calendar of Events Nos. 17, 18, 20 and 15
French Institute Alliance Française, New York
24 × 17.8 cm (9½ × 7 in.)
Typefaces: Myriad Pro, Minion
2010–13

Brochure
Cinématuesdays
French Institute Alliance Française, New York
12.8 × 18 cm (5⅛ × 7⅜ in.)
Typefaces: Myriad Pro, Minion
2012

Brochures
World Normads
French Institute Alliance Française, New York
17.8 × 12.8 cm (7⅛ × 5⅛ in.)
Typefaces: Myriad Pro, Minion
2008–09

F
A
SH
I
O
N
A
T
FI
A
F

fi:af

french institute
alliance française

A
Fresh
Look
at
Fashion

Calendar n° 20

January–March
2013

Calendar No. 15
April–August 2011

fi:af

french institute
alliance française

World Nomads
Morocco

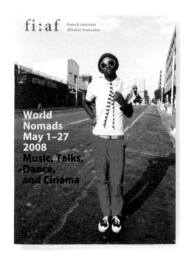

fi:af french institute
alliance française

World
Nomads
May 1–27
2008
Music, Talks,
Dance,
and Cinéma

fi:af

french institute
alliance française

World
Nomads
Haiti
May 2009
Music
Literature
Cinema
Visual Arts

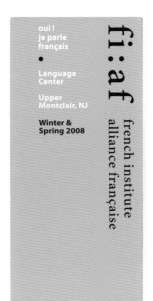

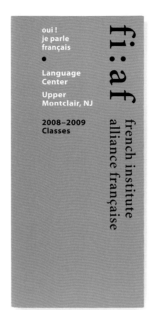

Magazine
FIAF Magazine
French Institute Alliance Française,
New York
17.8 × 12.7 cm (7 ⅛ × 5 in.)
Typefaces: Myriad Pro, Minion
2006

Leaflets
Language Center
French Institute Alliance Française,
New York
22.3 × 12.8 cm (8 ⅞ × 5 ⅛ in.)
Typefaces: Myriad Pro, Minion
2008–2009

Invitation cards
Trophée des arts
French Institute Alliance Française,
New York
17.8 × 12.8 cm (7 ⅛ × 5 ⅛ in.)
Typefaces: Myriad Pro, Minion
2008 – 09

Brochure
Language Center
French Institute Alliance Française,
New York
22.3 × 12.8 cm (8 ⅞ × 5 ⅛ in.)
Typefaces: Myriad Pro, Minion
2009

Signage, wall panel
**French Institute Alliance Française,
New York**
2005

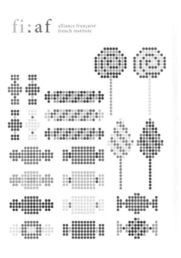

Crossing the Line
FIAF Fall Festival

Crossing the Line is an annual fall festival organized and produced by the FIAF in partnership with other cultural organizations in New York. It is conceived as a platform to present new developments in art and experimental practices from both sides of the Atlantic.

The 2010 poster is based on a kinetic effect achieved through successive repetition of the title, a visual allusion to musical and dance works. The letters are made up of numerous punctuation signs that make their lines irregular and out of focus. The letters and words undulate across the page, like brushstrokes or pencil marks.

For 2011, a minimal approach was used. The black program cover is bare save for the festival title set in white type and arranged in a single vertical line. The program is printed on ordinary paper using the French-fold system and Japanese binding: each sheet is folded in two with the folds all lining up at the book's edges to give it volume. The text is printed in red and black, while the inside of each folded page is a neon pink that is visible through the transparent paper, with intense bursts of color glimpsed at top and bottom.

Program
Crossing the Line,
FIAF Fall Festival 2011
French Institute Alliance Française,
New York
17.8 × 12.7 cm (7 × 5 in.)
Typeface: Myriad Pro
2011

Poster
Crossing the Line,
FIAF Fall Festival 2010
French Institute Alliance Française,
New York
150 × 100 cm (59 × 39⅜ in.)
Screen print
Printer: Sérica
Typefaces: original creation,
Myriad Pro
2010
See page 294

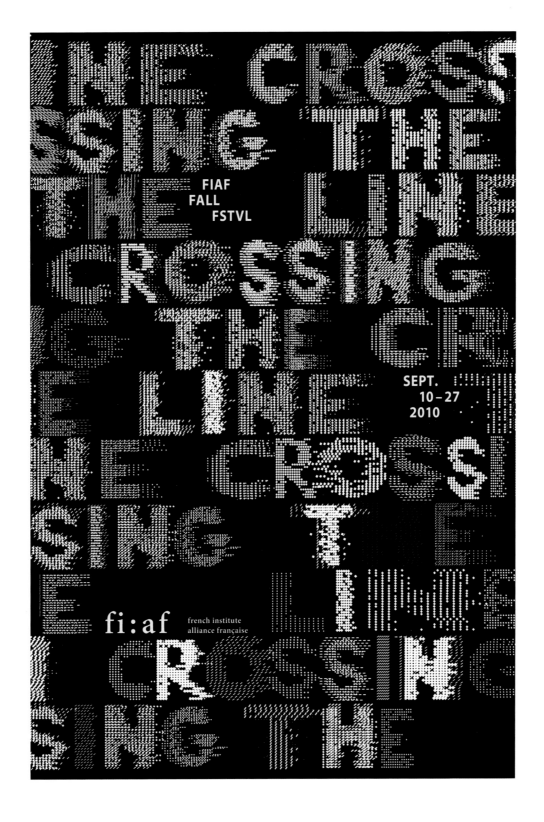

Moeller Fine Art

Established in London in 1972, Moeller Fine Art relocated to New York in 1984 and opened a second space in Berlin in 2009. Under the direction of owner Achim Moeller, the gallery sells paintings, drawings, and sculptures by Modern masters, with particular emphasis on German Expressionism, Dada, Surrealism, and the Bauhaus.

In 2002, Moeller Fine Art and Philippe Apeloig began to collaborate on the gallery's design aesthetic and approach. Together, they created a clean, functional identity and logo for the gallery's website, stationary, publications, and advertisements. The design evolved in several steps. Initially, the visual identity was based on the Frutiger font. But after Moeller moved into new spaces in New York and Berlin, Frutiger was replaced by Foundry Sterling, a modern sans serif typeface designed in 2002 by David Quay and Freda Sack with fewer historical undertones. The current logo design is a block filled with three evenly stacked lines that read "Moeller New York + Berlin." The positioning of the two cities alternates depending on the location of the exhibition or project. Throughout the evolution of the identity, a definite Modernist orientation prevailed. Economy of means, a reductive use of well-balanced typography, and an understanding of art are all evident in the design.

The publications that accompany exhibitions are created in the same spirit. For the most part, these consist of catalogs and some anthologies, which Achim Moeller oversees, as he did for the catalog on Lyonel Feininger, which is dedicated to Feininger's drawings and watercolors, and accompanied by a major illustrated biography. The cover features a cutout that exactly matches the framing the artist himself drew on a photographic portrait reproduced in the *Bauhaus Review* (No. 2/3, 1928).

Logotype
Moeller Fine Art, New York, Berlin
Typeface: Foundry Sterling
2008

Card
Celebrating 40 years
Moeller Fine Art, New York, Berlin
10.4 × 22.4 cm (4⅛ × 8⅞ in.)
Typeface: Foundry Sterling
2012

Moving card
Moeller Fine Art, New York
10.4 × 22.4 cm (4⅛ × 8⅞ in.)
Typeface: Foundry Sterling
2012

Folder
Blue Four Plus Five
Moeller Fine Art, New York
10.2 × 21.6 cm (4⅛ × 8½ in.)
Typeface: Foundry Sterling
2002

Card
Hubertus Gojowczyk
Gutenberg Labyrinth. The Book as
Object, Text and Situation since 1968
Moeller Fine Art, New York
21 × 15 cm (8¼ × 5⅞ in.)
Typeface: Foundry Sterling
2008

M O E L L E R
N E W Y O R K
+ B E R L I N

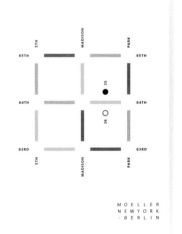

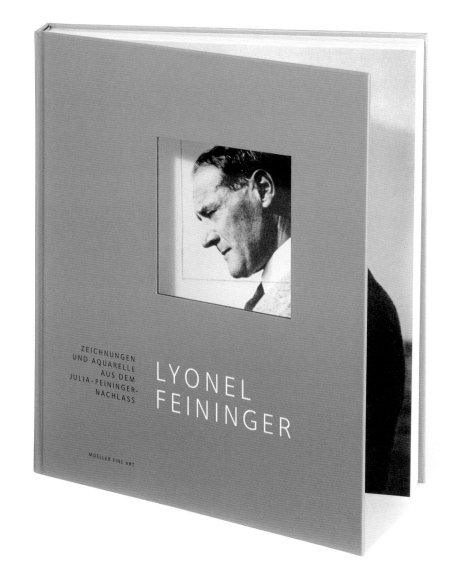

Book
Lyonel Feininger
Zeichnungen und Aquarelle
aus dem Julia-Feininger-Nachlass
Moeller Fine Art, Berlin, New York
27.9 × 21.6 cm (11 × 8½ in.), 192 pages
Printer: H. Heenemann GmbH & Co. KG
Typeface: Foundry Sterling
2008

HOWARD WISE GALLERY EXPLORING THE NEW

MOELLER BERLIN+NEW YORK

MOELLER

PIERO DORAZIO

watercolors and drawings 1957–1962

Brochure
Howard Wise Gallery
Exploring the New Moeller Fine Art,
Moeller Fine Art, New York, Berlin
20.5 × 25.5 cm (8⅛ × 10 in.), 16 pages
Typeface: Foundry Sterling
2012

Folder
Piero Dorazio
Watercolors and drawings 1957–1962
Moeller Fine Art, New York, Berlin
10.2 × 21.6 cm (4 × 8½ in.)
Typeface: Frutiger
2002

Invitation Card
Private Views
Lyonel Feininger and Mark Tobey:
Two Friends
Moeller Fine Art, New York, Berlin
10.2 × 21.6 cm (4 × 8½ in.)
Typeface: Frutiger
2003

MOELLER

Private Views

Lyonel Feininger and Mark Tobey: Two Friends

February 11–April 4, 2003
Achim Moeller Fine Art

167 East 73rd Street, NYC
by appointment

February 20–24, 2003
The Art Show

Seventh Regiment Armory
Park Avenue at 67th Street, NYC
Stand A12

Private Views

Lyonel Feininger and Mark Tobey: Two Friends

February 11–April 4, 2003
Achim Moeller Fine Art

167 East 73rd Street, NYC
by appointment

February 20–24, 2003
The Art Show

Seventh Regiment Armory
Park Avenue at 67th Street, NYC
Stand A12

Impressionism to Modern and Contemporary Art

Piero Dorazio: painter of light

In his vibrant, tense abstractions, Piero Dorazio has captured not life but rather a fleeting, emotionally charged glimpse of life in passing. Luminosity itself might be the subject of Air, a delicately textured, atmospheric grid from 1962, or a similarly green-tinged and untitled watercolor of the same year [1], had they not also embodied a lyricism that is both fragile and firmly, even classically constructed. Another grid dated 1962, Pink [2], is equally reticent in its imagery and elemental, subdued title. Instead of the woven textures and mossy natural hue in the untitled painting or in Air, Dorazio turned to a more shallow and crystalline structure as the basis for Pink, tethering its radiant bars of color to one another as if from some spontaneous evolution, or seemingly through the inspired efforts of a weaver working with tensile bands of pure color and light.

Yet the Italian artist's elegant abstractions are not merely atmospheric and ethereal, as is evident in such visceral works as an untitled 1957 gouache [3], whose tactile grid twists and writhes energetically across the surface, or the equally muscular Antibes, dated 1957, with its hot palette and firm, fluid gestures. Dorazio's approach at that early point in his career, informed by his close ties to the European avant-garde and familiarity with the New York School's angst-ridden style, revealed a taste for tempering the explosive postwar "tachisme" with the muted, meditative sensibility that was his heritage.

Born in Rome in 1927 and trained in traditional classical painting and drawing, Dorazio turned to architecture as a university student, in 1945. His interests weren't limited to architecture in that heady period at the end of World War II, when the defeat of fascism allowed young Italian intellectuals and artists to discover modernist advances that had been off limits. Dorazio became active in a variety of artistic and literary circles, creating delicate early abstract compositions that are reminiscent of Paul Klee, and that evoke the tone of Klee's statement that the modern artist must be a philosopher as well as a poet.

Dorazio was exposed to a wealth of artistic influences and intellectual currents, from the School of Paris and Surrealist biomorphism to Russian Suprematism, Constructivism and even Italian Futurism. He notably rediscovered the art of Giacomo Balla, whom he sought out in Rome in 1950 and visited often, studying the paintings and sketchbooks in the neglected Futurist's studio. At the same time, Dorazio became actively involved in design, printing silk-screens and creating furniture before his 1950 visit to Paris, which soon led to his collaboration with a number of fellow artists in organizing a notable avant-garde institution, L'Age d'Or.

That little gallery/bookshop became the Roman gathering place for the exchange of avant-garde ideas, attracting in 1950 a roster of distinguished visitors that included Mark Rothko, Rufino Tamayo, Matta and the Baroness Hilla Rebay. Dorazio forged connections at the same time through his membership in The Art Club, and his work was shown widely in group-exhibitions in Vienna, Milan and at the Museum of Non-Objective Art, which later evolved into the Guggenheim Museum in New York. During the late forties and early fifties, when he traveled throughout Europe and visited New York, Dorazio was evolving the approach that a decade later would establish his international stature.

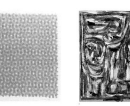

After abandoning architectural studies in 1951, he organized the Fondazione Origine with Matta and others, and the following year he wrote the first book published in Italy on international modern art, La Fantasia dell'Arte Vita Moderna. By 1953, after traveling to Harvard's International Summer Seminar and spending a year in the United States, where he met New York's leading artists and critics, Dorazio focused primarily on his own art.

Painting was primary but he explored other areas, among them the experimental ceramics he made in Rome in the mid-fifties and his collaboration in 1957 on a book published in New York, The World of Abstract Art. His invitation to present a lecture series at the University of Pennsylvania's Graduate School of Fine Arts in 1960, followed by his appointment to reorganize the university's Department of Painting, Sculpture and Graphics, led to a nine-year faculty tenure and further involvement with the art world's leading figures, among them Robert Motherwell, Herbert Ferber, Barnett Newman, Ad Reinhardt, Clyfford Still and David Smith.

Catalog
George Grosz
His visual and theatrical politics
Moeller Fine Art, New York, Berlin
20.5 × 25.5 cm (8⅛ × 10 in.), 112 pages
Printer: Snoeck-Ducaju, Gent
Typeface: Foundry Sterling
2005

Catalog
Matthew Sontheimer
Sent off and revealed,
counted down and sealed
Moeller Fine Art, New York, Berlin
20.5 × 25.5 cm (8⅛ × 10 in.), 32 pages
Printer: DDC NJ
Typeface: Frutiger
2005

Catalog
From Daumier to Matisse:
French Master Drawings from
the John C. Whitehead Collection
Moeller Fine Art, New York, Berlin
18 × 24 cm (7⅛ × 9½ in.), 56 pages
Printer: Finlay Printing,
Bloomfield, Conn.
Typeface: Foundry Sterling
2010

Catalog
Hubertus Gojowczyk
The Book as Object
Moeller Fine Art, New York, Berlin
20.5 × 25.5 cm (8⅛ × 10 in.), 24 pages
Printer: DDC NJ
Typeface: Foundry Sterling
2005

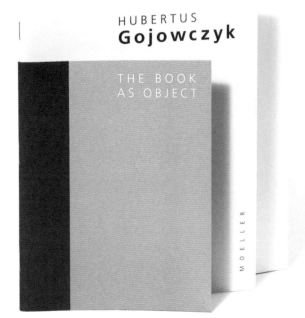

Espace Topographie de l'art

Espace Topographie de l'art (Gallery for the Topography of Art) shows three to four exhibitions per year. It opened in 2001 in Paris's Marais district in an industrial space that had originally housed a warehouse and a textile factory. The walls and floors betray their previous use, providing historical references and an aesthetic contrast with the art on display.

The gallery's identity was built around the typeface Letter Gothic, which is reminiscent of the old type-writer font. It has a format and elements composed of dotted lines that correlate with the physical roughness of the space, as does the offset paper selected for all the printed material.

Apeloig's global branding for Espace Topographie de l'art combines organic, low-quality materials, a vintage-looking typeface, and a sophisticated layout. Printed in sheets of twelve, business cards have to be individually detached before they can be used, which gives them irregular edges. Invitations are made from sheets folded in four to give a horizontal format that matches the envelopes. Inside, typographic designs or reproductions of works are arranged in dotted lines that recall the venue's visual image.

On the cover of photographer Vera Röhm's book on the Jaipur Observatory in India, the title is embossed in black on natural-colored cardboard with straight edges. The same approach was adopted for the graphics on the cover of a book celebrating the venue's tenth anniversary: the embossed letters stand out against the high-gram Kraft paper of the cover in a dynamic play on the words "Repères" (reference point) and "Dix ans de l'Espace Topographie de l'art" (Tenth Anniversary of the Gallery for the Topography of Art) that cross each others' paths. Inside, we find dotted lines that echo the ocher binding threads, which become lighter towards the top.

Stationary
Espace Topographie de l'art, Paris
Typeface: Letter Gothic
2004

Exhibition Catalog
Vera Röhm: Jaipur Observatory
Espace Topographie de l'art, Paris
21 × 21 cm (8¼ × 8¼ in.), 126 pages
Printer: Blanchard
Typeface: Letter Gothic
2004

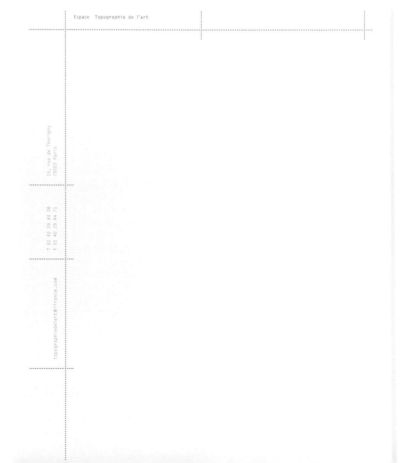

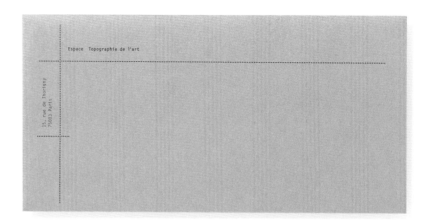

Invitations
Espace Topographie de l'art, Paris
21 × 10 cm (8¼ × 3⅞ in.)
Open: 42 × 20 cm (16½ × 7⅞ in.)
Printer: Jourdan
Typeface: Letter Gothic
2004 – 11

Exhibition Catalog
**Repères: dix ans de l'Espace
Topographie de l'art
Espace Topographie de l'art, Paris**
25 × 19 cm (9⅞ × 7½ in.), 182 pages
Printer: MM Artbook Printing & Repro
Typeface: Letter Gothic
2011

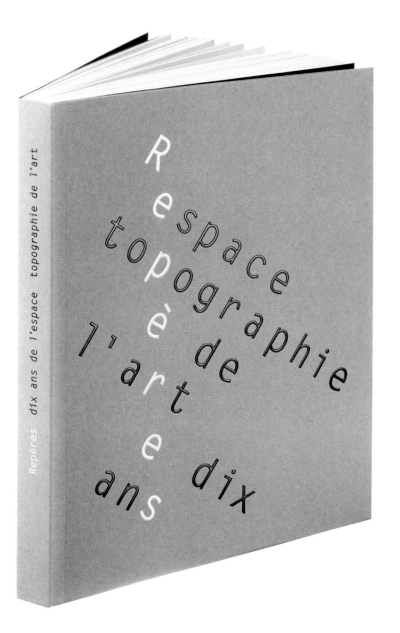

Projection est le titre de la pièce principale présentée dans
cette exposition réunissant des œuvres de l'artiste brésilien
José Damasceno. Constituée par une série de fauteuils
et par des amoncellements de semelles découpées en papier
coloré qui se répandent aléatoirement dans l'espace, l'atmosphère
de cette sculpture/installation est chaotique et dramatique.
Elle est la reconstitution fabulatrice d'une audience absente
dont le passage est évoqué par les traces en papier.
　En même temps qu'elle instaure un évènement figé d'une
matérialité puissante, elle évoque un caractère cinématique
intrinsèque aux matériaux utilisés et leur turbulence.
À la manière d'une narration apparemment sans déroulement ;
comme un *still* d'une séquence de film ; ou encore de la même
façon qu'un instant d'une action interrompue, cette œuvre
se réfère à un moment *avant* ou *après* de ce qui est vu.
Évènement *en transit*, comme d'ailleurs dans l'ensemble
de l'œuvre de Damasceno, *Projection* se projette dans l'espace-
temps de manière instable en créant un territoire spéculatif
sur la question du visible, de l'invisible et du devenir.
　Étant donné que l'énoncé principal du travail questionne
par exacerbation la notion de mouvement, il existe dans
l'œuvre une fixation et un mouvement à la fois potentiels
et oscillatoires. Cette «animation occulte» suggère la dilatation
du temps et de sa durée en puissante cinématique constante.
Dans ce contexte, tant la fixation quant le mouvement sont
abordés en tant qu'énergies oubliées dans la conscience
de l'espace, susceptibles de ressurgir l'une de l'autre à n'importe
quel moment.
　Chez Damasceno, la sculpture est aussi image. Elle dépasse
la présence matérielle des volumes et établit une relation
phantasmatique au-delà du caractère physique des choses.
Le représenté se transforme en une simple résonance
de l'«animation» des idées. L'artiste travaille l'image comme
s'il était possible de l'aborder physiquement en même temps
qu'il essaye d'extraire de la chose son potentiel d'image.
Il existe toujours un potentiel fluide et mouvant situé au-delà
du visible qui s'installe dans la psyché du spectateur.
Et Damasceno place cette résonance de l'œuvre dans notre
psychisme en tant que question visuelle.
　Machines imaginaires en action, les interventions
de Damasceno transforment la place habituelle et le temps
chronologique en une expérience fictive inusitée à partir
de distorsions poétiques de la réalité. Cela est le cas
non seulement pour *Projection*, mais aussi pour les autres œuvres
présentées dans cette exposition : l'organigramme intitulé
Hier, Aujourd'hui, Demain et le relief pariétal *Cinéma élastique*.
　Fasciné par les états *en transit* et par ce qu'active le flux
entre des mondes apparemment séparés, Damasceno produit
un revirement dans les dimensions souvent acceptées de temps,

d'espace et de rep
maintenaient les p
du réel, son intér
poétiques de maté
De ce fait, la dyn
un champ sensible
le sens de ce qui
　Des endroits
de la poésie, son
et élastique que p
irrégulière de l'i
de l'imaginaire su
des tensions entre
Il concentre et p
imprévues en faisa

Ligia Canongia
commissaire de l'expos

Projection

José Damasceno

15 novembre
–14 décembre 2008

avec le soutien de l'Ambassade du Brésil en France,
Thomas Dane Gallery à Londres,
Galerie Fortes Vilaça à São Paulo et the Project à New York

une exposition en collaboration
avec le festival d'Automne à Paris 37e édition

La Maison de Photo

La Maison de Photo, a publisher and gallery based in Belle-Île-en-Mer, Brittany, looks to the Far East for its inspiration. It represents traditional photographers who adhere to the use of black-and-white film and continue to create their prints by hand in the darkroom. Their black and white logo, inspired by a Japanese aesthetic, evokes Constructivism. The angular letters, similar to Kanji characters – especially the *A* and the *M* – embody the meeting of East and West. The vowels are underlined, making them the same size as the larger consonants. This variation in size creates a visual cadence similar to a music score.

Business cards continue this aesthetic. On a velvety-paper, the embossed logo letters are coated with a UV varnish. Playing with the idea of film negatives and darkroom technique, the back of the letterhead is printed with a black strip, from which the text reverses out. Thanks to the fineness of the paper, the logo looks like a watermark, an impression that is heightened by the varnish placed on the exact same spot on both front and back. This is more legible when held to the light. In their simplicity and rigor, the graphics for La Maison de Photo pay tribute to the endurance and power of the black-and-white photographic tradition and aesthetic.

Logotype
La Maison de Photo, Belle-Île-en-Mer
2010

Stationary
La Maison de Photo, Belle-Île-en-Mer
Offset and screen print
Printer: Jourdan et Silium
Typeface: Deck
2010

Litvak Gallery

The Litvak Gallery opened in Tel Aviv in 2008 in a space designed by Asaf Gottesman. The logo, designed for the opening event, features the six characters of "Litvak" using capital letters, strong diagonals, and exaggerated lines reminiscent of the gallery's architecture. The word "Gallery" is also set in this typeface but at a smaller point size. Although some of their parts are missing, the letters are still legible because their fundamental lines remain undisturbed. The letters of the logo come and go like as a metaphor for the wealth and complexity of the gallery's architecture.

The poster is a matte black silkscreen on a metallic celluloid material, giving the logo a chrome-like brilliance – a quality and contrast that reflected the luminosity of the works in the inaugural show dedicated to artist–glassmakers.

Poster
Litvak Gallery, Tel Aviv
150 × 100 cm (59 × 39⅜ in.)
Screen print
Printer: Sérica
Typefaces: original creation, Akkurat
2009

Association des bibliothécaires de France

Once its master, the book now shares the library's limited shelving with new media. In 2006, the poster announcing the one hundredth anniversary of the ABF (Association des bibliothécaires de France, or Association of French Librarians) featured a typographic logo that represented the modular, multi-use furnishings of modern libraries.

Logotype ABF

The visual identity developed by Apeloig concentrates the meaning of the library and its function in an original typeface, with three variations: ABF Petit, ABF Silhouette and ABF Linéaire. Five shapes – two rectangles and three rounded-down circles and ovals – compose almost all the letters of the alphabet in this typeface. ABF Petit is composed of rectangles and ovoid shapes that evoke worktables and chairs seen from above, as well as the outlines of their users. The same elements appear in negative within blocky black letterforms in ABF Silhouette (page 262). For ABF Linéaire (page 264), the shapes have been transformed into contours. The design of this typeface family and its visual identity communicate the message that today's library offers much more than books.

Demain la bibliothèque… 52ᵉ congrès

In addition to serving as a physical repository and place of conservation – "The memory of the whole world," as filmmaker Alain Resnais called them in 1956 – libraries are dedicated to study and research, and build a sense of community by hosting conferences and presenting exhibitions, film screenings, and performances. In 2006, the ABF organized the congress "Demain la bibliothèque…" (The library tomorrow…) in celebration of its one hundredth anniversary. The poster design revolves around the notion of space and expansion. This message is reinforced by the central semi-transparent pink rectangle. The poster's visual language encompasses perceptions of the library now, as well as an abstracted projection of its future form.

Logotype
Association des bibliothécaires de France, Paris
Typeface: ABF Petit
2006
See page 311

Poster
**Demain la bibliothèque… 52ᵉ Congrès
Association des bibliothécaires de France, Paris**
175 × 118.5 cm (68⅞ × 46⅝ in.)
Screen print
Printer: Sérilor
Typefaces: ABF Petit, Akkurat
2006

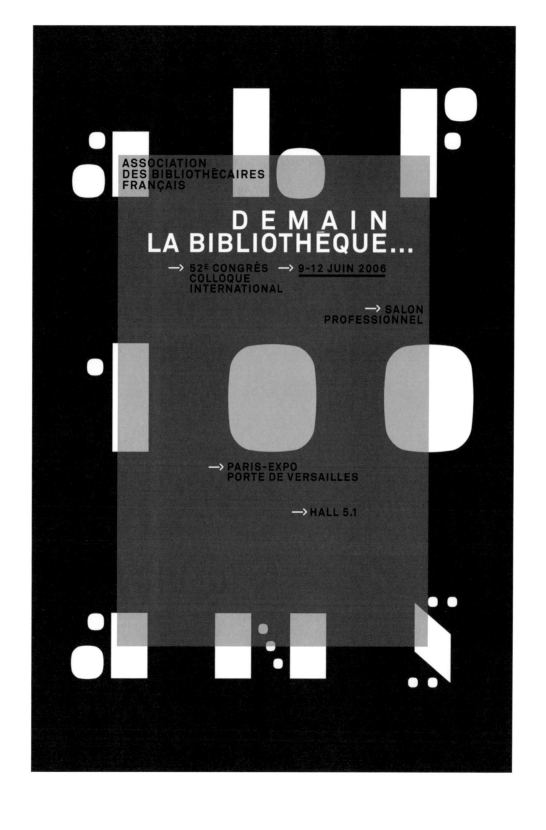

COLLOQUE INTERNATIONAL
SALON PROFESSIONNEL

ABF
55E CONGRÈS
11-14 JUIN 2009

PARIS
PORTE DE VERSAILLES
HALL 5.1

des

USAGES
ESPACES
ARCHITECTURES

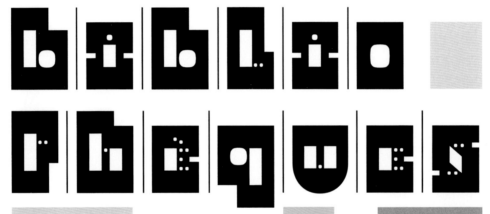

**biblio
thèques**

à vivre

ASSOCIATION
DES BIBLIOTHÉCAIRES
DE FRANCE

Des bibliothèques à vivre
Usages, espaces, architectures
55ᵉ congrès

For the poster for the 2009 ABF Congress, for which
the theme was "Des bibliothèques à vivre, Usages,
spaces, architectures" (Libraries to Live In: Uses,
Spaces, and Architecture), the ABF font was converted into silhouetted characters. For this version,
each white letter floats in front of its own "echo,"
a boldly geometric counterpart in black. The contrast
between the letters' soft organic shapes and their
block-like shadows is stark. This graphic focal point
is central to the function of these newly combined
typographic elements: inhibited by the near solitary
confinement of each letter, the reading process
becomes a game of decoding. The poster casts
reading in a new light, challenging the norm in
relation to text and space, as well as the form and
function of the modern library.

Poster
Des bibliothèques à vivre
Usages, espaces, architectures
55ᵉ congrès
Association des bibliothécaires
de France, Paris
175 × 118.5 cm (68⅞ × 46⅝ in.)
Screen print
Printer: Sérica
Typefaces: ABF Silhouette, Akkurat
2009

Agenda
Association des bibliothécaires
de France, Paris
15 × 10.7 cm (5⅞ × 4¼ in.)
Typefaces: ABF Petit, Akkurat
2009

Notepad
Association des bibliothécaires
de France, Paris
21 × 14.8 cm (8¼ × 5⅞ in.)
Typefaces: ABF Petit, Akkurat
2009

Program
Association des bibliothécaires
de France, Paris
24 × 17 cm (9½ × 6¾ in.)
Typefaces: ABF Petit, Akkurat
2009

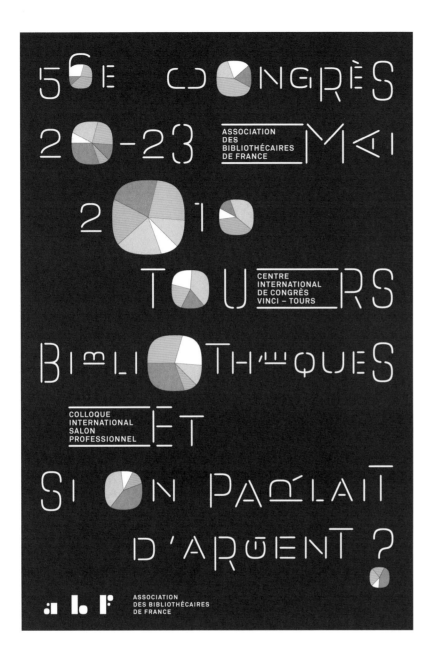

**Bibliothèques
Et si on parlait d'argent?
56ᵉ congrès**

In 2010, the theme of the fifty-sixth ABF Congress was "Et si on parlait d'argent?" (How about we talk money?). In the midst of an increasingly dire economic climate, candid discussions on this topic were crucial to the survival of libraries. On top of the monies required to process and maintain their holdings, acquire new books, and mount exhibitions, new emphasis on media formats now adds an even greater burden on the budgets of libraries. In the visual identity for this congress, the ABF font evolved yet again, this time into a new, very light design. The letters were defined by their contours only – thin fine lines delicately placed – hence the name ABF Linear. In addition, the numeral *0* and the letter *O* were transformed into pie charts that are traditionally used in statistics to depict percentages. Comprised of orange, blue, green, and gray slices, they were sized differently according to the scale of the typographic line, sometimes breaking out of that scale. A playful animation celebrating New Year's Eve and the launch of the new congress brought the letterforms and pie charts to life.

Poster
Et si on parlait d'argent?
56e congrès
Association des bibliothécaires
de France, Paris
175 × 118.5 cm (68⅞ × 46⅝ in.)
Screen print
Printer: Sérica
Typefaces: ABF Linéaire, Akkurat
2010

Animation
New Year's e-card 2010
Association des bibliothécaires
de France, Paris
Typeface: ABF Linéaire
Length: 30"
2009

Théâtre du Beauvaisis

The Théâtre du Beauvaisis in Beauvais, the largest city in northern France's Picardie region, offers a multidisciplinary program. In 2012, Apeloig refreshed the existing logo (design by Sevan Demirdjian in 2002) to create one that is visually dense and compact. It consists of four parallel lines arranged in rectangular formation, announcing the theater's name. The word "Beauvaisis" (the term for the region surrounding the city) has been divided in two and placed on lines three and four, highlighting the word "beau" (beautiful) at the center of the design. The letters are set in Argo, a contrasted sans serif typeface designed by Gerard Unger between 1988 and 1992. Like the earlier logo, the letters are cut on a fifty-degree angle. Small slashes interspersed throughout intensify the logo's vibrancy and solidity and act as a visual translation of a musical phrase.

On the program for the 2012–13 season, the numbers "12–13," composed of bright pink dotted lines, fill the visual field in a regular, geometric, angular matrix. These lines trace a fine path across the white cover, like whispers, and wrap themselves lightly around the central logo. Their apparent fragility contrasts strongly with the logo's black letters and their imposing, rounded silhouette – contrasts that evoke the ephemeral nature of the performing arts in a place that is permanent and brings people together.

Program
Saison 2012 – 13
Théâtre du Beauvaisis, Beauvais
29 × 19.5 cm (11³⁄₈ × 7⅝ in.), 80 pages
Typeface: DTL Argo
2012

Santarelli and CO

Santarelli and CO is a marketing and communications agency located in Paris. The firm's name derives from the family name of co-founder Christine Santarelli and the initials of her partner, Christopher Oldcorn, though the letters *c* and *o* can also be read as an abbreviation of "company."

The letterforms of the logo call to mind sculptures with the vitality of graphic characters. The four syllables of Santarelli are cut and placed on different lines, upsetting our reading patterns with alternating rows of three letters, then two, then three again. The logo is almost an architectural form with broken lines and open corners, no curves, and the same thickness throughout.

The logo's assemblage of forms creates a dissonance similar to that of Dadaism. Cut into segments, it playfully suggests that a complex problem can be analysed and solved if broken down creatively.

Stationary
Santarelli and CO, Paris
Offset and screen print
Typeface: Deck
2010
See page 295

```
20
rue Moreau
75012
Paris

01 44 67 96 13

www.
santarelli
andco.com
```

```
20
rue Moreau
75012
Paris

01 44 67 96 13

www.
santarelli
andco.com
```

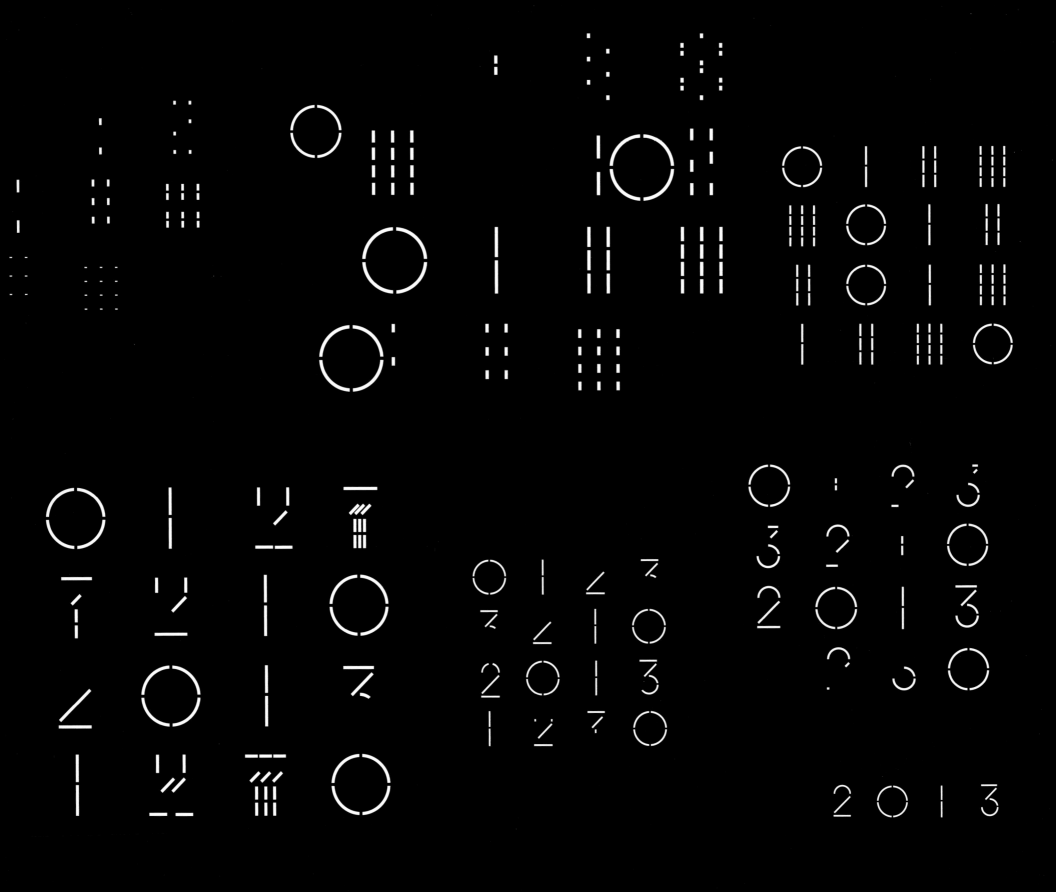

Claudine Colin Communication

Claudine Colin Communication is a public-relations agency that provides specialized consulting services for cultural events. The strategy behind the logo design was straightforward: to repeat the three Cs that are the initials of the company. Each *C* is composed of four elements: two black triangles, a black semicircle, and a white triangle that resembles an arrow. This arrow infuses the design with clear direction and perpetual movement, symbolizing the agency's commercial objectives.

Philippe Apeloig's New Year's greeting cards for the company take the form of graphic animations. Since 2006, he had produced a succession of ballets of geometric forms set to the music of his choice. In the 2011 animation, colored brackets – schematic images of the number *1* – transform into colorful squares, then shrink back into lines, forming the number *11*. The animation is set to the 1988 two-part percussion work *Rebonds* by Greek composer Iannis Xenakis. The morphing does not stop until the squares fill the screen. In 2013, fragmented straight lines and bits of circles, white on a black background, moved to the rhythm of Brazilian percussion.

Animation
New Year's e-cards 2013
Claudine Colin Communication, Paris
Length: 34"
2012

Logotype
Claudine Colin Communication, Paris
2008

Animation
New Year's e-cards 2011
Claudine Colin Communication, Paris
Length: 34"
2010

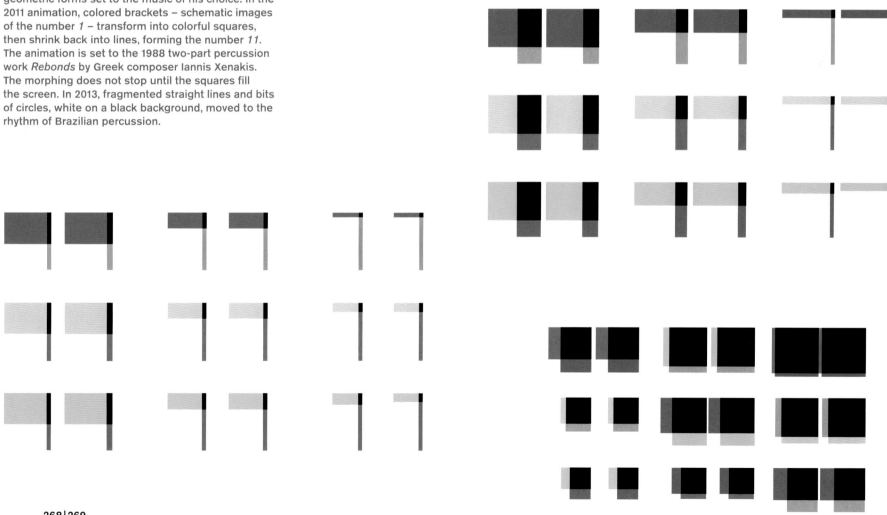

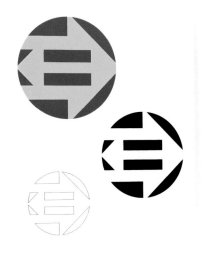

European Ombudsman
Médiateur européen

European Ombudsman
Médiateur européen

Press Pack

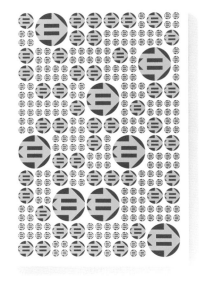

5.5.1
document bag
321 x 240 mm

Red Europea de Defensores del Pueblo
Europäisches Verbindungsnetz der Bürgerbeauftragten
European Network of Ombudsmen
Réseau européen des Médiateurs
Rete europea dei difensori (civici)

Médiateur européen

The European Ombudsman (EO), or Le Médiateur européen, investigates the bases of complaints concerning maladministration within institutions of the European Union (EU). Through it, any citizen, EU resident, business, society, or organization with its official headquarters in the EU can seek redress. Apeloig's logo, two arrows within a circle, communicates the EO's integral role in finding solutions to these problems.

The bidirectional arrows create an equal sign, reflecting balanced, two-way relationships and exchanges. The circle's unbroken line and abstract shape symbolize unity, an image understood by all member states, regardless of culture and language. The palette is yellow and blue, the colors of the EU flag. The extremely readable Frutiger Next font – a new interpretation of the well-known typeface Frutiger released in 2000 by Adrian Frutiger and Linotype – was chosen for its pureness and versatility in the Latin, Cyrillic, and Greek alphabets.

A complementary logo was created for an offshoot of the EO, the European Network of Ombudsmen (ENO), which brings together more than one hundred ombudsmen from across Europe to promote knowledge of European law and share good practices between mediators. For this logo, three arrows rotate in a circle, suggesting partnership and unity; the arrowheads symbolize possible meeting points for diverse factions. The logo is executed in a spectrum of vivid solid colors that represent the diversity of its members.

Design guide
Press release folder
Press release
Notepad
**Médiateur européen,
Brussels, Strasbourg**
Typeface: Frutiger Next
2009

Design guide
Press release folder
Press release
Notepad
European Network of Ombudsmen
Typeface: Frutiger Next
2009

Logotype
**Médiateur européen,
Brussels, Strasbourg**
2009

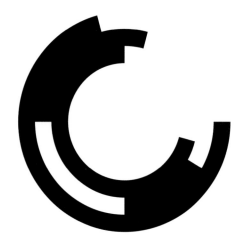

Icade
Foncière-développeur

Icade, a commercial property developer founded in 2003, is a major competitor in the French real estate market. Its logo represents the doorway of a large office building and an "open door" welcoming new business.

Shown slightly ajar, this "door" consists of a solid black parallelogram with a three-dimensional angle that creates a sense of spatial depth. It is also transformed, in the final logotype, into the letter *i* (for Icade) through the placement of a square dot above. This structural design, with its illusion of figurative imagery and implied narrative, establishes a virtual microcosm that invites the viewer to "push the door" and come discover what's inside.

Domaine
de Chaumont-sur-Loire

The Domaine de Chaumont-sur-Loire, acquired by France's Région Centre (Central Region) in 2008 and expanded in 2012, includes a famous fifteenth-century chateau and its vast grounds, along with a public arts center devoted to the relationship between artistic creation and nature, and a large exhibition space. The Domaine is renowned for its annual International Garden Festival, its role as a testing ground for the gardens of the future, and its ambitious policy of commissioning contemporary works of art.

The logo embodies the Domaine's architectural and historical heritage and its outstanding setting. The design is a stylized view of the castle entrance flanked by its two massive towers. The ever-longer dashed horizontal line evokes both the ongoing expansion of the site and the organic renewal of nature. The dash lengths and intervals are derived from the Fibonacci sequence, a mathematical concept that has fascinated artists. Allowing for the imagination – and the impression of light – to complete the undefined volumes and empty spaces, the logo represents the Domaine's history and mission with striking simplicity.

SAEM
Val-de-Seine aménagement

Val-de-Seine is one of the most important business districts in the greater Paris area. Located in the southwest of the city, it spreads along the bend of the river Seine, mainly in the municipality of Boulogne-Billancourt, the former site of the Renault car factory. The area encompasses the Île Seguin (Seguin Island) and a large trapezoidal section of land that is ear-marked for a multipurpose development with amenities for living, business, parks, and public and cultural spaces. The Val-de-Seine Aménagement (SAEM) manages this urban development plan.

The design for the SAEM logo is based on an aerial view of this suburban landscape as traversed by the curve of the Seine. The perfectly round shape —a circle one third open – with imperfect edges symbolizes the importance of the river to the area. A second visual component is the white curved shape inside the incomplete circle, an abstract representation of Seguin Island that is immediately recognizable to the region's inhabitants.

Logotype
Icade, Paris
2003
See pages 320 – 21

Logotype
Domaine de Chaumont-sur-Loire
2012
See page 289

Logotype
Val-de-Seine aménagement
Boulogne-Billancourt
2005

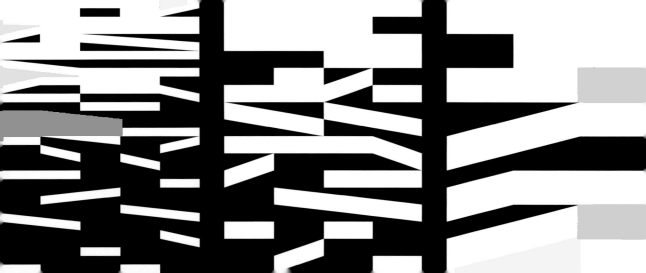

Voies navigables de France

Founded in 1991, the Voies navigables de France (VNF; Waterways of France) exploits, maintains, modernizes, and develops French waterways. Its role also includes the promotion of goods transport and waterways tourism. In 2013, VNF became a much larger entity with 4,700 employees. For that occasion VNF commissioned the Apeloig studio to create a new design that would enhance the existing logo and shape its new identity. Inspired by light reflecting from the surface of water, the logo is composed of horizontal and softly angled particles in a palette of soft blue, dark blue, and green against a white background. The particles appear in three sets of light, medium, and bold, representing long, mid-range, and close-up views. Each set is arranged within its own visual field and follows a grid that has a different number of columns: five, four, and three. They can be shown together or individually, creating a versatile system.

The design has multiple connotations: the geographic disposition of rivers, streams, and canals in France; the navigation of barges and boats; the light-reflecting qualities of water; and the fluid movement of rivers and tributaries. The new identity emphasizes VNF's mission of environmental preservation.

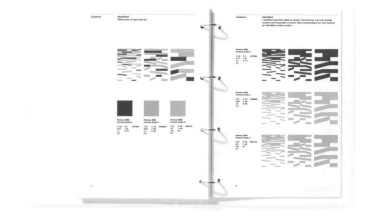

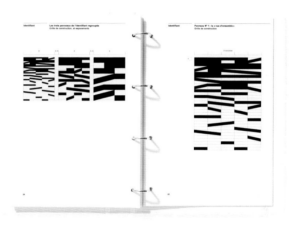

Symbol
Voies navigables de France
2013
See pages 286 – 287

Design guide
Voies navigables de France
32 × 25 cm (12⅝ × 9⅞ in.)
Typeface: Fakt Pro
2013

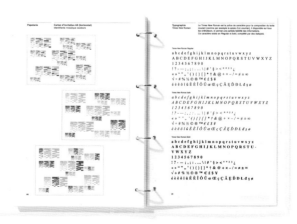

Puiforcat

Philippe Apeloig was invited to work on the brand redesign for Puiforcat, a Parisian silversmith active since 1820. Puiforcat is a brand that straddles tradition and modernity and is renowned for producing both functional and artistic pieces in a classical, historical style, as well as in Art Deco or contemporary styles. The logo has three stacked elements: a pictogram, the company name, and the word "Paris."

One of the masterpieces in the collection of Louis-Victor Puiforcat, the father of Jean – who established the company – is the Anne of Austria beaker (now kept at the Louvre). For his logo redesign, Apeloig revived this symbol in a stylized version that shows the reflection of light on metal. The result is a contemporary pictogram that respects the traditional proportions of the object. As the word "Puiforcat" has an equal number of letters on either side of the letter *O*, Apeloig established the middle of the pictogram as a vertical axis.

Apeloig updated and customized the font to be graphically dynamic, taking subtle cues from the Art Deco movement and from technical drawings in the company archives. He was inspired by forms such as the cube, sphere, and cone, which are central to many Puiforcat pieces, as well as by the original drawings of Jean Puiforcat, whose monogram designs were very geometric. Apeloig redesigned the Puiforcat logo in this spirit, with the *O* a pure circle, the *A* a triangle, and the *U* a square.

Logotype
Puiforcat, Paris
2012
See page 288

New Year's greeting card
Puiforcat, Paris
21 × 14.8 cm (8¼ × 5⅞ in.)
2012

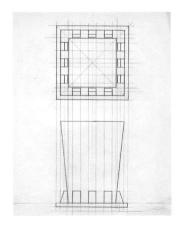

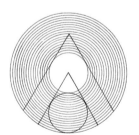

Jean Puiforcat (1897 – 1945)
Cup Drawing
Graphite and ink on paper
Collection Puiforcat, Paris

Jean Puiforcat (1897 – 1945)
Monogram OA
Ink on paper
Collection Puiforcat, Paris

Louvre Abu Dhabi

The Louvre Abu Dhabi, designed by Jean Nouvel in the capital's vast cultural district, Saadiyat Island, right beside the sea, is an example of architectural and aesthetic prowess combining modernity and echoes of great Islamic architecture, notably that of palaces. The dome, 180 meters in diameter, filters the sun's rays like an enormous *mashrabiya*. The space is bathed in a shower of constantly shifting light that spreads over the geometric forms sheltered by the dome and incites meditation and discovery.

For the museum's logo, Philippe Apeloig chose to symbolize the building's spiritual dimension and recreate its very particular climate. The challenge was to evoke the mysterious whiteness and lightness of this exceptional space, including the region's warm temperatures. The logo's flat outline alludes in an abstract fashion to the horizontality of the building's architecture, which is accentuated by its proximity to the sea. A thick straight line, like a hyphen between two cultures (East and West), hatched with black lines in different directions, illustrates and gives form to the kinetic effects of light. These, in turn, are the starting point for the pictograms. Depending upon the optical perception, this line is made up of a series of yphens of different widths that embody the link between the cultures and two scripts used in the logo. The typography combines Frutiger, a modern font widely used for signage, and LAD Arabic, a classical-looking *naskh*-style font with its pronounced calligraphy, which Kristyan Sarkis, a young Lebanese typographer, designed in 2013.

Logotype
Louvre Abu Dhabi
Typefaces: Frutiger, LAD Arabic
2013
See pages 282–83

Pictograms
Louvre Abu Dhabi
2013
See page 283

LOUVRE ABU DHABI ▮▮◢◤◢▮ اللوفر أبوظبي

Sketches

LOUVRE ABU DHABI

LOUVRE

LOUVRE ABU DHABI

LOUVRE   اللوفر

LOUVRE ABU DHABI   اللوفر ابوظبي

Logotype
Pictograms
Louvre Abu Dhabi
2013
See page 279

LOUVRE ABU DHABI
اللــوفر أبــوظبي

SAUT
HERMÈS

SAU
SAUT
SAUES
HERMÈS

12 13 14
AVRIL
SAUT
HERMÈS
GRAND
PALAIS
PARIS

TYPO D'AVENIR

SAUT
HERMÈS
12 13 14
AVRIL 2013
GRAND
PALAIS
PARIS

12 13 14
AVRIL 2013
SAUT
HERMÈS
GRAND
PALAIS
PARIS

JUMPING
INTERNATIONAL
CSI 5
12 13 14
AVRIL 2013
AU GRAND
PALAIS
PARIS

WWW.SAUTHERMES.COM   RÉSERVATION: FNAC, VIRGIN ET POINTS DE VENTE HABITUELS.

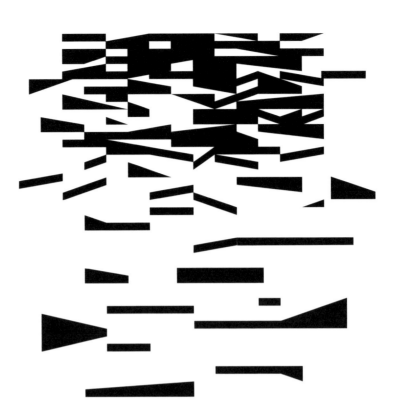

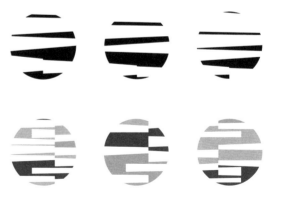

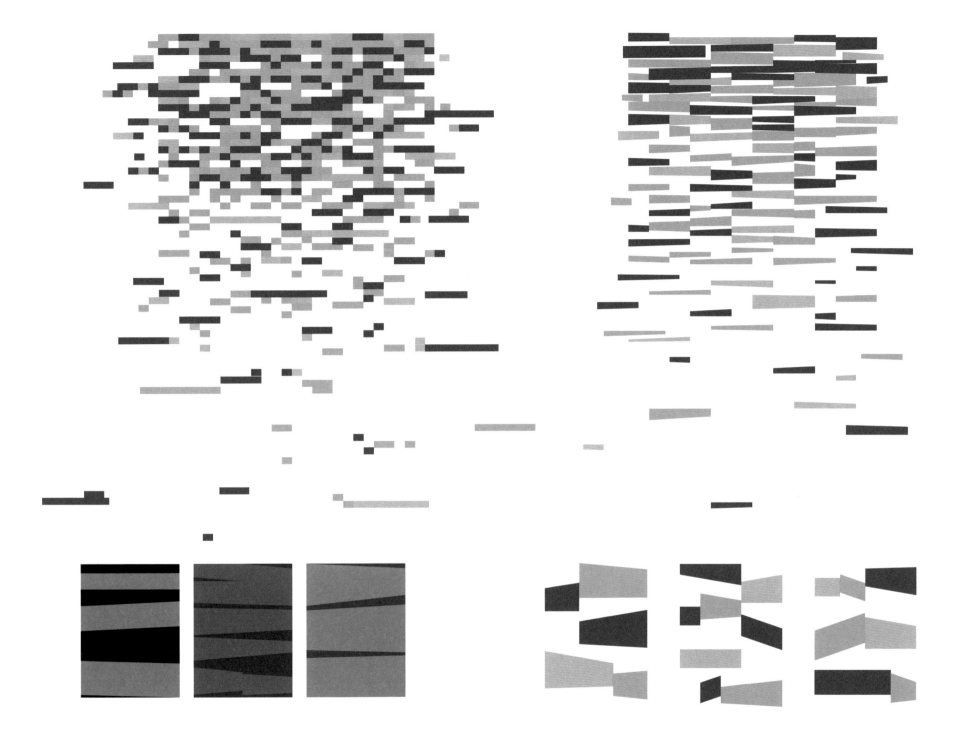

Logotype
Puiforcat, Paris
2012
See page 276

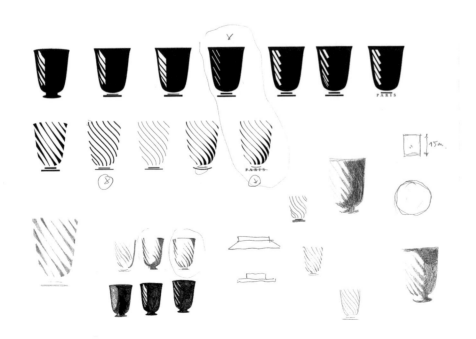

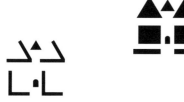

THÉÂTRE
NATIONAL
DE
TOULOUSE

MIDI-
PYRÉNÉES

SAISON
2012-13

Poster
Saison 2012–13
Théâtre national de Toulouse
Midi-Pyrénées
2012
See page 105

Poster
Geoffroy Tory.
Imprimeur de François Ier
Graphiste avant la lettre
Musée national de la Renaissance,
Écouen
2011
See page 64

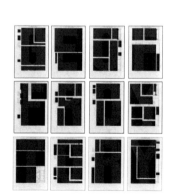

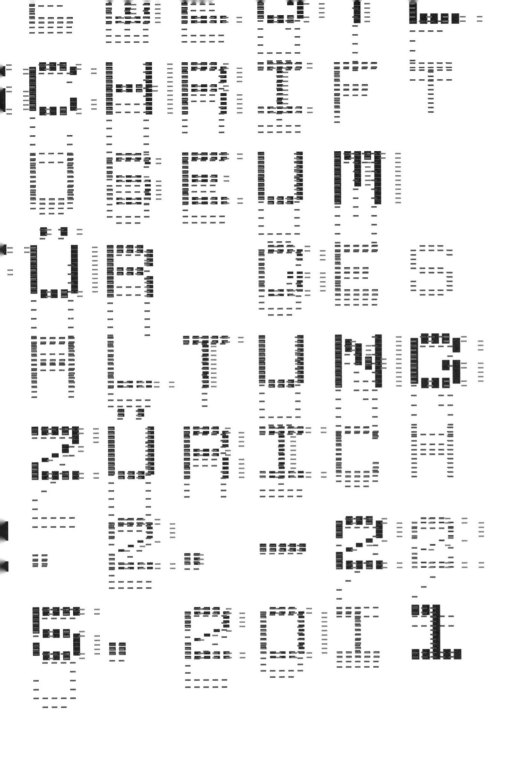

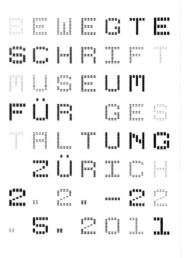

Poster
Bewegte Schrift
Museum für Gestaltung, Zurich
2011
See page 206

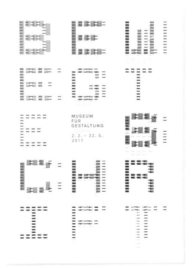
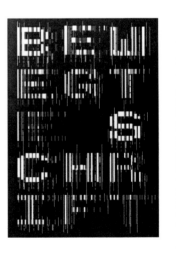

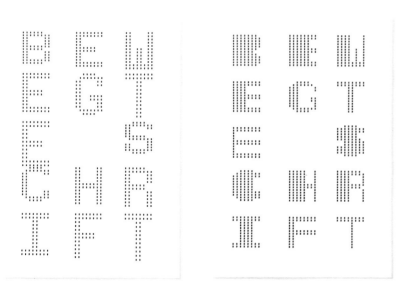
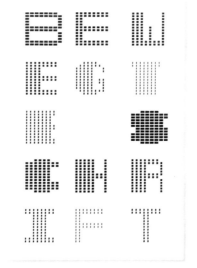
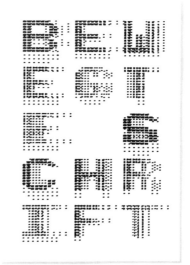
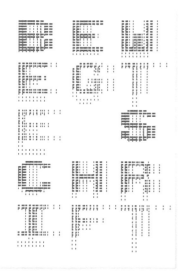

MUSEUM
FÜR
GESTALTUNG
ZÜRICH
2.2. –
22.5.2011

Poster
Crossing the Line,
FIAF Fall Festival 2010
French Institute Alliance Française,
New York
2010
See page 248

Logotype
Santarelli and CO, Paris
2010
See page 267

Poster
Radical Jewish Culture
Scène musicale New York
Musée d'art et d'histoire
du Judaïsme, Paris
2010
See page 203

CULTURE
SCENE
MUSICALE
NEW
YORK

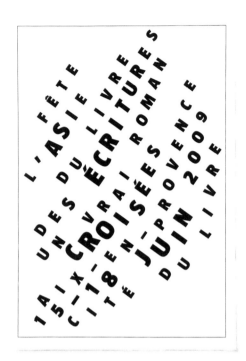

Poster
**L'Asie des écritures croisées,
Un vrai roman
Fête du livre, Aix-en-Provence**
2009
See page 187

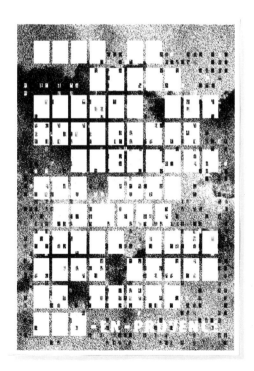

Poster
**Frida and Diego
A Creative Love
AGI, Alliance Graphique Internationale**
2008
See page 199

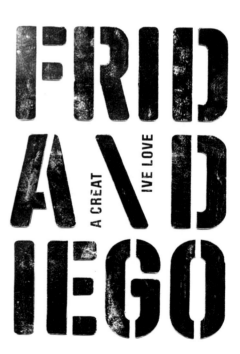

Exposit...

alfred
NOBEL

au servi...

de l'innovation

du 7 octob...

...al aie au 11 janvie...

Poster
Alfred Nobel
Au service de l'innovation
Palais de la découverte, Paris
2008
See page 200

Poster
Wole Soyinka,
La maison et le monde
Fête du livre, Aix-en-Provence
2007
See page 184

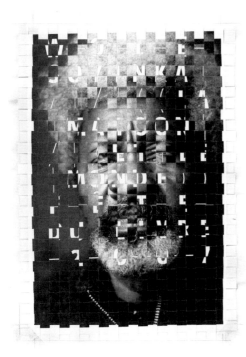

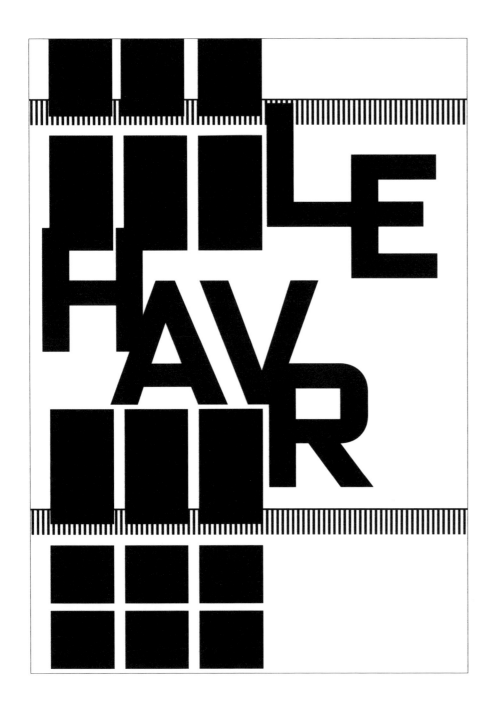

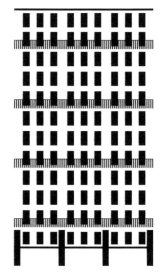

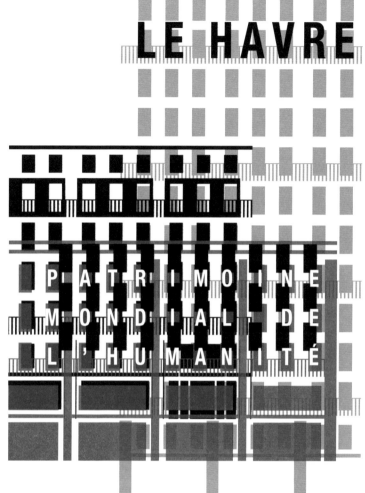

Poster
Le Havre,
Patrimoine mondial de l'humanité
2006
See page 194

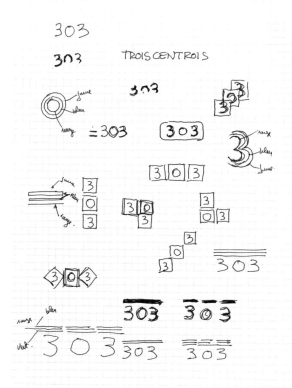

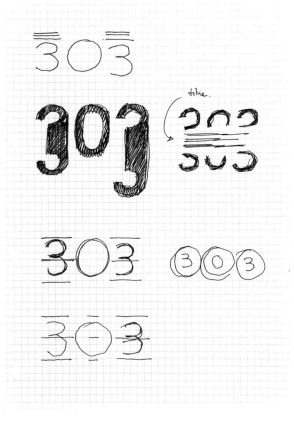

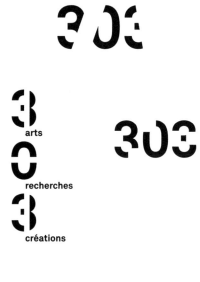

Logotype
303, Arts, recherches et créations, Nantes
2006
See page 120

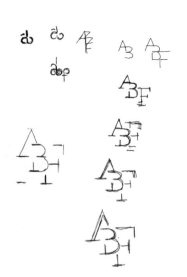

Logotype
**Association des bibliothécaires
de France, Paris**
2006
See page 260

Poster
Kenzaburō Ōé
Je suis de nouveau un homme
Fête du livre, Aix-en-Provence
2006
See page 183

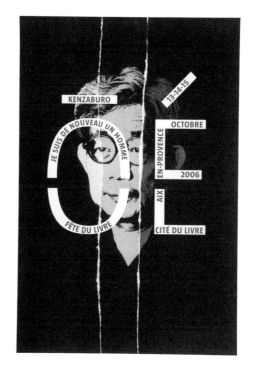

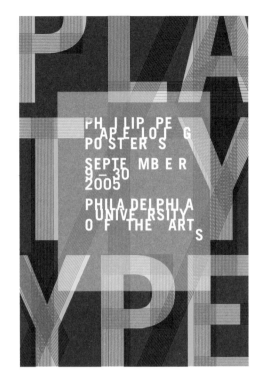

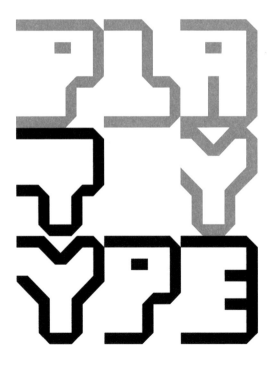

Poster
PlayType
University of the Arts, Philadelphia
2005
See page 165

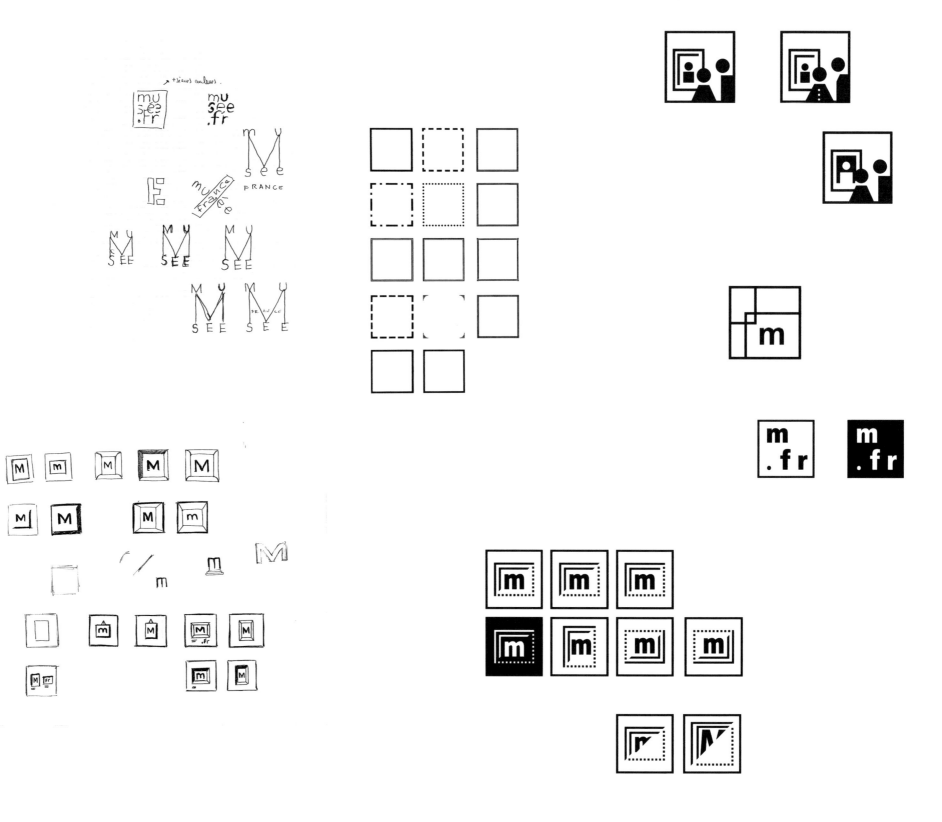

 musée de France

musée.fr

Logotype
Direction des musées de France, Paris
2004
See page 226

Logotype
BrésilBrésils
Association Française
d'Action Artistique
2005
See page 239

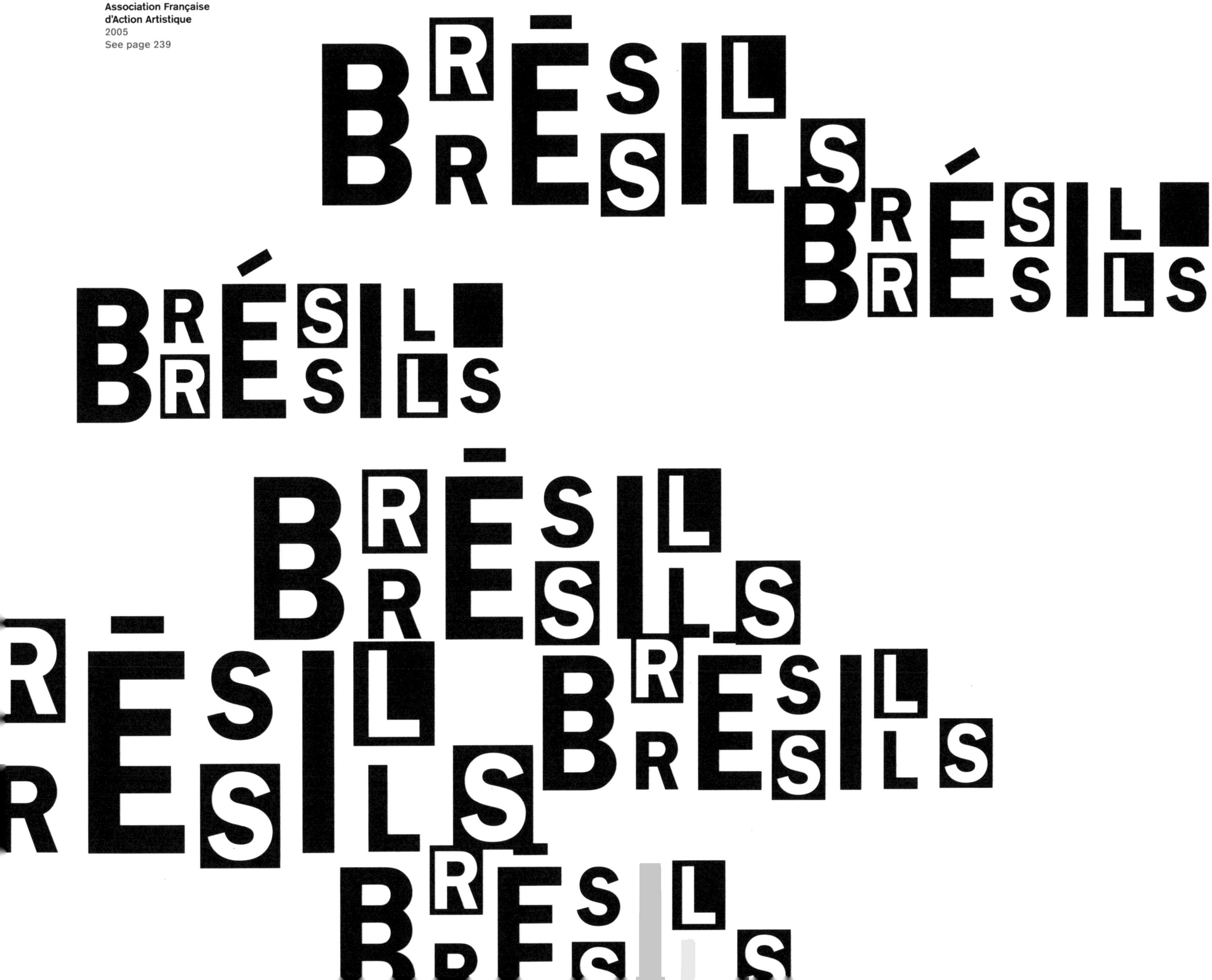

BRÉSIL
BRÉSILS
BRÉSIL
BRÉSILS
BRÉSIL
BRÉSILS
BRÉSIL
BRÉSILS
BRÉSIL
BRÉSILS
BRÉSIL
BRÉSILS

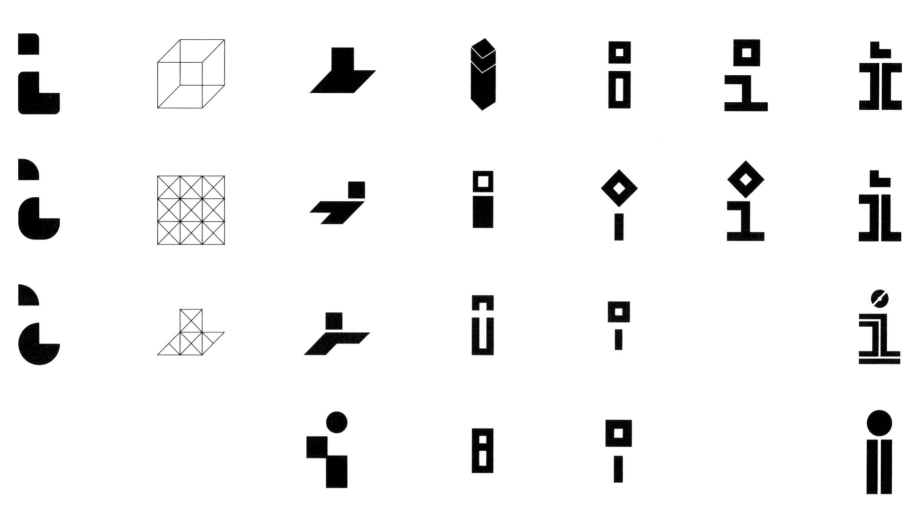

Logotype
Icade, Paris
2003
See page 273

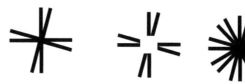

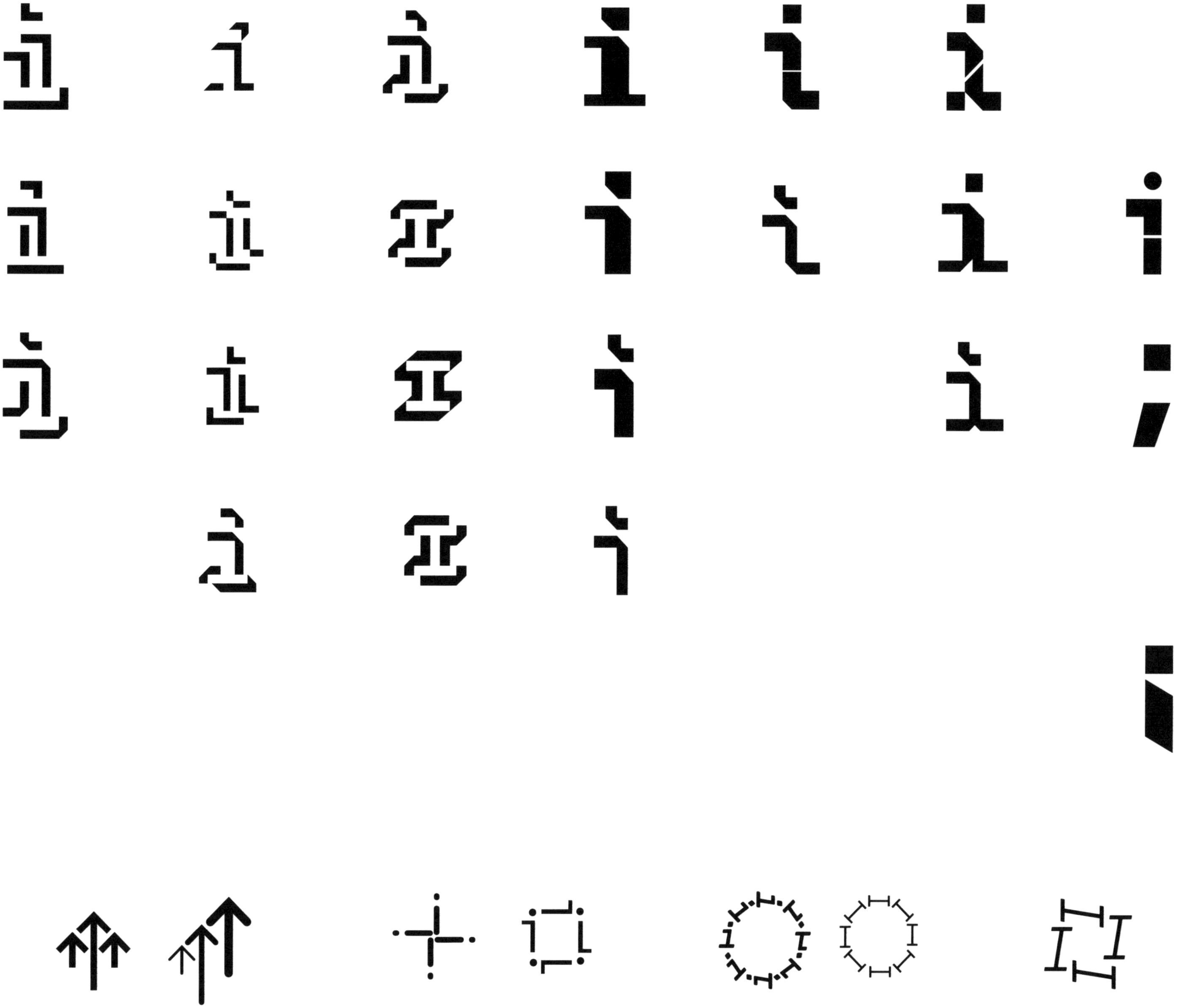

Poster
Une autre Amérique
Fête du livre, Aix-en-Provence
2004

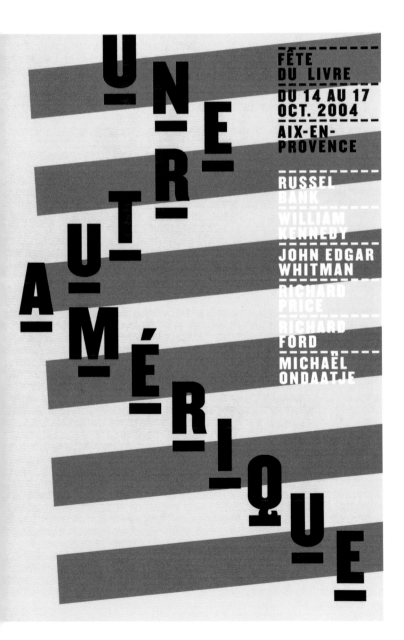

Logotype
Compagnie Régis Obadia, Paris
2004
See page 88

Poster
Vis pour nous/Vis sans nous
2003
See page 27

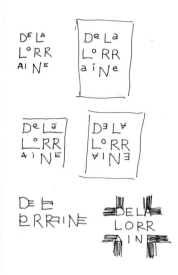

Poster
**De la Lorraine,
Histoires, mémoires, regards
contemporains
Musée des Beaux-Arts, Nancy
Musée de la Cour d'Or, Metz**
2003
See page 169

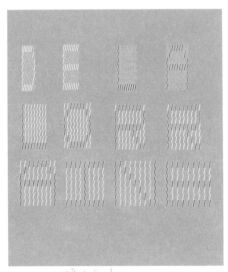

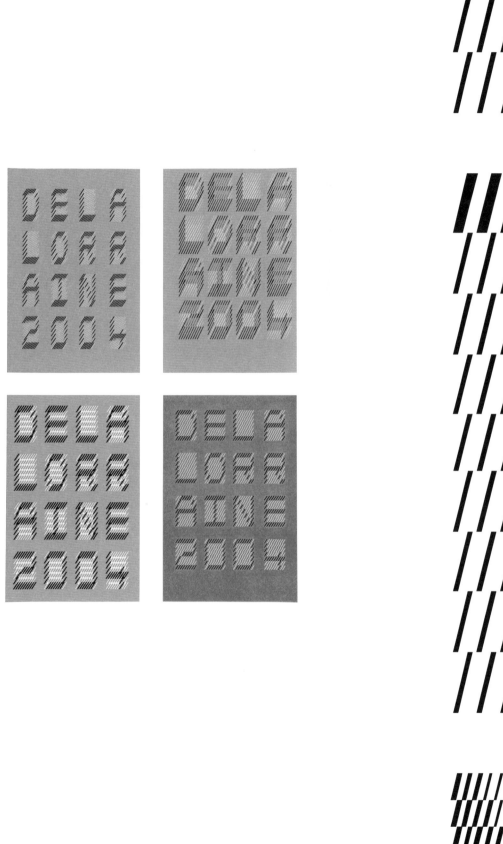
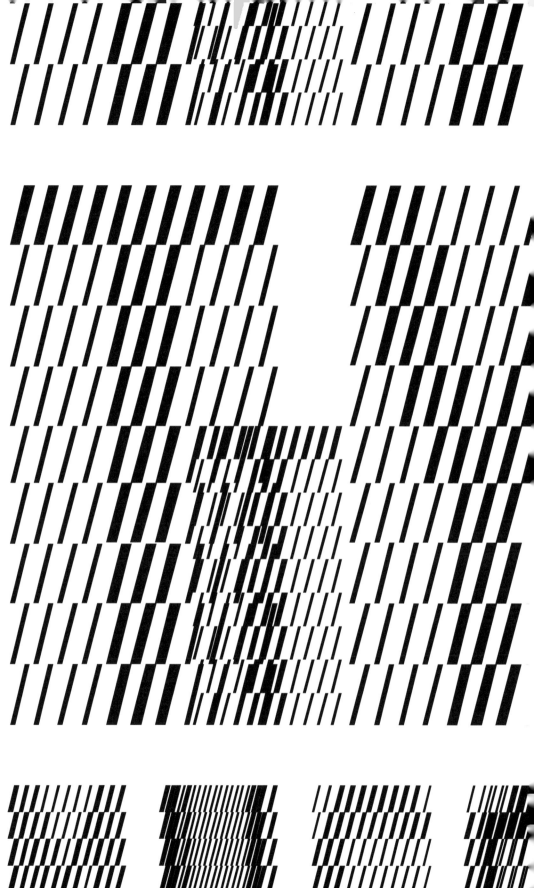

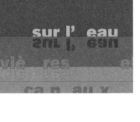

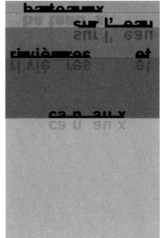

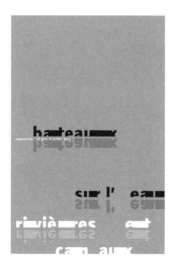

Poster
Bateaux sur l'eau, rivières et canaux
Armada de Rouen
Voies navigables de France
2003
See page 192

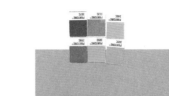

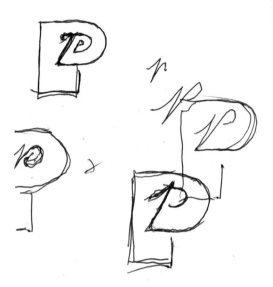

Logotype
Petit Palais
Musée des Beaux-Arts
de la Ville de Paris
2004
See page 232

Logotype
Festival Rose et Fafner
Flamanville
2003
See page 87

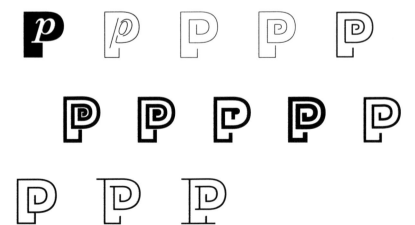

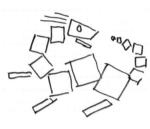

#6

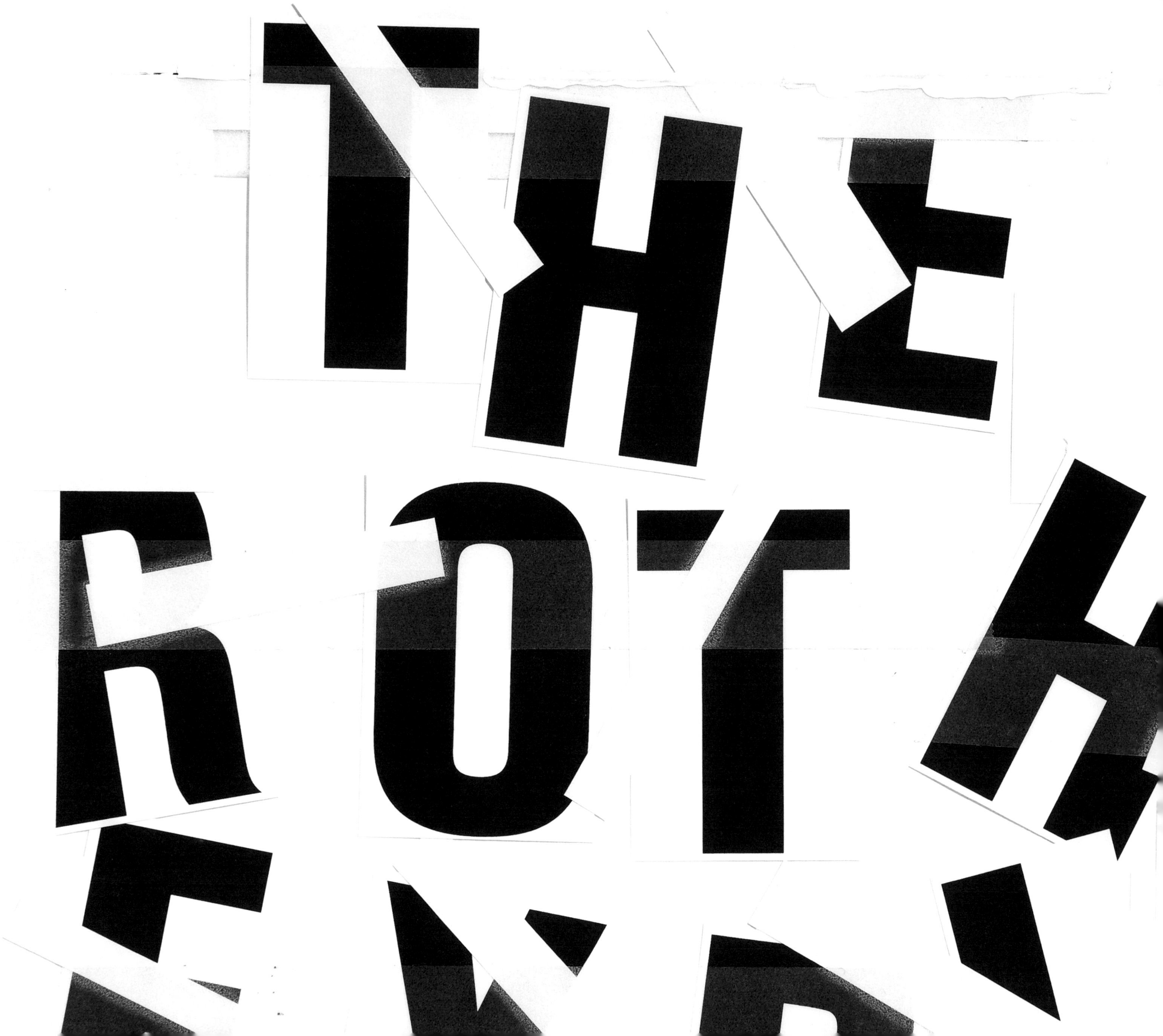
THE
ROT

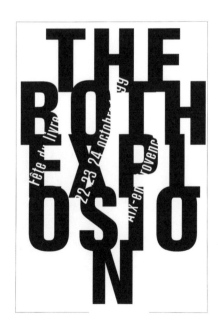

Poster
The Roth Explosion
Fête du livre, Aix-en-Provence
1999
See page 181

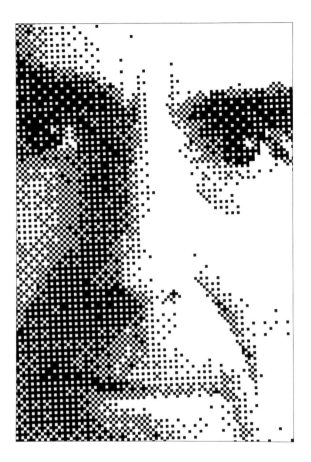

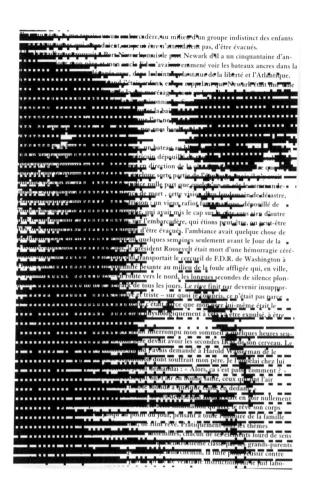

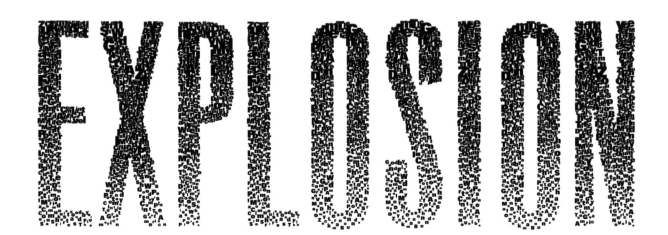

Poster
Louvre
Dix ans de la pyramide
Saison 1998–99
1998
See page 54

Card
New Year's greeting card 1998
Philippe Apeloig, Paris
1997

Leaflet
New Year's greeting card 1999
Philippe Apeloig, Paris
1998

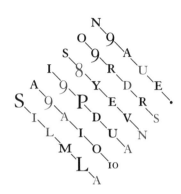

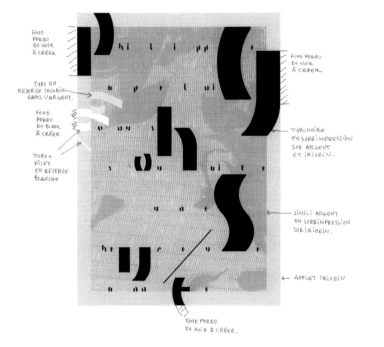

VERSION "VOEUX AVEC DATES"

philippe apeloig vous souhaite une heureuse année

Poster
Naissance et Renaissance
Octobre en Normandie, Rouen
1998

Poster
Lire la Caraïbe, Haiti, Cuba
Fête du livre, Aix-en-Provence
1998
See page 179

Lire Haïti
Caraïbe
Cuba la

Logotype
**Musée d'art et d'histoire
du Judaïsme, Paris**
1997
See page 230

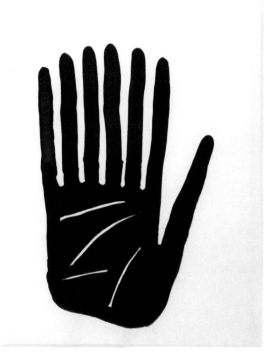

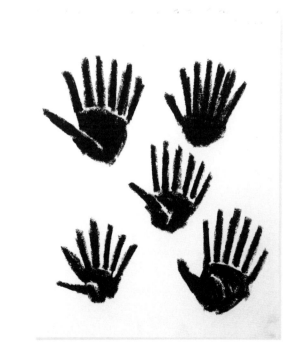

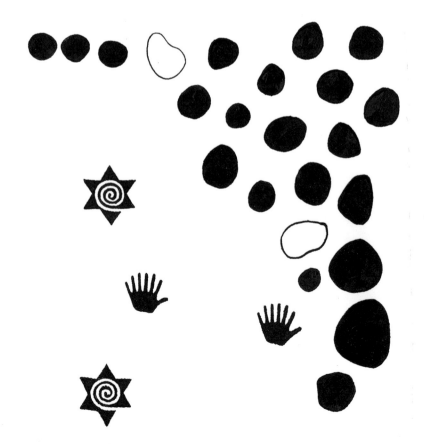

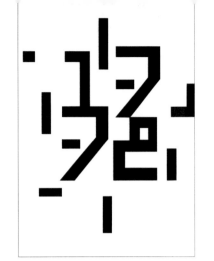

Folded poster
New Year's greeting card 1998
Philippe Apeloig, Paris
1997
See page 218

Poster
La ville en fête
La ville blessée, la ville sonore
Octobre en Normandie, Rouen
1997

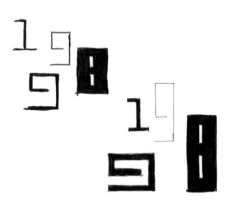

la ville blessée

la ville blessée

la ville blessée

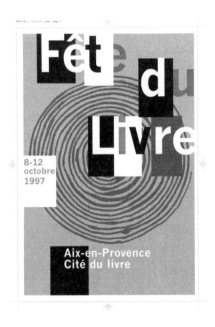

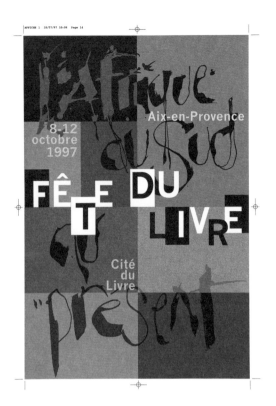

Poster
L'Afrique du Sud au présent
Fête du livre, Aix-en-Provence
1997
See page 176

l'Afrique du Sud
au présent

Leaflet
New Year's greeting card 1997
Philippe Apeloig, Paris
1996
See page 218

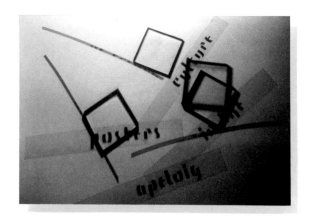

Invitation
Philippe Apeloig:
Posters in the Context of French Culture
GGG Ginza Graphic Gallery, Tokyo
1998
See page 164

a b c d e f g
h i j k l m n
o p q r s t u
v w x y z

1 2 3 4 5 6 7
8 9 0
A B C D F

Typeface
Aleph
1993–94
See page 164

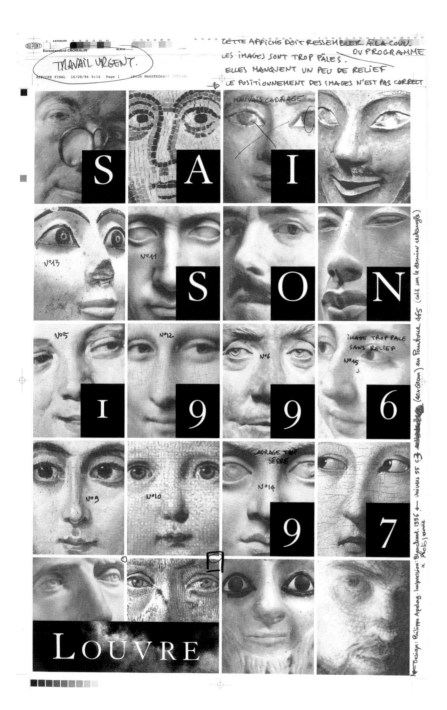

Poster
Saison 1996–97
Musée du Louvre, Paris
1996
See page 51

Poster
Octobre ouvre la saison en musique
Octobre fait danser la saison
Octobre en Normandie, Rouen
1995
See page 84

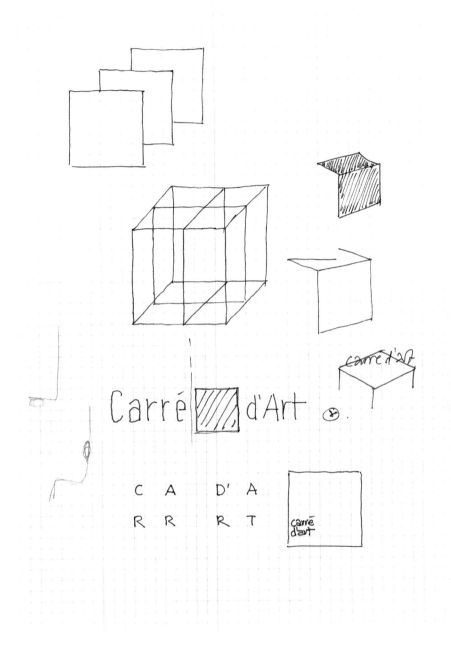

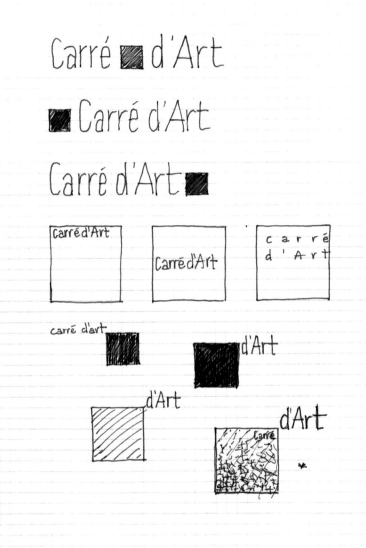

Logotype
Carré d'Art, Nîmes
1993
See page 224

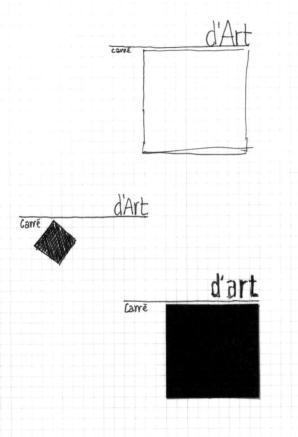

Carré d'Art

Carré d'Art

Carré d'art

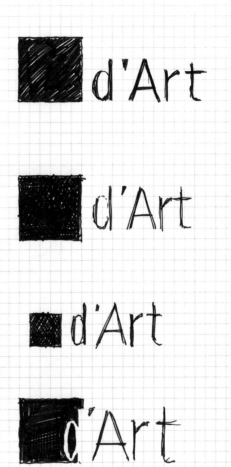

d'Art

d'Art

d'Art

c'Art

Typeface
Octobre
1993 – 94
See page 84

Leaflet
Approche Philippe Apeloig
Institut français, Barcelona
1995
See page 162

Poster
**Théâtre national populaire,
Villeurbanne**
1993

Didier Imbert
19 avenue Matignon
Paris

701

7 Panneau "façade de la maison"   1 Panneau Format: Largeur 1125 / Hauteur 640 cm
Avec une découpe particulière

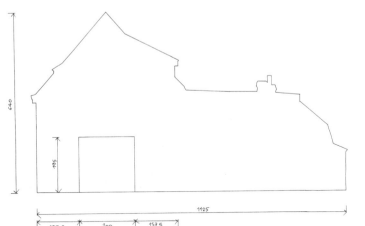

Didier Imbert
19 avenue Matignon
Paris

Moore intime
3 avril-26 juillet 1992

Moore intime

Trianon de Bagatelle
Rond-Point des Champs-Elysées

12 avril-26 juillet 1991

Didier Imbert Fine Art
19, avenue Matignon. Paris 8ème

Didier Imbert Fine Art

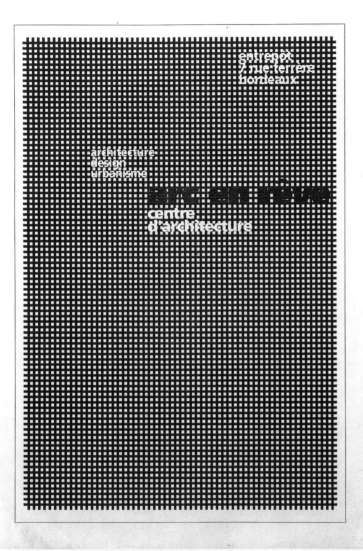

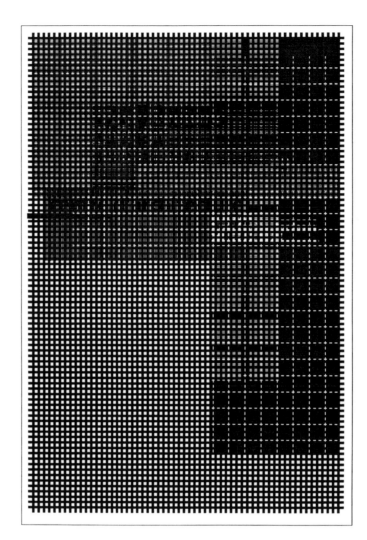

Poster
Arc en rêve
centre d'architecture, Bordeaux
1992
See page 161

octobre

octobre

octobre

octobre

octobre

octobre

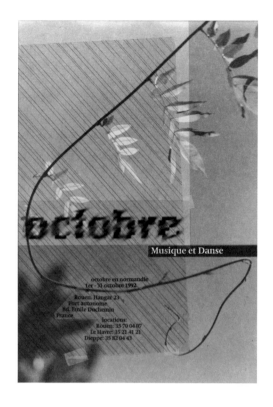

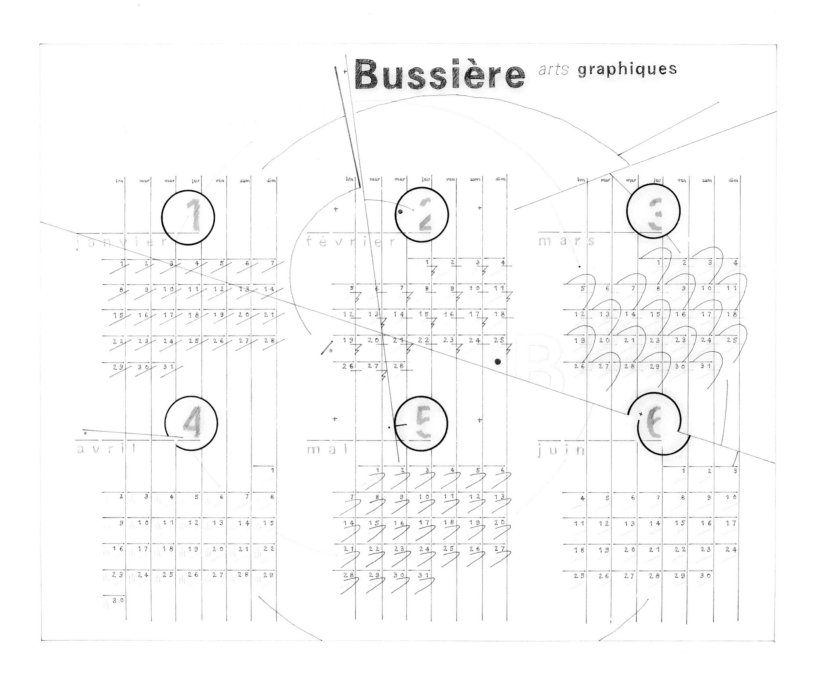

Bussière *arts* graphiques

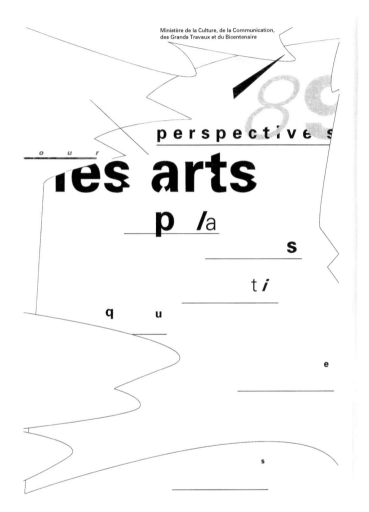

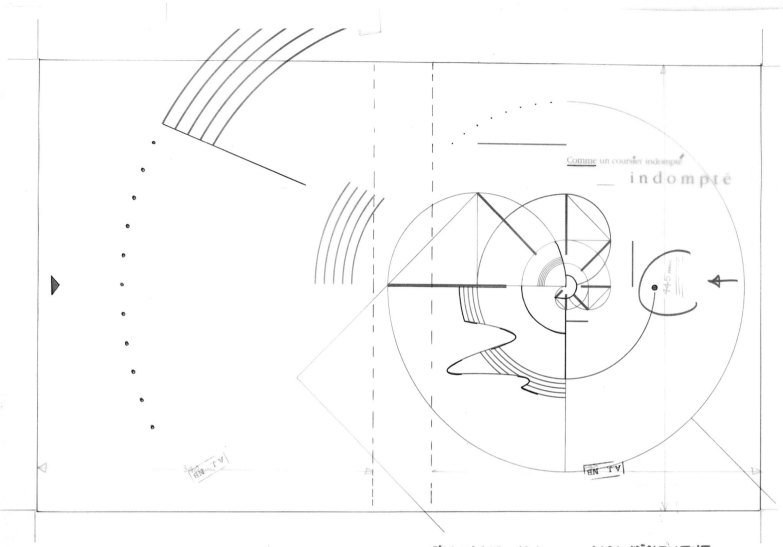

Comme un coursier indompté
indompté

DOCUMENT N° 1   AGRANDISSEMENT
SUR BROMURE POSITIF

PHILIPPE APELOÏG.
42.71.54.43.

Slipcase
Comme un coursier indompté
Imprimerie nationale
Centre national des arts plastiques
1989
See page 110

Poster
Musée d'Orsay, Paris
Project for the opening of the
museum (not realized)
1986

Poster
Quai ouest de Bernard-Marie Koltès
Théâtre des Amandiers, Nanterre
(not realized)
1983

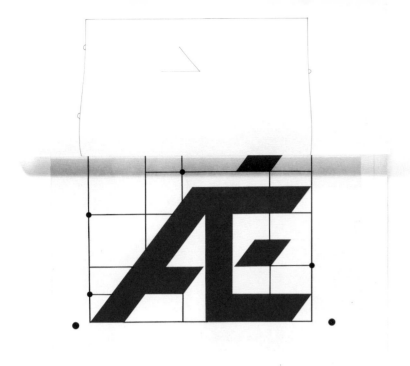

Poster
Chicago
Naissance d'une métropole
1872 – 1922
Musée d'Orsay, Paris
1987
See page 36

Resources

Philippe Apeloig
Born in Paris in 1962

**Permanent studio staff
since 2009**
Anna Brugger
Yannick James

**Principal staff,
post-1990
In chronological order**
Sebastian Peetz
Tobias Keller
Daniel Utz
Ben Salesse
Ellen Zhao
Jurgen Waidelich
Manija Emran
Élamine Maecha
Matthias Neuer

Occasional staff
Graphics (Paris)
Sevan Demirdjian
Léo Grunstein
Jean-Benoît Lévy
Benoît Perrier
Clovis Vallois

Graphics (New York)
Marion Bizet
Alexandra Brand
Carin Fortin
Ronny Quevedo
Mathilde Roussel-Giraudy
Damien Saatdjian

Animation
Vadim Bernard
Jean-Patrice Blanc
Matthias Orsi

Typography
Benjamin Gomez
Anton Studer
and Clovis Vallois
(Apeloig Type Library,
www.nouvellenoire.ch)

and
Jean-Charles Bassenne
James Bolton
Pascal Guédin
Gaël Le Maître
Olivier Marcellin
Joël Renaudat
Domitille Roblot
Edith Wilsdorf

Interns
Paramdeep Bahia, Alexandra Bauch,
Marie Bertholle, Bastian Bischoff,
Andrée Blattner, Antje Booken,
Pascal Botlik, Sybille Bucher,
Maruxa Carranza, Charlotte Cohen,
Delphine Cormier, John Crawford,
Benjamin Dennel, Franklin Desclouds,
Julien Dhivert, Katrin Dittmann,
Amélie Doistau, Sébastien Dragon,
François-Romain Dumont,
Marine Duroselle, Léo Favier,
Carin Fortin, Severin Frank, Lorenzo
Geiger, Nicolas Girard, Léo Grunstein,
Bianca Gumbrecht, Laura Gutz,
Anja Haas, Adrien Hofer, Steffi Holz,
Young Jin, Erwann Kervadec,
Maryse Khoriaty, Anja Krohne,
Loïc Lévèque, Julie Linotte,
Diana Lischer, Hadrien Lopez
Caquelard, Sylvestre Lucia,
Xavier Majewski, Amélie Manac'h,
Susanne Markovski, Juliane Mars,
Claudia Martinez, Nicolas Merlhiot,
Philippe Millot, Sébastien Millot,
Mikaël Mourgue, Alexandre Müller,
Caroline Pauchant, Samuel Perroud,
Mari Pietarinen, Virginie Poilièvre,
Nicolas Portnoï, Olivier Pouzet,
Simon Renner, Valentin Robinet,
Nour Sabbag, Simon Santschi,
Oliver Schmid, Laura Schmitt,
Sebastian Schmitt, Karen Schmutz,
Christian Schwentke, Roman Seban,
Edgard Sisto, Julie Soistier, Michaela
Spohn, Aleksander Struczyk, Irène
Thomas, Nadine Unterharrer, Clovis
Vallois, Rémy Valton, Klaartje Van Eijk,
Alexandre Viault, Elena Vieillard,
Svenja Voß, Irmi Wachendorff,
David Watson, Kristina Wießner,

And Camille Dupaquier,
Jackie Sweeney.

Apologies if anyone has inadvertently
been missed.

Main exhibitions

1990
"Philippe Apeloig, Affiches,"
Impressions Gallery, Paris

1990 – 91
"Philippe Apeloig, Affiches," Arc en rêve
centre d'architecture, Bordeaux

1998
"Posters in the Context of French Culture,"
DDD Gallery, Osaka, organized by Dai Nippon
Printing Company

"Posters in the Context of French Culture,"
GGG Gallery, Tokyo, organized by Dai Nippon
Printing Company

1999
"The Lingering Memory," Houghton Gallery,
Cooper Union School of Art, New York

2000
"Le musée s'affiche/Posters for Museums,"
La Maison Française,
New York University, New York

2001
"Au cœur du mot," Galerie Anatome, Paris

Second International Poster Exhibition
(group exhibition), Ningbo, China

2003
"Affiches Philippe Apeloig," La Médiatine,
Brussels, organized by the École Supérieure
des Arts de l'Image "Le 75"

"Affiches Philippe Apeloig," Galerija Avla NLB,
Ljubljana, organized by *Emzin Arts Magazine*

2004
Nineteenth International Poster Biennial
(group exhibition), Wilanów Poster Museum,
Warsaw

International Istanbul Graphic Design Week,
Institut français, Istanbul

"À la croisée du visible et du lisible,"
Dawson College, Montreal

2005
"Typo/Typé," Carré Sainte-Anne, Montpellier,
organized by the Galerie Anatome, Paris

"PlayType," Rosenwald-Wolf Gallery,
University of the Arts, Philadelphia

"Typo/Typé," Museum of Russian Art, Kiev,
organized by the Institut français of Ukraine

2006
"Typo & Konstrukcja" (group exhibition),
Miejska Galeria Sztuki, Łódz, Poland

2008
"Vivo in Typo, Affiches et alphabet animé,"
Espace Topographie de l'art, Paris

2009
"La typographie animée/ Animated
Typography," University of Quebec
in Montreal (UQAM), Montreal

2010
"Gravures, Portes," Atelier Didier Mutel, Paris

"OrienTYPOccident"
an exhibition of posters with Reza Abedini,
Centre Culturel Français, Damascus

2011
"Graphisme et création contemporaine"
(group exhibition), Bibliothèque nationale
de France, Paris

"Bewegte Schrift" (group exhibition),
Museum für Gestaltung, Zurich

"Graphic Design: Now in Production," Walker
Art Center, Minneapolis, group exhibition
organized by the Walker Art Center,
Minneapolis, and the Smithsonian
Institution's Cooper-Hewitt, National Design
Museum, New York

2013
"Matisse à l'affiche" (group exhibition),
Galerie des Ponchettes, Nice

Public and private collections
with Philippe Apeloig holdings:

Stedelijk Museum, Amsterdam
Les Silos, Maison du livre et de l'affiche,
  Chaumont, France
Deutsches Plakat Museum, Museum
  Folkwang, Essen, Germany
Poster Museum, Lahti, Finland
Smithsonian's Cooper-Hewitt,
  National Design Museum, New York
Merrill C. Berman Collection, New York
Museum of Modern Art, New York
Ogaki Poster Museum, Ogaki, Japan
Collection Emmanuel Bérard, Paris
Bibliothèque nationale de France, Paris
Les Arts Décoratifs, Paris
Poster Museum, National Museum, Wilanow
Museum für Gestaltung, Zurich

Main Awards

1988
Mention in the Grand Prix de l'Affiche
Culturelle de la Bibliothèque nationale
de France for the exhibition poster
"Chicago, Naissance d'une métropole,"
Musée d'Orsay, Paris

1992
Silver Award, International Computer
Graphics Art Exhibition, Tokyo, for the
exhibition poster "Henry Moore intime,"
Galerie Didier Imbert, Paris

1995
Gold Award, Tokyo Type Directors Club,
for the posters for two events held as
part of the Octobre en Normandie festival:
"Octobre ouvre la saison en musique"
and "Octobre fait danser la saison."

1997
Philippe Apeloig becomes
a member of the Alliance Graphique
Internationale (AGI)

2004
Premier Award, International Typographic
Awards, International Society of Typographic
Designers (ISTD), London, for the exhibition
poster curated by the voies navigables
de France (VNF) "Bateaux sur l'eau, rivières
et canaux," Armada de Rouen

Golden Bee Award (poster category),
Golden Bee 6, Moscow International Biennial
of Graphic Design, for the exhibition poster
"Vis pour nous/Vis sans nous"

2006
First Prize, Five Star Designers' Banquet,
International Invitational Poster Biennial,
Osaka, prize organized by the University
of the Arts, Osaka, along with an exhibition
featuring Philippe Apeloig's entire *oeuvre*

2007
Gold Award (Promotion of Cultural
Events category), Hong Kong International
Poster Triennial, for the exhibition poster
"Kenzaburō Ōé, Je suis de nouveau un
homme," Fête du livre, Aix-en Provence

2008
Golden Bee Award (poster category),
Golden Bee 8, Moscow International Biennial
of Graphic Design, for the exhibition poster
"Vivo in Typo," Espace Topographie de l'art,
Paris

2009
Overall Winner, International Typographic
Awards, International Society of Typographic
Designers (ISTD), London, for the three
posters "Bintou Wéré, Un opéra du Sahel,"
"Festival de danse" and "Roy Hargrove et
RH Factor," Châtelet, Théâtre musical de Paris

2011
Chevalier de l'ordre des Arts et des Lettres

Authors

Alice Morgaine

Alice Morgaine was artistic director of the Verrière-Hermès gallery in Brussels from 1999 to 2012, and previously worked as a journalist with *L'Express* (1962–78) and *Jardin des modes* (1979–97). She is now an advisor to the artistic director of Hermès.

Ellen Lupton

Ellen Lupton is the curator of contemporary design at the Smithsonian's Cooper-Hewitt, National Design Museum in New York and the author of several books, including *Thinking With Type: A Critical Guide for Designers* (2004), *Skin: Surface, Substance, Design* (2007) and *Graphic Design: The New Basics* (2008).

Tino Grass

Tino Grass, born 1979, is a Cologne-based graphic designer. Since 2008 he has been teaching visual communication and typography in several universities for art and design. His publication *Schriftgestalten – über Schrift und Gestaltung* (2008) is dedicated to typography.

The commentaries of the work of Philippe Apeloig were written by Ann Holcomb based on the descriptions and projects submitted by Philippe Apeloig, with the guidance of Ashley Banks. They were reviewed, supplemented and adjusted by Michel Wlassikoff for the final version in French.

This book is the product of many years of work and personal investment from all of them, but it would not have happened without Anna Brugger and Yannick James.

A number of people have helped in different ways to get this publication off the ground. We would like to thank:

Camille Dupaquier
Ann Holcomb
Andreas Körner and his team
Marcel Meesters,
MM Artbook Printing & Repro
Cécile Niesseron
Michel Wlassikoff for his shrewd advice.

Marie-Laure Bernadac
Wim Crouwel
Marie Descourtieux
Daphne van Peski
Valérie Marin La Meslée
Lydie Leroy
Frans Lieshout
Massin
Rudi Meyer
Philippe Mugnier
Nicole Savy
Alberto Del Saz
Hala Warde

We would finally like to express our heartfelt thanks to Béatrice Salmon at Les Arts Décoratifs, who has supported the project from the outset.

This book was published on the occasion of the exhibition "Typorama: Philippe Apeloig Graphic Design," held at Les Arts Décoratifs, Paris, from November 21, 2013 to March 30, 2014.

The exhibition was made possible with the support of Fedrigoni, Nord Sud Matériaux, the printers Stipa, the Théâtre du Châtelet, and the Théâtre national de Toulouse Midi-Pyrénées.

It was also supported by:
Achim Moeller, Moeller Fine Art, New York and Berlin
Connery Pissarro Seydoux
French Institute Alliance Française (FIAF)
Fondation d'Entreprise Hermès
Fondation Pierre Bergé–Yves Saint Laurent
Voies navigables de France (VNF)

This publication received support from:
Voies navigables de France (VNF)
The Barki Agency and Lessebo Bruk

Acknowledgments
For their untiring support throughout
the years, Philippe Apeloig would like
to give particular thanks to:
Ida and Marcel Apeloig
Évelyne Apeloig

And, in chronological order, to:
Léone Nora
Michel Laclotte
Jean Jenger
Henri Loyrette
Richard Peduzzi
Jacques London
April Greiman
Francine Fort and Michel Jacques
Alice Morgaine
Anne-Marie Sauvage
Pierre Rosenberg
Annie Terrier
Ellen Lupton
Marie-Anne Couvreu and Henri Meynadier
François Bordry
Achim et Colette Moeller
Marie-Monique Steckel
Adon Peres
Jean-Luc Choplin and Jean-François Brégy
Nikiforos Diamandouros
Agathe Mélinand
Pierre Bergé
Hélène Dubrule
Pierre-Alexis Dumas

**He would also like to express
his gratitude to his friends:**
Katrin Adam and Keith Godard
Corinne Bacharach
Agnès Benayer
Emmanuel Bérard
Hélène and Michel Bonneau
Emmanuelle Boulestreau
Marie-Claude Bugeaud
Raymonde Caloghiris
Valérie Caillon-Gervier
Marlyse Courrech
Nathalie Elemento
Nathalie Fiszman
Julia Hasting and Kobi Benezri
Sagi Haviv
Yehuda Hofshi
Aïcha Kherroubi
Françoise Lazare
Didier Mutel
Ivan Nunez
Sebastian Peetz
Sandrine and Lionel Pissarro
Chantal Polier
François Roussel

Index

Numerals in *italics* refer to references in captions.

Photographic credits

l = left, r = right, c = center, a = above, b = below

The works of Philippe Apeloig were photographed by Andreas Körner, except: Michael Konrad: 38; Prisca Martaguet: 250 bl, 282, 283 a, 285 r, 290 c, 290 r, 292 c, 292 r, 293 a, 293 bl, 293 bc, 298, 299, 301 b, 338 lb, 338 r, 342 b, 343 ac, 343 ar, 343 br, 345 © Les Arts Décoratifs, photo Jean Tholance: 40 l, 41, 44 l

© Adagp, Paris, 2013/Philippe Apeloig/Max Bill: 23 l/Constantin Brancusi: 236/Marc Chagall: 230 l/Roman Cieślewicz: 29 b/ Gerrit Rietveld: 14 ar/Sol Lewitt: 23 cb, 46 br/Josef Müller Brockman: 31 b/Jean Puiforcat: 276/William Verboven: 31 al/ Jean Widmer: 20 al; © Succession H. Matisse: 23 a; 11 l: Cat's Collection/Corbis Standard Droits gérés (DG); 11 ar: Impex Film; 11 r: Gaumont Pathé archives; 12 l: Paris-Match/Service Scoop; 12 r: RMN-Grand Palais (musée du Louvre)/Thierry Le Mage; 13 al: akg-images; 13 lc: Barbara Morgan Archive/Courtesy of Bruce Silverstein Gallery, New York City; 13 bl: Pantin, médiathèque du Centre national de la danse/Fonds Albrecht Knust-Donation Roderyk Lange; 13 ra: Ulli Weiss; 13 rc: Photographie de Fred Hayes/Ririe-Woodbury Dance Company; 13 br: MIRISCH-7 ARTS/United Artists/The Kobal Collection; 14 al: Wolfgang Weingart; 14 bc, 14 br: Collection Stedeljik Museum, Amsterdam; 14 c: DR; 14 ac, 14 ar: Les Arts Décoratifs; 17 l: Manuscripts and Archives, Yale University Library; 17 ar: April Greiman; 17 br: Frans Lieshout; 19 l: Roger Ressmeyer/ CORBIS Standard Droits gérés (DG); 19 c: Emigré Inc/Rudy VanderLans; 19 ar: April Greiman; 20 al: Jean Widmer; 20 r: Peter Keller; 20 bl: Rudi Meyer; 23 a: DIGITAL IMAGE © The Museum of Modern Art, New York/Scala, Florence; 23 cb: DIGITAL IMAGE © 2013, The Museum of Modern Art, New York/Scala, Florence; 23 br: Photo © Victoria and Albert Museum, London; 23 bl: Museum für Gestaltung Zürich; 27 l: Diaphana Productions Paris; 28: Jean Widmer; 29 a: Bruno Monguzzi; 29 b: Roman Cieślewicz; 30: NKS (Nederlandse Kunst Stichting) and Total Design, Daphne Duijvelshoff; 31 b: Museum für Gestaltung Zürich; 31 al, 31 r: Frans Lieshout; 32 ar: Mairie de Beaune/Direction du patrimoine culturel; 36: Burnham Library of Architecture, The Art Institute of Chicago; 42: Musée d'Orsay; 43: Musée d'Orsay; 46 l: RMN-Grand Palais (musée d'Orsay)/image RMN; 46 r: Sol Lewitt Collection; 54 l: Yann Weymouth; 54 r: Pyramide du Louvre, arch. IM Pei, musée du Louvre; 60 l: Yves Saint Laurent SAS; 60 c: Pierre Boulat/Cosmos; 60 r: Fondation Pierre Bergé – Yves Saint Laurent/photo Alexandre Guirkinger; 64: Imprimerie nationale, Paris; 69: Les Arts Décoratifs; 80: Tate, London, Dist. RMN-Grand Palais/Tate Photography; 84: 2013 Kunsthaus Zürich; 158: Reproduced by permission of The Henry Moore Foundation; 174: Catherine Rebois; 179: Alex Webb/Magnum Photos; 184: musée du quai Branly, Paris, photo Claude Germain/Scala, Florence; 187: Paolo Pellegrin/Magnum Photos; 192: RMN-Grand Palais/Christian Jean; 194 l: Francis Fernez/ Archives municipales du Havre fonds Tournant 80W4-7; 194 r: Lucien Hervé, September 2013; 199: Werner Bischof/ Magnum Photos; 202: Alex Jay, 2005; 207: Zürcher Hochschule der Künste; 208: Collection Stedeljik Museum, Amsterdam; 230 l: Collection Stedeljik Museum, Amsterdam; 230 r: Photo © The Israel Museum, Jerusalem by Elie Posner; 236: Centre Pompidou, MNAM-CCI, Dist. RMN-Grand Palais/Jacques Faujour; 243: akg-images/André Held; 276: Collection Puiforcat, Paris

First published in the United Kingdom in 2013 by Thames & Hudson Ltd, 181A High Holborn, London WC1V 7QX

www.thamesandhudson.com

First published in 2014 in hardcover in the United States of America by Thames & Hudson Inc., 500 Fifth Avenue, New York, New York 10110

thamesandhudsonusa.com

Original edition copyright © 2013 Les Arts Décoratifs, Paris This edition copyright © 2013 Thames & Hudson Ltd, London

Concept, design and typesetting: Tino Grass

with assistance from Anna Brugger and Yannick James for the Philippe Apeloig Studio

Cover design: Philippe Apeloig Set in ABF Linéaire

Translator: Philippa Richmond

Curator: Amélie Gastaud

Photo-engraving and printing: MM Artbook Printing & Repro

Typeface: AkzidenzGrass (based on Akzidenz Grotesk designed by H. Berthold AG in 1898 and modified by Luc(as) de Groot in 2008)

Paper: Phoenix Motion Xenon 150 g/m^2 Lessebo Design Smooth Natural 150 g/m^2 made by Lessebo Bruk and distributed in France by Barki Agency (www.barki.com)

British Library Cataloguing-in-Publication Data A catalogue record for this book is available from the British Library

Library of Congress Catalog Card Number 2013945213

ISBN: 978-0-500-51722-2

Printed and bound in Germany